My 10 Strategies for Integrative Coaching

Vincent Lenhardt

My 10 Strategies for Integrative Coaching

Co-constructing the Journey from Freedom to Responsibility

Vincent Lenhardt
Transformance Pro/VL EURL
Puteaux, Paris, France

Translated by Guy Bullen

ISBN 978-3-319-54794-7   ISBN 978-3-319-54795-4 (eBook)
DOI 10.1007/978-3-319-54795-4

Library of Congress Control Number: 2017945901

Cover Design by Samantha Johnson

Printed on acid-free paper

This Palgrave Macmillan imprint is published by Springer Nature
The registered company is Springer International Publishing AG
The registered company address is: Gewerbestrasse 11, 6330 Cham, Switzerland

Foreword

Being and becoming, for and through the other.

This is how I aspire to position myself, as I relate to my clients.

Positioning oneself as "being and becoming for and through the other" requires a particular set of convictions, values, attitudes and competences—the attributes of a profession that also requires deep expertise: I speak of the coaching profession.

At the same time, anyone who wishes to create the conditions of unconditional acceptance, where the other is deeply and truly the center of attention, can aspire to these attributes in the context of a helping relationship.

When I say "for and through the other", I also speak of the irreducible complexity of the helping relationship and its dynamics.

"I is another",[1] wrote the French poet Arthur Rimbaud. It is also the title of one of Father Maurice Zundel's most beautiful books on spirituality (one can guess who the "Other" is for Zundel).

My identity develops and is continually transformed through my contact with the "other"—this alter ego, similar to me but never the same. As I open myself up to this "otherness" that envelops and penetrates me, I enrich myself as much as I enrich the other. This inter-subjective dynamic lies at the heart of the helping relationship in general, and coaching in particular.

Accepting and opening up to the "other" in this way deeply changes the helper's view of himself and the client. It can also radically change the way the client sees both himself and his own relational ecosystem. A number of complex,

---

[1] "Je est un autre."

psychological dynamics are at work[2] that the helper can, to a large extent, analyze and bring to conscious awareness. Yet the essential quality of a relationship—and hence its richness—comes from somewhere deeper: an alliance forged through the encounter of two beings who, respecting the mystery of the "other", dare to open themselves up to that mystery. The alliance they forge with one another not only enables each one to draw upon resources from within themselves, but also empowers them together to free up an energy that emerges through their relating, transcends them, and radiates beyond them.

This book revisits a number of concepts and tools described in my earlier books, and adds this expanded perspective. It significantly reshapes and deepens my previous writings, based on my experience in recent years. It also introduces notions that are either new, or were previously only outlined, such as third-order listening, the DRCR (Deconstruction-Restoration-Construction-Reconfiguration) model, the meaning molecule or the autonomy development tree. It also describes four identity strategies and the culminating Crystallization strategy, a meta-strategy that underpins all nine others.

Above all, this book seeks to provide a structured framework for the vast theoretical and practical body of coaching which is now available, and to draw out its fundamental principles. It aims to help the coach find the right stance as he stands at the crossroads of multiple complementary and interacting strategic and tactical options. Articulating these around "ten strategies" enables the reader to place the approaches, rules, models, tools, techniques and intervention modes that make up the coaching paradigm, within a global, coherent and comprehensive framework.

This book will be of value to both seasoned coaches and those starting on the coaching journey. Both will value this book, as they "inform their practice with theory, and their theory with practice".

The coach's stance also shares the same essence (one might even say "is consubstantial") with that of other practitioners of the helping relationship. I dare to hope that all those involved in the helping relationship—be they therapists, trainers, teachers, sports coaches, social workers or consultants—will find sustenance in these pages.

May I be so bold as to venture further: understanding these strategies, and thereby understanding the culture of an integrative approach to coaching, will be valuable to any person engaged in relationships through which they develop

---

[2] Such as projections, introjections, transference, counter-transference. These are explained in the main body of the book and in the glossary.

others, enhance their competences or resolve their problems—from mother or father, to manager or medical doctor, to HR director.

Dare I even say that this book contains a message that concerns us all? By definition, are we not all *beings in relationships*, with a deep, partly conscious desire to become *beings in fellowship* with each other?

Each and every one of us lives in a world that is transforming at an exponential rate. The groundswell of globalization, digitization and virtualization has not only affected economics and politics, but has also swept away many of our old ways of thinking. This "Third Industrial Revolution" so eloquently described by Jeremy Rifkin, and whose principles I will apply to coaching in this book, calls forth radically new modes of management: with respect to how we communicate, how we use our energy and how we organize all aspects of our lives. Five major trends underpin this intellectual, cultural and societal revolution:

- increasing *complexity*, generating renewed search for meaning;
- ever-increasing *uncertainty*, that calls for new ways of thinking and acting;
- the affirmation of *individuality*, along with the claim to be master of one's own destiny;
- the spread of *interdependence* at all levels—individuals, companies, organizations, and states—which requires increasing cooperation in the face of increasing overlapping of the stakes involved;
- above all, *generations Y and Z* bursting in on the scene at the outset of the third revolution in human culture described by Michel Serres[3] (digitalization, following on from writing and printing) concurrently with the outbreak of the Third Industrial Revolution—the emergence of "homo numericus" at the same time as Jeremy Rifkin's "homo empatheticus". These generations embody the post-modern era, and are the symptoms of a new global civilization that is changing not only society but also business, compelling it to change paradigms and to break out of its prisons of status, hierarchy and procedures.

In business, the Collective Intelligence needed for growth, or at the very least survival, requires that those involved not only "liberate" business from its past, but also take responsibility for giving it a better future.

---

[3] Michel Serres and Bruno Latour, *Conversations on Science, Culture, and Time*. University of Michigan Press, 1995.

Many fear this paradigm shift to a new world. The focus on local identities, the retreat into closed communities and the rejection of those who are different make tragic headlines in the news; all speak of the difficulty of breaking away from frames of reference that belong to a past age.

In spite of the crises we are living through, I am convinced that a new era is emerging, where social bonds are generated in new ways. The sharing economy, a caring culture, Collective Intelligence, awareness of the planet and our common good—all supported by the development of networks—are emerging as the foundations of the new global consciousness identified by Jeremy Rifkin (and spoken of by many before him[4]) when he speaks of the advent of the empathetic civilization.

In order to be at ease in this complex environment, in order to discover and fully exercise their freedom, and then to progress from freedom on to responsibility, those involved in this transformation need structure. This book offers such a structure for the practice of coaching.

I believe that spreading a culture of coaching will contribute to the emergence of this new era, as our world as a whole goes through the process of "being and becoming".

My heartfelt hope is that this book will contribute to its emergence. If it does, my joy will be full.

---

[4] For example, Martin Luther King Jnr: "I refuse to accept the view that mankind is so tragically bound to the starless midnight of racism and war that the bright daybreak of peace and brotherhood can never become a reality... I believe that unarmed truth and unconditional love will have the final word."

Preface by Patrick Litré, Bain & Company

It's lonely at the top. The pressure on executives to improve performance has never been stronger. Every step up in the hierarchy, every new challenge brings more rewards and recognition but also higher expectations. "People warned me it would be a shock, but nothing could prepare me for this: it's been a lot harder than I ever expected" is what I hear from most newly appointed CEOs.

New leaders don't have much time to learn and adapt: regardless of level, they must immediately set their agenda, build a strong team, make key decisions, and manage up while trying to adjust to their new role, without transition… Under such pressure, even the most brilliant and powerful executives can suffer from some form of "imposter syndrome". Deep inside they think "I am not sure I can do this…I have been able to make it through until now, but will it work this time?"

That's why leaders need help. Like the best athletes, they increasingly surround themselves with people who will push them and help to accelerate their development to their full potential. Ideally these are people who are completely on their side, who know how to listen but "tell it like it is", without imposing a personal agenda. That is why high quality coaching has become such a precious form of support for leaders.

My personal experience reflects this: after 30 years as a CEO and management consultant, I finally understood, thanks to Vincent Lenhardt, the difference between coaching and consulting, and the powerful complementarity between the two approaches. I find McGregor's[5] "Theory X and Y"

---

[5] Douglas McGregor, *The Human Side of Enterprise*, McGraw-Hill Professional; Annotated edition, 2006.

particularly relevant: Leaders with an "X" posture assume that people are neither naturally motivated nor competent. Leaders with a "Y" posture assume that people have the ability and motivation to solve complex problems and create solutions, given the right support. A coach takes a "Y" posture and this has transformed how I practice my profession, with surprising results. I was fortunate enough to have Vincent as my coach to help me make this transition: it turns out I also needed help.

The impact has been transformational for me, my clients, and my colleagues. At Bain & Company, we have built a Leadership Center of Excellence that runs executive coaching "black belt" sessions in every part of the world to help the firm's partners coach their clients and develop cohesive leadership teams based on Vincent's approach. Moreover, this effort is only a part of the firm's broader investment in Results Delivery®, a proprietary approach to help clients execute transformative change while building their internal capability.

Let me illustrate this with one of my experiences: a few years ago, the newly appointed CEO of a global Biotechnology Company knew he needed to transform the company. After years of extraordinary growth, the company had become slower, more complex, and less efficient. The pipeline was strong, but it took 15 years to bring a molecule to patients. From the start, the CEO set out to build a better company not just reduce cost. He wanted to use the transformation as the training ground to develop a new generation of leaders who could re-energize the company. This required a fundamental shift in posture at the top to tap into the "collective intelligence" of the organization. We combined the Bain transformation toolkit with the 10 strategies described in this book and the results have been extraordinary: not only has the stock price doubled in two years, but the 200 leaders who led this work have formed critical mass and created a new culture that has fundamentally changed the way people collaborate and solve problems. The executive who ran the transformation program reflected: "Now I can't imagine my career without this experience. It was a good reminder to always stay open to changes and never stop growing."

Why are Vincent Lenhardt's 10 coaching strategies so effective?

- Based on his eclectic and extensive experience, he has drawn from the best schools (transactional analysis, psychoanalysis, Organizational Development, Gestalt...) and integrated them into a coherent body of work that is as solid in its theoretical foundation as it is original in its articulation.

- His work is infused by a positive, optimistic and humanistic worldview. As a result, it is vibrant and soulful. It creates energy and possibilities wherever it is applied.
- These strategies are practical and operational without ever falling in the traps of simplistic, mechanistic or reductionist formulas.

And ultimately, they work and help deliver results, while developing leaders and making organizations a better place to work.

Partner, Atlanta   Patrick Litré
Global Leader of Bain's Results Delivery® practice

A Note on Pronouns and Definitions

For conciseness, I use the pronoun "he" in the text without prejudice, since the same situations could be described with the pronoun "she". Varying "he" and "she" might be confusing to the reader, and the use of "they" as a singular pronoun is not universally accepted.

Terms that may be unfamiliar to the reader are marked with an asterisk* the first time they occur in a section, to indicate that they are defined in the glossary at the end of the book. For ready reference, a text box also explains the term in the body of the text when the term first occurs in the book.

Contents

Introduction   1
  Some Preliminary Thoughts   1
    Why This Book, Now?   1
    Yes to Tools and Techniques ... within the Context of a Strong
    Coaching Culture   2
    Navigating Frontiers   3
    Coaching—an Unavoidable Paradigm for Developing People
    and Organizations   4
    Collective Intelligence—the Number One Challenge   6
  Please Give Me a Strategy!   9
    Effective or Efficient?   10
    What to Do, and What Not to Do   10
    A Contract or an "Alliance"?   10
    Complicated or Complex?   11
    Beware of Icebergs!   14
    Leading by Influencing   14
    A Metaphor: the Hostage Taker   15
    Which Game—Chess or Go?   17
    Meaning and Purpose First   19
    A Humanizing Perspective   19

The Ten Strategies—An Overview   23
  A Set of Dynamic and Interconnected Strategies   23
    Operational Strategies   23
    Identity Strategies   25
    Crystallization: The Meta-strategy   27

Key Considerations around the Ten Strategies   28
  A Constructivist Space   28
  Expanding Awareness   29
  The Satnav Metaphor   32
  Strategies for Helping the Coach Become
  a True Professional   33

Strategy 1: The Person-centered Approach, or Rogerian Alliance   35
  The Client at Heart   35
    Prince(ss) meets Prince(ss)   37
    A Matrix of Empathy   40
    From Personal to Organizational Development—Pygmalion
    at Work   43
  Levels of Change   44
    The Princes(s)' Alliance   47
    Being Able to See the Prince(ss)   48
    Masculine/Feminine   49
    Third-Order Listening   49
    From Socrates to Frankl, towards Modes of Generative
    Questioning   50
  A Code of Ethics for a Princely Alliance   51
  Key Points and Pause for Reflection—the Rogerian Alliance   53

Strategy 2: Fish/fishing Rod—His Frame/My Frame   55
  Fish/Fishing Rod   55
    Giving the Client a Fish   56
    Providing a Fishing Rod   56
    Which Approach, When?   57
  His Frame/My Frame   59
  Metacommunication: The "Listening Word"
  and the "Eloquent Ear"   61
    So What is Third-order Listening?   67
  Autonomy and the Paradox of Education   69
    Degrees of Autonomy   71
    Degree 1: Dependence (Deviant Form: The "Doormat")   72
    Degree 2: Counter-dependence (Deviant Form:
    The "Hedgehog")   72
    Degree 3: Independence (Deviant Form: The "Rascal")   73
    Degree 4: Interdependence (Working in "Unison")   74
    Degree 5: Alter-Dependence (The "Alter Ego")   74

Spiraling Growth—the Coach's Stance   75
Degree 6: The Dimension of Meaning at the Heart
of the Spiral   78
Autonomy in Summary   81
Key Points and Pause for Reflection—Fish/Fishing Rod
and His Frame/My Frame   82

Strategy 3: RPNRC (Reality-Problem-Need-Request-Contract)   83
Building a Relational Ecosystem   84
Five Facets of the Same Issue   86
  Identifying the Client's Reality   86
  Identifying the Problems, Issues
  and Stakes Involved   86
  Identifying the Need   87
  Clarifying the Request   87
  Developing the Contract   88
  A Comprehensive Approach to the Relationship
  and its Ecosystem   89
  The RPNRC Radar   90
Beyond RPNRC: The Coach's Fifteen-Parameter Dashboard   93
  The Fifteen Parameters   94
  A Shared Change Agenda   97
Key Points and Pause for Reflection—RPNRC
and the 15 Parameters   99

Strategy 4: Contextualization and the Intervention Zones   101
Putting the Problem and the Stakes
into Perspective   102
A Work Plan to Enable Step-by-Step Contextualization   108
Behind the Problem, a Complex Interplay of Identity Stakes,
and the "Seeding Effect"   111
Parallel Processes—When an Uneasy Relationship Reveals
an Uneasy Client   112
  Why Worry About Parallel Processes?   115
  The Coach Who Uses the Parallel Process is in Fact Resorting
  to a Powerful Transformational Lever   117
  Eight Steps to Manage and Guide the Parallel Process   117
  Access to Meaning and Restoration: The Path
  of Humanization   119
  Key Points and Pause for Reflection—Contextualization   120

**Strategy 5: Interventions: Categories
and Options**   123
  The Coach, an Acupuncturist?   123
    Three Main Intervention Categories   126
  Coach-Centered Interventions   126
    Silence   126
    The Coach's Stance   128
  Client-Centered Interventions   129
    Questioning   129
    Endorsements   129
    Challenging—Where and When to Challenge?   130
    Diagnosis   130
    Options, Protections and Permissions   131
    Decisions and Re-decisions   132
  Relationship-Centered Interventions   133
    Parallel Processes   133
    Chairwork   133
  Key Points and Pause for Reflection—Intervention
Categories and Options   134

Strategy 6: Access to Meaning   137
  The Meanings of Meaning   137
    Creating Meaning in Complexity   138
    The Secret of the Golden Goose   140
  The Identity Backbone   142
    Access to Renewed Coherence   145
  The Meaning Molecule   148
    The Object of Love   149
    The Capacity to Relate   150
    The Infinite Dream   153
    Energy   153
    From Ego to Self: Connecting Anew
with the Spark of the Divine   154
  Key Points and Pause for Reflection—Access to Meaning   156

Strategy 7: The Client's Path   159
  A "Waypoint" in the Client's Personal Journey   159
  Inevitable Losses   161
    Third-Order Suffering: the Price of the Return to Life   162
  The Space-Time Dimension   164
  The Transition Space   166

A Constructivist Logic   168
Points and Pause for Reflection—The Client's Path   169

Strategy 8: Identity Construction   171
The DRCR Model   172
  A Relationship of Equals   175
Envelopes of the Self: The Four Identity Zones   176
  Linking to the Identity Backbone   178
Balancing Action, Meaning and Relationships—the Autonomy
Deployment Tree   179
  Integrating Different Perspectives   181
What Is Important: Managerial Stances   182
  From Expert to Manager to Leader   183
  From Order-Giver to Resource-Provider to Meaning-Bearer   184
  Adjusting the Cursor: the Art of Contingent Management   188
What is Essential: Self-Transformation   190
  Spiritual Openness   192
Key Points and Pause for Reflection—Identity Construction   193

Strategy 9: Humanization   195
Death As Stage of Growth: Accepting Our Finiteness   196
An Empathetic Consciousness   198
Identity in Three Dimensions   199
At Ease in the Midst of Chaos   201
The "Scarlet Thread" of Responsibility   204
Individuation: Uniqueness in Universality   207
Key Points and Pause for Reflection—Humanization   209

Strategy 10: Crystallization   211
Taking the Risk of Opening up the Future   212
A Meta-Strategy: The Stance of Crystallization   214
The Necessary Ethics of Change for the Coaching Profession   216
  An Obligation of Means   216
  Giving up the Illusion of Omnipotence   217
  The "Out of bonds" Field of Therapy   217
  The Alliance for Change   218
  Cleaning One's Spectacles   219
What Should One Expect from a Coaching Course?   219
The Paradox of Power   220
Key Points and Pause for Reflection—Crystallization   223

Appendix: Training, The "Coach & Team" Way   225

Glossary   229

Bibliography   235

Index   239

List of Figures

Fig. 1   Logical levels in a coaching culture   3
Fig. 2   Four dimensions of a coaching strategy   12
Fig. 3   Summary of the ten strategies   24
Fig. 4   Key questions for each of the 10 strategies   28
Fig. 5   The 10 Strategies seen as holomorphic   30
Fig. 6   Conscious, unconscious and the transcendent unconscious   31
Fig. 7   Levels of change   44
Fig. 8   Levels of change and the Princes(s)' Alliance   47
Fig. 9   The Princes(s)' Alliance   48
Fig. 10   Fish/fishing rod   58
Fig. 11   His frame/my frame   59
Fig. 12   One…or two cubes?   63
Fig. 13   Boring's figure   64
Fig. 14   Metacommunication and black boxes   65
Fig. 15   The iceberg and third-order listening   67
Fig. 16   Alter-dependence   75
Fig. 17   The autonomy spiral   78
Fig. 18   Meaning at the heart of, and passing through autonomy   80
Fig. 19   The coach as "relationship expert"   85
Fig. 20   RPNRC in summary   89
Fig. 21   RPNRC in context   91
Fig. 22   The RPNRC radar and its five screens   92
Fig. 23   The coach's 15-parameter dashboard   98
Fig. 24   The 15 parameters over time (the spinning top)   99
Fig. 25   RPNRC with the intervention zones   103
Fig. 26   The eight main intervention zones   104
Fig. 27   Key steps in the intervention zones strategy   109
Fig. 28   The parallel process   113

Fig. 29   The identity backbone   143
Fig. 30   The existential model of life between birth and death   146
Fig. 31   The meaning molecule   149
Fig. 32   Weighted integrative therapy   157
Fig. 33   Simultaneous deconstruction, restoration, construction
          and reconfiguration   172
Fig. 34   The four identity zones, or four "envelopes"   176
Fig. 35   The autonomy deployment tree   180
Fig. 36   Summary of identity construction   181
Fig. 37   Stages of management development   187
Fig. 38   Managing the cursor between McGregor's theory X and theory Y   188
Fig. 39   Transformance   189

Introduction

Some Preliminary Thoughts

Why This Book, Now?

This book represents the culmination of my journey as consultant, therapist and coach over four decades and the ten or so books I have published during that period, two of which have been translated into English. My early books dealt with the practice of therapy using approaches based on humanistic psychology* and psychoanalysis. Other books focused on management, with coaching as a specific mode of the helping relationship in the context of managing organizations. Finally, I co-authored three books with business leaders whom I had had the privilege of coaching. Through their testimonies and my reflections on the consequences of their practice for coaching theory, these books explore a notion I believe to be of major import—the Collective Intelligence* of organizations. My work with these business leaders brought home to me that the potential for development of a company, or any other form of organization, is proportionate to the development of the potential of its people, in particular that of those governing it. Yet again and again I was led to reconsider the stakes, the challenges, and the ways people construct their identities when one takes account of **all** the stakeholders in a given human community—not just the leaders who are its key players.

© The Author(s) 2017
V. Lenhardt, *My 10 Strategies for Integrative Coaching*,
DOI 10.1007/978-3-319-54795-4_1

Humanistic psychology

Not to be confused with humanism. Humanistic psychology studies the whole person, and the uniqueness of each individual. The humanistic approach emphasizes the personal worth of the individual, the centrality of human values, and the creative, active nature of human beings.

Collective Intelligence

is a dynamic of co-responsible players, interconnected culturally and organizationally through an alliance around a shared vision. It is described in detail later in this introduction.

The following chapters are a fresh synthesis of what I have learned over the years. The ten coaching strategies pull together the main concepts, tools and models (both theoretical and practical) that guide an integrative approach to the helping relationship to which I have contributed through my writing, teaching and practice.

Yes to Tools and Techniques ... within the Context of a Strong Coaching Culture

A helping relationship cannot be reduced to operational method. Though a professional coach needs to master a certain number of tools and techniques, and to integrate them into organized strategies, the key question is how to embed all this into a culture. For me a coaching culture is a combination of:

- **A philosophy.** What identity, and what view of human nature as applied to management does the coach embody, and promote with his clients?
- **An attitude**. What values and explicit or implicit belief sets—about themselves, about others, and about relationships—does the coach represent?
- **A set of behaviors.** How can the coach demonstrate deep listening, exemplify nonviolent communication, build an alliance with the client, and be at ease in both individual and group relationships.
- **A set of framing procedures.** How to establish and evolve contracts, how to manage multiple interfaces, how to guarantee a code of ethics in both

individual and group coaching through "coaching charters" that are adapted for the specific culture of the institution where the coaching occurs.

Above and beyond all this, a coach requires solid and ongoing training, regular supervision, and a code of ethics that is constantly reassessed.

We are indeed talking of culture, and this culture can be expressed in each of a number of logical levels, as Fig. 1 shows.

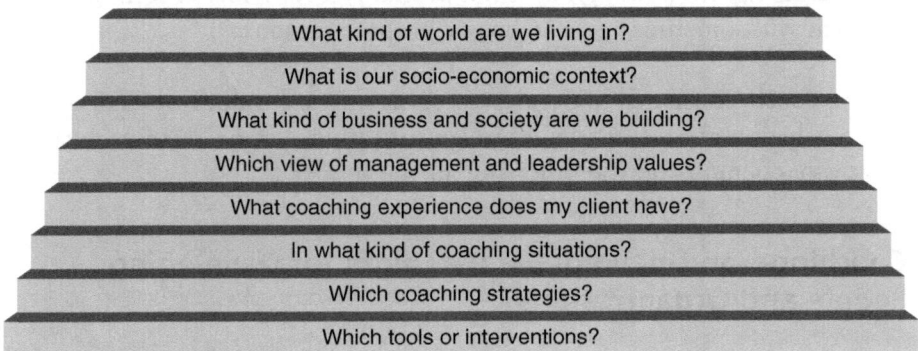

What kind of world are we living in?

What is our socio-economic context?

What kind of business and society are we building?

Which view of management and leadership values?

What coaching experience does my client have?

In what kind of coaching situations?

Which coaching strategies?

Which tools or interventions?

Fig. 1 Logical levels in a coaching culture

Navigating Frontiers

The coach continually operates at the frontiers of a number of domains. Since these domains involve human relationships, he needs to take account of other domains of knowledge such as individual psychology, group psychology, the psycho-sociology of organizations, sociology and politics. His prime material is reality in the "here and now" as perceived by individuals living out their intersubjectivity*. This "reality" is not objective, but is made up of the perceptions constructed and lived out by them as they interact. A purely "objective and rational" approach to coaching is simplistic and misses the point.

Intersubjectivity

The sharing of their subjective states (emotions, attention, intention...) by two or more people. A focus on intersubjectivity gives primacy to reality as experienced by subjects, rather than attempting to define "objective reality".

Coaching involves all that makes us human, and the coach needs to take account of the whole person in all its complexity. As such, coaching shares certain essential properties of (or is consubstantial with) a number of other disciplines:

- **Humanistic therapies and psychoanalysis.** The coach is not primarily focused on listening to the unconscious, but cannot completely disregard it.
- **Training.** Though he does not define himself as a teacher, the coach brings knowledge and a new way of learning to the client, thus contributing to the client's development by enriching his frame of reference.
- **Consulting.** Even though he is not primarily a "provider of solutions", the coach will sometimes give advice or propose options.

The coach constantly navigates these frontiers: he does not cross them without legitimate reasons or ethical justification, yet he remains aware of what is happening "on the other side of the border".

Coaching—an Unavoidable Paradigm for Developing People and Organizations

We have come a long way since 1988, when in the United States the practice of coaching was in its infancy and in France it was practically unknown. Through my activities as a helping professional (therapist, trainer, Organization Development consultant, coach and trainer of coaches) I have seen at close quarters—and indeed lived through—the upheavals of management with the massive emergence of the post-industrial world.[1]

Business has evolved from the age of industry-commerce to the age of service, and to the instantaneous universal distribution of information. In this new paradigm, management principles inherited from the Second Industrial Revolution*—part of which remains with us—no longer suffice to function effectively. The vertical organization of work, centralization of power, and "command and control" management have not been abolished and remain with us. However, the logic behind them is both inadequate to deal with the complexity of a world in which change continually expands and accelerates, and unable to meet the needs of organizations confronted with the multiple challenges of the Third

---

[1] I refer the reader who would like to explore this theme in more depth to the works of Peter Drucker (*Management Challenges for the twenty-first century*, Routledge, 2007), Gary Hamel (*The Future of Management, Harvard Business Review Press, 2008*) and Jeremy Rifkin (*The Zero Marginal Cost Society: The Internet of Things, the Collaborative Commons, and the Eclipse of Capitalism*, Palgrave Macmillan, 2014).

Industrial Revolution*: globalized exchange, dramatic margin reduction, the Internet of Things, the culture of the millennials, social networks and the volatility of industry players. Organizing work has become deeply complex: traditional hierarchical management needs to be combined with matrix management, and even networked management. The old pyramids have not just been turned on their heads, but flattened, and new forms are ready to emerge.

Second Industrial Revolution

The Second Industrial Revolution came about with the discovery of oil and the combustion engine, electricity and the telephone. All of these required significant capital, and implied central, hierarchical organization of materials and labor.

Third Industrial Revolution

The coming together of peer-to-peer communications through Internet with peer-to-peer energy through distributed energy generation, an intelligent infrastructure through the Internet of Things, and distributed production through 3–D printing.

The deal of a "job for life" in return for compliance has all but disappeared. For employers and employees alike, the challenge has become employability, with its paradoxical consequences: to attract and keep the best in the war for talent, employers offer future employees the opportunity to enhance their employability (competence, reputation, experience, etc.) and to be better equipped to find a job elsewhere. Extrinsic motivation factors, such as salary, health cover or security, are no longer the only parameters involved: intrinsic motivation factors,[2] such as belonging, recognition, personal development and self-actualization, are moving up the priority list for the brightest and best. As generations Y and Z permeate the workforce, and take up positions of responsibility, they will reinforce the need for companies to consider the requirement for a sense of meaning in work, the need for trust and creativity, and the opportunity to become a creator in a context of collective responsibility. Failing this, they will simply go elsewhere, create their own start-ups, or go freelance.

---

[2] See Abraham Maslow's hierarchy of needs (*A Theory of Human Motivation*, Wilder Publications, 2013) and Frederick Herzberg's motivation-hygiene theory (*Motivation to Work*, John Wiley & Sons Inc, 1959) for a more detailed discussion on intrinsic motivation.

Collective Intelligence—the Number One Challenge

Along with many informed observers of today's management revolution, I am convinced that the transformation is only just beginning. In high-performing businesses that have survived and thrived during the recent crises, even more radical aspirations and values are beginning to make their mark: parity, self-management, wholeness and evolutionary purpose, to name but a few. These trigger a dynamic that the static documentation traditionally describing company strategy sadly lacks.

We are experiencing a deep and broad movement that aims to "free enterprise"[3] and in doing so fundamentally questions previous management models. Through my encounters with business leaders as a coach, and through my role as expert in the EVH CEO Club[4] I have discovered the amazing power of Collective Intelligence for myself. Wherever it blossoms, it is nurtured by those leaders who are convinced they need to change the way they position themselves if they are to transform their company and ensure that it becomes sustainable.

As Senior Advisor to a number of international strategy consulting organizations where I have worked with senior Partners and their clients in Europe, the United States and Asia since 2010, I have seen at close quarters how it is no longer enough to tell clients what to do. As Jim Collins[5] and Simon Sinek[6] have shown, in high-performing companies the players have moved from the "What?" or the "How?" to the "Why?". The questions asked here are: "What is the meaning of what we do? What final purpose are we pursuing? In the name of what common vision are we going to commit ourselves, go into action, take risks and thereby take hold of our freedom and our responsibility?"

In this new paradigm, there is an ever more pressing need to develop and implement a strategy "by and for" the whole organization. There is no point

---

[3] Tom Peters' *Thriving on Chaos*, Harper Perennial, 1989, was a seminal book on the subject. See also Carney and Getz *Freedom Inc: Free Your Employees and Let Them Lead Your Business to Higher Productivity, Profits, and Growth*, Crown Publishing Group, 2010, Vineet Mayar *Employees First, Customers Second: Turning Conventional Management Upside Down*, Harvard Business Review Press, 2010, and above all Frédéric Laloux *Reinventing organizations: A Guide to Creating Organizations Inspired by the Next Stage of Human Consciousness*, Nelson Parker, 2014.

[4] EVH stands for *Entreprises Vivantes par et pour des Femmes et des Hommes Vivants* (Living Enterprise for Living Women and Men). It was founded in 1992 by Bertrand Martin, CEO of CCM Sulzer, with whom I wrote *Oser la confiance (Dare to Trust)*, Insep editions, 1997 (not translated into English).

[5] Jim Collins, *Good to Great*, Random House Business, 2001.

[6] Simon Sinek, *Leaders Eat Last: Why Some Teams Pull Together and Others Don't*, Penguin, 2014.

in advocating and managing change if those in the human community that makes up the organization have not understood its final purpose. This is where the priority becomes the "Who?"—Getting the right players and giving them the opportunity to freely and fully express their potential through what they do, how they innovate and how they share responsibility with others.

What is Collective Intelligence?

Collective intelligence is a constantly moving, dynamic process.

The **players** are proactive and inspired by a common vision.

The notion of **shared responsibility** goes far beyond emancipation, and involves the notion of commitment by free players to a common goal.

Players are **interconnected**, and have moved from being a collection of individuals to an effective team motivated by a common spirit.

They have formed an **alliance** to achieve this common goal, and

this takes them beyond the differences, contradictions, suffering and frustrations they may encounter.

Their **shared vision(s)** reflect the common goal and stakes involved, and enable the team to navigate complexity and give meaning to events, including the losses and failures on the way.

A dynamic of
co-responsible players
who are interconnected
culturally and
organizationally
in an alliance
around shared
vision(s)

Along with these new modes of governance and decision making, new relational contracts are emerging, based on subsidiarity* (no longer just delegation), co-responsibility and consequence-sharing. Without completely abandoning their previous modes of thinking and doing, individuals are becoming aware of the need to integrate new ways of functioning, both individually and collectively. This radically changes the status and responsibility of management. The traditional "order-giving" function of the leader is not completely abolished but, leaders also become "managers-as-resource-providers" at all levels, from the executive team to department heads to project managers and first-line managers. Their authority no longer resides principally in their hierarchical position or their expertise, but in their capacity to develop fully the energy and the competences of those under their responsibility.

> **Subsidiarity**
>
> The principle that decisions should be taken at the lowest possible level or closest to where they will have their effect, for example in a local area rather than for a whole country. It differs from delegation in that the local decision maker has full authority and does not need to refer up the chain or report the decision to a higher authority for any aspect of a decision domain.

In a business that has developed Collective Intelligence*, managers no longer experience themselves as "locomotives pulling carriages". They think and act as "talent developers", sometimes even as a "meaning bearers"; they use each project as an opportunity to develop individuals, and hence the organization as a whole. These leaders of a new kind define themselves as "leaders of leaders"[7] those who know how to co-construct a shared vision with others, and generate a dynamic that incites each and every person to leave behind their "monologic" (a logic that excludes others' points of view) to enter, not just into a spirit of "dialogic" (a collaborative logic that includes contradiction), but into "teleologic" end purpose (from the Greek *telos*, final purpose). In an organization that has developed Collective Intelligence, each and every member is a standard bearer for its vision, its values, its challenges, its projects and its collective goals.

As a result, more and more leaders at all levels have turned to coaching. For the most part, they have reached the limits of traditional management. They have experienced first-hand how 80% of the difficulties in an organization or a team are, at heart, human issues. They have come to understand that any project that delivers real change involves a transformation of those involved, their relationships with each other and their relationship with reality. In this context, the culture of coaching, and its practice using the array of competences involved in Collective Intelligence, are, in my view, indispensable.

*
* *

---

[7] See Warren Bennis, Steven B. Sample, Rob Asghar, *The Art and Adventure of Leadership. Understanding Failure, Resilience and Success*, John Wiley & Sons, 2015.

Please Give Me a Strategy!

In 2008, twenty years after I had introduced coaching in France and founded the first coaching school that trained certified coaches,[8] I was asked by my students to explain the coach's frame of reference in the form of coaching strategies. This is what they said:

Do one or more specific strategies exist that a coach can apply, with situational intelligence*, to help our clients move forward?

Situational intelligence

Knowing what to do in a given situation, then doing it, based on understanding what is going on, rather than applying ready-made solutions.

This question challenged me to explain my own practice more clearly, to use my experience to inform the theory I was teaching, and to pull together in a more coherent manner the different concepts, techniques and coaching approaches taught during the course. This finally led me to draw up the framework consisting of the ten strategies in this book.

Before looking at these strategies in more detail, let me define what I mean by strategy in this book, and explain what that definition implies. The sense in which I use the term strategy is:

A structured, way of organizing, that brings one or more objectives into a coherent, systemic* and/or holomorphic* perspective, along with the means to achieve them. A strategy will include specific values in a given culture. It may also be more or less explicit.

Systemic

A manner of understanding how things influence each other within a complex entity, or larger system, by taking into account the relationships and interactions between its parts (as opposed to an analytical approach that breaks up the object in order to analyze its individual component parts).

---

[8] The "Coach & Team" (CT) course in coaching, team building and organizational development given through the organization TransformancePro. It has been followed by several thousand coaches in France, Belgium and Morocco. Today seven schools in the French-speaking world teach the CT curriculum.

> **Holomorphic**
>
> From the Greek *Holos* "whole" and *Morphos* "form". When the parts have the same form as the whole, in the same way that each cell of a living organism contains all the genetic information of the organism of which it forms a part.

The above definition entails the following considerations.

Effective or Efficient?

If it is to align objectives and means, a strategy needs to meet the criteria of effectiveness and efficiency.

- Effectiveness in achieving the objectives, even though, paradoxically, in coaching (as in all types of helping relationship), the coach is not accountable for the results, only for the means he provides for his client to achieve those results.
- Efficiency in achieving these objectives with the greatest economy of means.

What to Do, and What Not to Do

Adopting a strategy means deciding what to do…and what *not* to do. It is as important for the coach to think through what he should *not* do, as to think about what he *should* do. As Eric Berne once said: "The difference between professionals and amateurs in any game [is that] the professional knows when to stop".[9]

Once he has identified the possible scenarios, the coach not only chooses certain strategic options, but also discards others that he has determined are inadequate, thus avoiding pitfalls and dead ends.

A Contract or an "Alliance"?

Coaching strategies depend on a quality of relationship where the power of each party supports and reinforces the other, rather than contradicting or canceling the other out. The two parties forge an alliance based on their relationship, their common goal, and the means to achieve it. This co-constructed alliance is more

---

[9] Eric Berne, *Games People Play*, Ballantine Books, 1964. His comment on the game "the alcoholic".

important and engenders more commitment than the formal (though necessary) contract whose commitments are often illusory.

Complicated or Complex?

Complicated vs. Complex

A complicated problem can be resolved by analytical methods has "a solution", and its future states can be predicted, given enough time, work and analytical power. An airplane is an example of a complicated system. A complex system has multiple autonomous parts interacting in many ways, and constantly adapting to each other. The relationship between cause and effect cannot be discerned, nor can future states be predicted. The behavior of the whole is different to that of the sum of the parts. Social groups or the coach/client relationship are examples of complex systems.

The ten strategies in this book inform a specific stance by the coach within a systemic and multipolar relational space. These strategies do not primarily apply to the domain of the "complicated" (which can always be controlled with sufficient means), but to that of the complex, and it is there that their real value can be seen. The coach works across a number of domains that constitute the ecosystem of his client: the client's organization, his professional domain, or his social, political or cultural environment. All these condition the client's identity as a social agent, as a unique person and as a "relational being".

In this sense, the coaching process extends far beyond the rational realm. Emotions, the body, the unconscious, relationships—all these are part of the coaching relationship, which needs to be able to welcome the mystery that lies within every individual.[10] The coach thus acts in an environment that has at least four poles (Fig. 2).

1. The person of the coach and his stance that condition the relationship.
2. The particular intersubjective space called the "helping relationship", which, as we will see, is a paradoxical relationship.

---

[10] François Varillon, a Jesuit priest author of several books which have deeply nourished me among which *Joy of Faith, Joy of Life* (Paulines, 1993), invites his readers to distinguish between mystery and enigma. The latter can be understood and resolved, while the former may be understood, but is never fully comprehended.

Among these paradoxes is the fact that since the coach is a mystery to himself, and realizes that the client is also a mystery who will never be fully comprehended, he remembers that "to keep some sort of control over the situation, he needs to partially let go of control".

3. The coach's client(s)—in all their complexity.
4. The overall context in which both the client's experience and the coaching relationship exist.

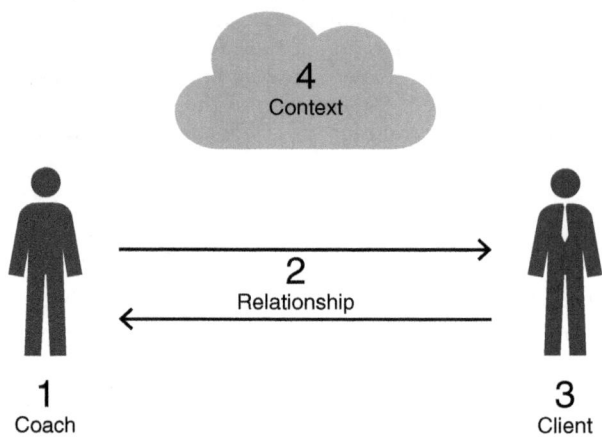

Fig. 2   The four dimensions of a coaching strategy

The key is the coach's ability to optimize the energy of these four elements.

The "Interdividual" Space

Psychoanalysis brought to light the complexity of intersubjective* processes as well as transferential* and counter-transferential phenomena.[11] But from the 1990s onwards, the discovery of mirror neurons considerably enriched our understanding of how we relate to each other. These neurons play a specific role, both in learning through imitation, and also in emotional processes, in particular empathy. The neuro-psychiatrist and

---

[11] Transference, counter-transference and parallel processes are covered in more detail in strategy 4: *Contextualization*.

neurologist Jean-Michel Oughourlian[12] has built on research by René Girard on the role of mimesis in relationships and identity development and linked them to findings on mirror neurons. He has shown that the relational space is composed not only of intersubjectivity in the traditional sense, but also of an **interdividual*** space defined by the interaction between mirror neurons. A relationship also has a mimetic dimension in that each player considers the other as a model, a rival, or an obstacle, with the ensuing consequences.

Interdividual

According to Oughourlian, "Interdividual psychology is the study of the types of interaction that take place between psychological entities". This interaction, and the relationship between people, is characterized mainly by mimesis, where each party imitates the other.

Transference and counter-transference

Transference is a phenomenon characterized by unconscious redirection of feelings from one person to another. It involves a reproduction of emotions relating to a client's previous relationships onto the coach. For example, a young client may reproduce emotions relating to father or mother figures if the coach is older.

Countertransference is where the transference of the client generates emotions in return by the coach. For example, the coach might remember problems with his adolescent son and project those feelings into the coaching relationship.

Implementing a coaching strategy means consciously taking up a stance in this intersubjective and interdividual space. This involves dealing with ambiguity, ambivalence and paradox, as well as managing situations involving transference, counter-transference, and parallel processes. Integrative coaching as described in this book takes into account the emotional, existential and unconscious dimensions, as well as the more "objective" elements in the client's ecosystem. In this, it differs from other coaching approaches based on mechanical or even systemic analyses.

---

[12] Jean-Michel Oughourlian, *Notre troisième cerveau (Our Third Brain)*, Albin Michel, 2003 (only available in French). See also his book *The Genesis of Desire (Studies in Violence, Mimesis, and Culture)*, Michigan State University Press, 2010.

Beware of Icebergs!

Even if the client tries to steer the coach towards the role of a therapist, the coach never confuses his role with that of a therapist. The coach will recognize the different identity levels (for example professional, personal, social, existential or spiritual) for both the client and himself, and the stakes for each party at each level. Though the coach takes them all into account, including the client's private life and intimate psychology, he does not directly address them. He has neither the means nor the intent to treat them. This ambiguity is part of the inherent complexity the coach has to deal with!

The coach and the client can be compared to two icebergs whose visible surface represents only a minute part of who they are. What occurs below the surface partly escapes them. The coach may listen with the ear of a therapist (like the sonar that captures what is happening under the surface), in order to understand the client's "here and now", and to help the client bring subconscious processes to the surface. But he will not attempt to intervene and heal the past (the "there and then")—this is the domain of the therapist. The coach navigates the surface of the ocean, and takes account of what emerges from the depths, but he avoids drowning in the ocean of the client's intimate personal psychology.

Leading by Influencing

The coach is neither accountable for the results of the coaching, nor does he have a hierarchical relationship with the client. But he is accountable for the relationship, and it is up to him to put a coaching framework in place and manage the coaching process. The coach's stance and practice thus contain a dimension of leadership—that of a leader who is a "resource provider", and whose domain of intervention is not content (the "What?"), but process (the "How?"), meaning ("Why?", and "What for?"), and subjective experience ("Who?").

The coach's responsibility is to establish a healthy structure for the intervention. This structure sets aside times and places to guarantee respect and autonomy for the client, and to protect the coaching process from interferences that might perturb or pervert the relationship—be they financial, social, political, institutional or organizational. Though he navigates the frontiers of several disciplines—and these frontiers are sometimes hazy or ambiguous—the coach guards himself against from taking up the formal role of a therapist, or a spiritual, ideological or political guide. If he takes up the role of a therapist, he moves into an open-ended relationship without clear goals. If he becomes a guide, he loses an essential quality of the coach's stance: that of refusing to encroach on the other's freedom by imposing another frame of reference. By staying within the boundaries of coaching, the coach structures the intervention so that it becomes an example for the client, and enables the client to integrate a kind of "internalized coaching" into his leadership that he can then apply when running his team or organization.

Indeed, coaching practice and culture open the doors to a special kind of leadership that supports, structures and guarantees relationships that are secure enough to create the conditions where people can fully exercise their freedom and shoulder their responsibility. This view of leadership, which coaching develops and reinforces, is not focused on developing and amassing the leader's competences, but on his ability to position himself as an enabler with respect to those under his responsibility. He is no longer confined to a hierarchical function, and the effectiveness and power of his leadership as "resource provider" or "meaning bearer" no longer depend on deploying his own competences. All the leader's competence and energy are deployed in the service of the competences and energy of others. He not only transmits his energy, he also activates the energy and potential of all those under his responsibility, and provides them with a model to do likewise.

This is what is really at stake in coaching. Bob and Mary Goulding[13] wrote of therapy that "the power is in the patient". In any coaching situation the coach looks for the client's power. As a coach, I exercise a certain kind of leadership with my client, since I am accountable for the relationship (with the client's agreement, and in alliance with him). Nevertheless, I take care to do this in a way that serves, and is centered on, the person's potency. This potency, as I understand it, is based on the optimization of two energy systems: that of the client and that of the coach.

A Metaphor: the Hostage Taker

George Kohlrieser's work on hostage taking can broaden our thinking on the links between leadership and coaching. I had the privilege of being closely supervised by George, a great psychologist and consultant, who is

---

[13] *The Power is in the Patient*, Barnes & Noble, 1979. Bob and Mary Goulding embody an American school that integrates Transactional analysis and Gestalt Therapy.

also one of the world's leading specialists in negotiation with hostage takers. In his works[14] Kohlrieser develops a model of the stance required, and the relationship that needs to develop with the hostage taker, by exercising a particular kind of leadership. Negotiating in these circumstances means developing a relationship with someone who has placed himself in a situation of extreme control over human lives, whom he believes he can dispose of at a whim. Through dialogue, the negotiator will try to convince the hostage taker to make a decision that is contrary to his original objective: freeing his captives, giving up his power over others, being condemned and put in prison, instead of killing or being killed. The art of such negotiation resides in the negotiator's ability to create a bond, full of paradoxes, between the parties, along with a common goal. Through this process, the hostage taker discovers that it is in his interest to give up his morbid blackmail and to make a new decision totally contrary to his original demands. By accepting handcuffs and prison he chooses life over death.

All other things being equal, hostage taking as a metaphor for leadership dilemmas can be extremely enlightening for a coach. A coach is in a relationship with a client who may imagine himself as "hostage" to his organization or his situation. The client may in turn replay that situation with the coach, and attempt to take him hostage. *He thus becomes, in his imagination, simultaneously a hostage victim and a hostage taker.* A hostage victim in the sense of being prisoner of an ideology, beliefs, repressed drives, or stress, victim of the situation in which he finds himself, or decisions he is unable to take; a hostage taker, because he tries to free himself from his chains by taking the coach hostage.

To be able help the client to free himself from this quandary, the coach needs to be free, with a secure base that ensures he is not engulfed in this hostage-taking spiral. He does this, like Kohlrieser, by creating a bond with his client. It is this bond that enables the client to break out of his spiral and enter a relationship defined by freedom and parity—two of the fundamental qualities of the coaching relationship. The relationship between coach and client then becomes the encounter between two freedoms, and leads to the responsibility of both parties.

---

[14] See *Hostage at the Table: How Leaders Can Overcome Conflict, Influence Others, and Raise Performance*, John Wiley & Sons, 2006, and his latest book, co-authored with Susan Goldsworthy and Duncan Coombe: *Care to Dare, Unleashing Astonishing Potential through Secure Base Leadership*, Jossey-Bass, San Francisco, 2012.

Which Game—Chess or Go?

Through his own fully assumed freedom, his active listening and his non-directiveness, the coach offers a holding space where the client can express himself and find his freedom. This creates the conditions that enable the client to call on resources from within himself to resolve issues and deal with the stakes at hand. Even though there may be times when the coach will provide information or advice relating to the situation, he is always careful not to lock the client into his own frame of reference. The coach never loses sight of the fact that all his words and actions are those of a person accompanying others on their journey. The coach needs constantly to wipe his own spectacles, and remind himself that his reality is not that of the client, and that the client's reality is neither more nor less "true" than his own. This leaves the relationship open to emergence and change.

In this sense, the coaching approach is closer to Eastern wisdom than the world vision forged in the main currents of Western philosophy. From the Greek mathematicians and geometers through to Descartes, the idea that it is possible to "model reality" has influenced the way we think and act, whether to explain what we do not understand, to draw maps to guide us in unknown lands, or to understand and manage change.

Eastern philosophy, notably Chinese thinking, considers change to be permanent and invisible (you cannot see trees growing or children growing up...). It generally escapes our understanding, and we have no other choice but to accommodate ourselves to the emergence of a reality we cannot control. The philosopher and sinologist François Jullien[15] contrasts these two methods of efficacy in the following way:

- According to the Western world view, efficacy depends on projecting our will onto the world, translated in terms of objectives, means and ends, or goals that we must achieve.
- Efficacy in Chinese thought proceeds from the stance that "learns to let the effect come [...], in other words to take advantage of how the situation evolves so as to let oneself be 'borne along' by it".

---

[15] François Jullien, *A Treatise on Efficacy*, University of Hawaii Press, 2004.

Comparing the game of chess with the game of Go can help to illustrate the difference between the two. In chess,[16] the strategy is to win by eliminating one's adversary—kill the king and take possession of the whole board. The Sino-Japanese game of Go is completely different. The objective is not to eliminate the enemy or wield absolute power over the "Go-ban" (board), but progressively to consolidate co-existing territories.[17] To achieve this, players roll out a strategy of "immobile movement" (once placed, the stones no longer move) that follows the shape of the empty spaces and the lines of force of the figures that both players co-construct across the Go-ban.

The coach is more of a Go player than a chess player. The integrative coaching approach, particularly in Europe, is based on a constructivist* stance that focuses on emergence, happenings, scenarios, inventing and building possibilities, rather than a planned implementation of means designed to achieve a predefined objective. This stance underpins the whole of my strategic reflection on integrative coaching as described in this book.

Constructivist

Based on the belief that people construct their own realities and find meaning based on life experience. In other words, experience constructs reality, affecting our knowledge and understanding of the world and our place in it. Constructivism focuses on human meaning making and promotes a person's proactive participation in his or her life in order to create change.

In my work alongside very senior consultants, I see for myself, day in and day out, how they achieve good solid results. They know how to capitalize on models they have built through their experience across the planet, in order fulfil, effectively and efficiently, the expectations of the leaders they advise. My stance is complementary and respectful of their approach, but is based on logic that comes from the opposite direction to the "answer first" approach that underpins their success.

---

[16] Even though it was invented in India in the sixth century, chess was mainly developed in the Western world.

[17] In the game of Go, victory is measured by the number of empty intersections between the territories bordered by the stones of each player. Since there are dozens of intersections, the supreme art of the Go Master is to "beat" his opponent by having more empty spaces than he—in other words, to build territories of almost the same size for each territory.

Meaning and Purpose First

I start from the premise that it is up to the client to create his solution. The client—by himself, or with his teams as long as they are not disenfranchised—will implement a solution so much better if he has been its author, or at least its co-author. The only thing the coach needs to do—and this is the entry point to the whole panoply of coaching strategies—is to help him mobilize the energy needed to create and implement his solution.

The stance I take is like that of an ethnologist for whom the other person is the only one who is able to give meaning to his acts and beliefs, even if an outside perspective can help to reveal that meaning. It could also be compared to the specialist in alternative or genetic medicine, who heals by anticipating disease rather than by treating it when it has been confirmed, as allopathic medicine often does. However, though the coaching approach may be fundamentally different from traditional management, it does not exclude other perspectives. We are not in a logic of "either … or", but in an inclusive "both…and" logic which admits contradictions and paradoxes. As such it can articulate and integrate the "complicated" into the "complex" and vice-versa, as long as the appropriate tools are used.

Fundamentally the coach, like the "leader" described by Jim Collins or Simon Sinek, defines himself by centering on the question of meaning—what has meaning for the client, and gets him going. The coach does not neglect the content (the "What?") or the means (the "How?") of the engagement, but he knows that it is by focusing on causality ("Why?") and final purpose ("What for?") that people find within themselves the powerful motivators that enable them to fully express their potential and even surpass themselves. The coach certainly does not ignore problems, but as the saying goes: "Plants grow towards the light, not towards the dirt". Though we should always learn from one's mistakes, it is by nourishing ourselves on our past successes, our desires and dreams, and the future we wish to construct, that we generates within ourselves the enthusiasm and dynamics that lies at the heart of all real change. "Let us beware of walking backwards into the future", said the French poet Paul Valéry.

A Humanizing Perspective

The path that has led me to this integrative vision of coaching is neither linear nor unambiguous. It is the fruit of 40 years of experience in which I have integrated humanistic psychology*, systemic therapy, management and change management in companies, personal coaching, team building and Organization Development.

May I take here the liberty of mentioning another major source of inspiration for me: my spiritual and denominational commitment? My journey has been mainly within the Roman Catholic Church—I spent two years as a "guest seeker" at Fleury Abbey, near Orleans (though I was not a monk). I was also the disciple of a Hindu master in whose Ashram I lived for a number of months in the Netherlands, and I continue my yoga practice almost daily. During the 1990s I hosted, along with Father Minguet, several dozen management seminars involving high-level business leaders organized by the Business Centre at the Benedictine monastery at Ganagobie. In these seminars, we shared deeply on management from a spiritual perspective. This continued through the work that I undertook with the leaders of the EVH Christian CEO movement in France and internationally.

When I speak of awakening a person's conscience, the words have a spiritual resonance for me. My faith remains a strictly personal affair—the ethics of my practice as coach and trainer require me to scrupulously respect my duty of reserve. Nonetheless, the reader should be aware that spirituality and my Christian beliefs permeate my view of human nature, and all I say and do.

I remain deeply convinced that whatever our beliefs, convictions, values, or vision of the world, we all share the idea that we are "beings in becoming", in the sense of becoming who we really are.[18] This is a fundamental premise of this book.

Another fundamental premise of this book is that meaning, human growth, autonomy, freedom and responsibility are more important than material success, financial results or "productive value-add". I believe that leadership and management models need to be reconfigured from the point of view of this humanizing perspective. The "manager as resource-provider" is neither Superman nor Robocop. He is plunged headlong into complexity, and is deeply aware that he will never be able to control everything. Though he is supposed to maintain a certain mastery of events, he is no more able to do so than the surfer is able to master the wave that carries him. He navigates by continually adjusting the cursor of his action: towards the logic of control when he assumes the role of order-giver and towards the logic of subsidiarity* when he positions himself as a "meaning-bearing leader".

---

[18] As per the title of Carl Rogers' book, *On Becoming a Person*, Constable, 2004.

This is where leadership and coaching come together. Whether he plays the role of coach, manager or director, the "manager as resource-provider" sees himself as a "linkman", or "facilitator" who helps people open up to what is deepest inside them, thereby opening themselves up to change, to complexity and to the profound cultural transmutation that is needed in today's world.

What is involved in integrative coaching as described in this book is truly transformational: far beyond implementing management methods or leadership techniques, coaching is about creating the conditions under which people become conscious of the fact that to change the world around them they first need to undergo a transformation of their own identity. This implies questioning not only the role and position of leaders, but also the way they represent the world, others and themselves.

Working on identity development presupposes a certain ontological security*. This implies an ease of being, self-esteem and self-knowledge, as well as the acknowledgment of one's limits and capabilities.

> **Ontological Security**
>
> Being secure at the core of one's being (ontology is about the nature of being). This security is a key anchor for the coach when faced with complex and sometimes difficult coaching situations.

These qualities are vital in order to transcend the tensions, paradoxes, ambiguities, ambivalences, and contradictions inherent in the growth of a human community towards Collective Intelligence*. It is not only desirable, but also possible and highly profitable, to both people and organizations, to train individuals to live out this kind of relationship that combines deep humility with high ambition, as Jim Collins[19] says of "Level 5 leaders"*.

> **Level 5 leaders**
>
> Leaders who build enduring greatness for an organization. Such leaders are characterized by their humility and altruism, combined with an ambition that is first and foremost for the organization, not themselves, and a total commitment to achieve results.

---

[19] Jim Collins, *Good to Great*, pp 17–40.

At heart, the way a coach considers his client is similar to the way the coach educates his client to consider his own people. A leader is not formally a coach: his functions and accountability are different, and the very notion of "manager-coach" is based on an irreducible paradox. Nevertheless, every manager can instill a philosophy, attitude, behaviors and procedures that reflect the coaching culture, and thereby achieve a kind of "internalized coaching".

In an organization that has been set up to work in Collective Intelligence, this "knowing-how-to-be-with" is a fundamental management competence.

The coaching strategies in this book are modelled on this paradigm change of moving from order-giver to resource-provider, and provide a blueprint for those wishing to experience this kind of transformation.

The Ten Strategies—An Overview

A Set of Dynamic and Interconnected Strategies

Below is a summary of the 10 strategies that make up this book. This will enable you to see the order in which they appear, think through their intrinsic dynamics and reflect on the ways in which they interweave with each other. They are presented in logical order, but this in no way implies a hierarchical or chronological structure (Fig. 3).

- Five of the strategies are mainly "operational", and help answer questions like "what to do?" and "how to do it?"
- The next four strategies are about identity and deal with personality construction.
- The tenth strategy is special: it is a meta-strategy which underpins and encompasses all the others.

Operational Strategies

1. The **person-centered (or Rogerian) approach** is based on a stance, in the context of a trusting relationship, which is centered on the client, on his energy, his identity, his dynamics and his potential. This strategy gives pride of place to active listening, and reveals its full potential when the coach integrates a number of different approaches of humanistic psychology*, such as Frankl's focus on meaning, Kohut's focus on empathy, Transactional Analysis, and the more recent approach of Appreciative Inquiry (AI).

© The Author(s) 2017
V. Lenhardt, *My 10 Strategies for Integrative Coaching*,
DOI 10.1007/978-3-319-54795-4_2

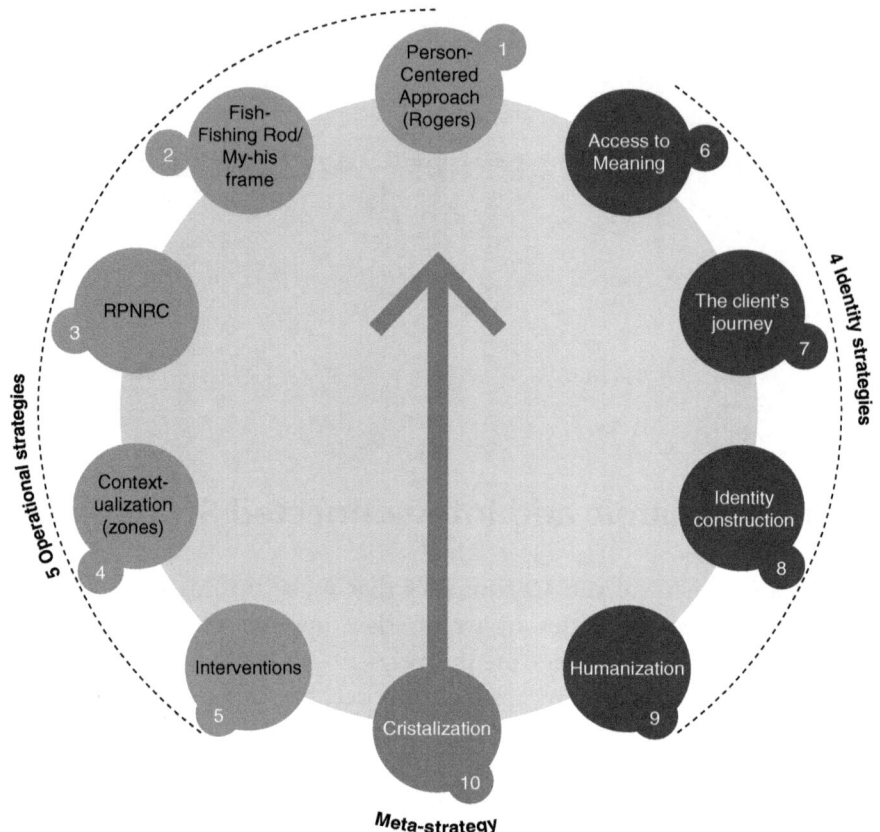

Fig. 3   Summary of the ten strategies

2. The dual alternatives that make up the strategy of **Fish/fishing rod— His frame/my frame** deal with the constant adjustments of the coach's intervention modes. Do I give my client a helping hand (a "fish") or remain in the background and help the client discover what he needs to do ("build his own fishing rod")? Do I use his frame of reference or my own? The practice of metacommunication—communicating about how we are communicating—helps the coach reach into the client's frame of reference, and also enables the client to reach into the coach's frame of reference.

3. The **RPNRC (Reality-Problem-Need-Request-Contract)** strategy highlights how a coach takes the consulting model into account when he identifies a situation, understands the stakes involved (or the problem), and identifies a need. It shows how he goes further, and differs from the consultant by engaging

in the complex undertaking of clarifying the client's request and turning this into a contract. All this occurs in the context of a peer-to-peer relationship that guarantees the client's freedom through a mutually-agreed contract.

4. Through **contextualization**—or the "intervention zones"—the coach is able to understand the client's situation, both in the light of the client's multiple interfaces, and with respect to his issues of identity. Parallel processes* will come to light in the relationship with the coach, and transferential* phenomena will occur. Contextualization makes it easier to identify the stakes, and to define a plan of work so that each coaching session finds its place within an overall timeframe and coaching framework that integrates the client's challenges, whether they relate to operations, relationships, or to his own identity.

Parallel process

A parallel process occurs when the client's unease or issues in relation to his ecosystem are reproduced in his relationship with the coach. The client "relives" the problems he has in his own relational system by projecting them onto his relationship with the coach.

5. **Intervention options** are more or less infinite, so I mention only a few broad categories: options to get a clearer diagnosis of the situation; options to gain understanding of covert elements; options to reinforce the client's ontological security*, for example by providing him with protections* (from possible dangers) or permissions* (encouragements); or options that focus on the coach's stance and his function as role model.

Protection, Permission, Potency

From Transactional Analysis. A coach provides protection when he ensures that the client is not putting himself at risk. He gives permissions by giving the client new messages about the client's resources and potential. He thus releases the client's potency.

Identity Strategies

6. Through the strategy of **access to meaning** the coach helps the client realize that the stakes involved in a given situation have a number of different logical levels. Among the models that help to identify these levels I particularly value the identity backbone*. It can be used in a

number of ways: to address the symptom; to examine the chain of causality between an event and the symptom and thus unblock the situation; to clarify a final purpose and transform the client's view of the situation by revealing a totally different, and liberating, perspective. As the coach deploys the strategy of access to meaning, the client grows in his awareness that he is a participant in a reality that is in constant movement, and this realization may bring to light a latent need, of which he had not previously been aware. He may suddenly become aware of a dysfunctional behavior, see a causal link that unblocks a situation, or even come to an understanding of a purpose in life that enables him to see the situation in a new, and liberating light.

Identity backbone

This is a tool I have developed for the coach to help align the different levels of a client's identity. It is fully discussed in Strategy 6, *Access to meaning*. At the base is the client's social identity, on which rests his organizational, then managerial and professional identities. Above that, the identity he has in his private or family life, then his intimate psychological identity. Finally there are the existential, spiritual and denominational levels of identity. The coach will help the client align these different identities, like the osteopath realigns a patient's spine.

7. The **client's journey** positions the client in the time and space continuum within which he formulates his request and is coached. The objective is to help him contextualize the change he is undergoing in the "here and now" in a manner consistent with his past, and especially with his future. Within the perspective of the client's past and future, the coach focuses on the transition the person is going through in the "here and now", helps the client clarify what he really needs, the stages he needs to go through as he changes, and the resources he can call upon to succeed in this transition. The coach also helps the client confront uncertainty, fear of change, and the inevitable bereavements that occur in all significant change.

8. **Identity construction** proposes a number of models that coach and client may draw upon to "transform the caterpillar into the butterfly". We know that in order to change the world around, a person first needs to undergo his own transformation. This strategy describes the dynamics of helping a client work on his own identity, paradigm and

frame of reference as a prerequisite for transforming the identities and range of possibilities of those around.

9. **Humanization** represents the profound final purpose of the coaching process. This strategy is about the client breaking free from his psychological fetters, his limiting beliefs or his hang-ups due to a life **script***,[1] his sense of belonging to social, ideological or professional communities, family, institutional and other ecosystems. As he becomes free, he discovers himself and takes full responsibility for his life.

> **Script**
>
> Each person decides in early childhood how he will live and how and how he will die, and that plan, which he carries in his head wherever he goes, is called his script.

Crystallization: The Meta-strategy

10. Finally, we come to **Crystallization**, a meta-strategy that continually irrigates the coaching process. Throughout his interventions, the coach remains constantly on his guard to ensure the conditions are met to enable the client's freedom to emerge, to be sustained, and then to develop into a state of responsibility, where he makes adult and autonomous choices. In other words, the client reaches the place where he takes his own decisions and finds his own solutions, even though the coach has, at certain moments, has been there to assist him.

Throughout the process, the coach pays constant attention to his stance. His management of the relationship is subtle but nonetheless fundamental to its success: he is neither consultant nor teacher, but someone who continually moves between challenging, directing and standing back in a non-directive manner. This "action-listening" attitude enables the client to gain access to his own sense of responsibility and the autonomy to make choices that are genuinely his (Fig. 4).

---

[1] See Eric Berne, *What Do You Say After You Say Hello?* Corgi Books, 1975, p 51.

1. THE PERSON-CENTERED APPROACH (Rogerian alliance)
Am I truly centered on my client's potential?

2. THE ALTERNATIVES OF FISH/FISHING ROD—HIS FRAME/MY FRAME
Should I propose a solution (give my client a fish)… or help my client build his own fishing rod?
Am I centered on my client's frame of reference or my own?

3. RPNRC (Reality-Problem-Need-Request-Contract)
What problems is my client facing? What are the stakes? What is he asking for? What does he want to do with me in this session? What does he want from me? Do we have a clear contract? Over and above the contract, are we "in alliance"?

4. CONTEXTUALIZATION (Intervention zones)
Where do the problems and stakes really lie in my client's ecosystem? In which "zones"?
Where should I focus? How might I plan the intervention as a result?
What is being played out in my relationship with the client?

5. INTERVENTIONS: CATEGORIES AND OPTIONS
In concrete terms, what should I do when I am with my client? What mistakes should I avoid?

6. ACCESS TO MEANING
What is the meaning of the work I am doing? At what level of meaning are my issues and my stakes (professional, family, personal, spiritual…)?

7. THE CLIENT'S PATH
How does the current stage fit in my client's journey? Where is my client coming from? What is his past? Where is my client going? What does the future hold for him? What transition space should he consider?

8. IDENTITY CONSTRUCTION
What does my client need in terms of his identity? Deconstruction? Restoration? Construction? Reconfiguration? All four? What balance between actions, relationships and searching for meaning? How to align what is important (profession) with what is essential (personal life)?

9. HUMANIZATION
How can I help my client become more aware of his finiteness, his limits, and become more himself in all his fullness? How can I help him find himself by developing his empathy and his capacity to accept otherness? How can I help him become freer, fully accept that freedom, and become more responsible?

10. CRYSTALLIZATION
How can I help my client become the architect and owner of his solutions and decisions?
And avoid doing things in his place!

Fig. 4   Key questions for each of the 10 strategies

Key Considerations around the Ten Strategies

A Constructivist Space

Presenting the ten strategies in a linear, step-by-step manner enables the reader more easily to identify the right point of entry at the right time. However, the strategies are not independent approaches: they form a synchronic, systemic* and holomorphic* whole—the part generates the whole, and the whole generates the part—whose causality is recursive and circular. Each strategy both influences, and is influenced by the others; each triggers, and is triggered by the others.

For example, if I have taken a Rogerian, person-centred approach, and I believe that the person in front of me possesses in himself the solution to his problem, I will consider using the strategies of *Humanization* and *Identity Construction*. If, I decide to give my client a pill to swallow ("give him a fish" in terms of the *Fish/fishing rod—His frame/my frame* strategy), my interventions and their consequences will not be the same as if I decide to insert a needle like an acupuncturist to free up the energy in my client so he can find a solution for himself.

Each strategy can link to another, use its tools or mirror it. Each one contains all the others, and is contained by them—which is what I mean by holomorphism. They are dynamic, and evolve within a constructivist* approach: the coach welcomes the thoughts, words and emotions of his client, and thereby assists the passage from latent to explicit awareness that is generative of action. The coach holds the different interrelated strategies continually in his mind and is able to welcome whatever emerges and is continually constructed for the client and coach in the space of their relationship that represents the "betweenness" of their alliance (Fig. 5).

Expanding Awareness

Strategy 2: *Fish/fishing rod—His frame-my frame* describes in detail what I have called third-order listening. For the moment, suffice to say that it describes the way the coach listens to what occurs within himself (thoughts, behaviors, bodily or emotional manifestations) during a coaching session. I believe third-order listening is one of the keys for keeping an overall perspective on the various strategies so as to use them wisely. To use the metaphor of the iceberg again, I intervene for the most part on the visible part of the iceberg, but am conscious of the hidden part underwater: the unconscious, the emotions, effects on the body, and everything in the client's internal ecosystem. These elements come and speak to the underwater part of my own iceberg. Using third-order listening, I become aware of what is happening within myself, and in turn use the appropriate strategy to help my client become aware of what is happening within himself. Part of my role as coach is to take into account the totality of the "iceberg-to-iceberg" interactions in our relationship.

When I speak of the "underwater" part of the iceberg I mean not only the unconscious structures that gradually reveal themselves to our awareness, but also what Viktor Frankl[2] calls the "transcendent unconscious": a domain of

---

[2] Viktor Frankl, *The Unconscious God*, Simon & Schuster, 1976.

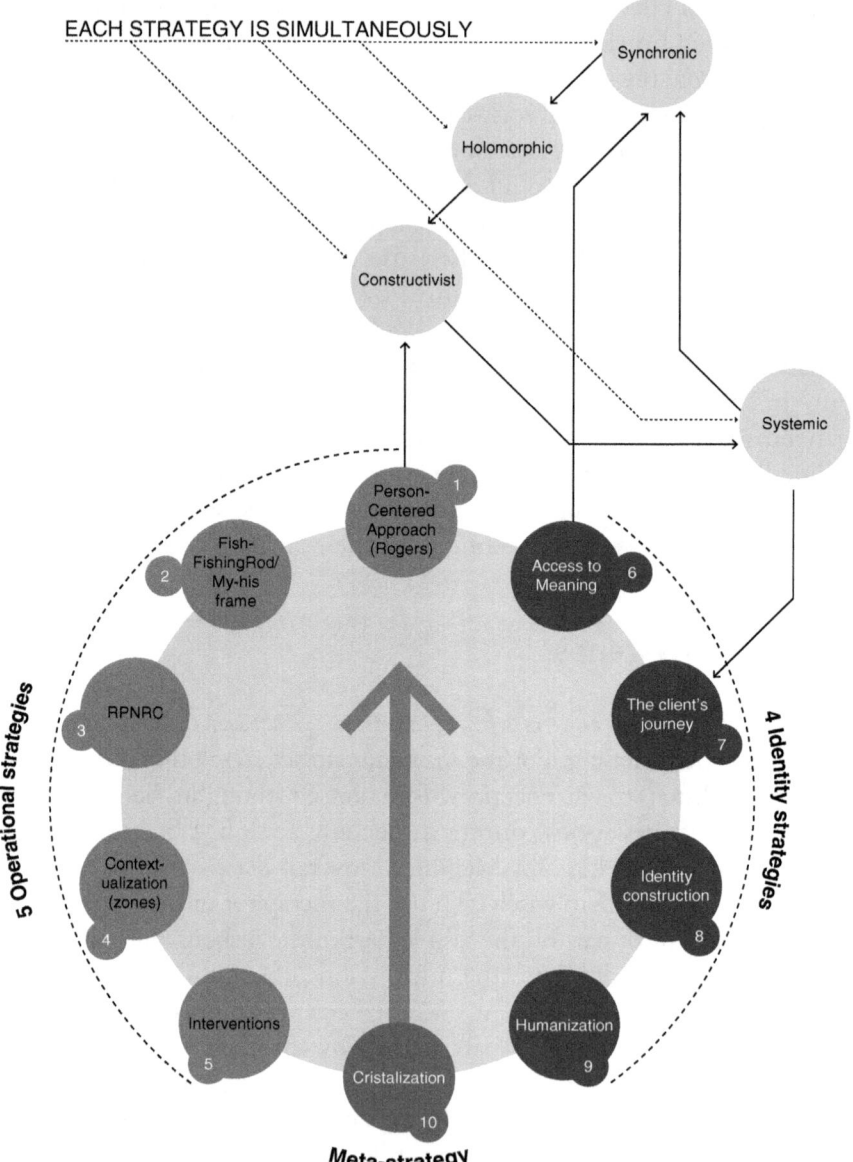

EACH STRATEGY IS SIMULTANEOUSLY

Synchronic

Holomorphic

Constructivist

Systemic

5 Operational strategies

4 Identity strategies

Person-Centered Approach (Rogers) 1

Fish-FishingRod/My-his frame 2

Access to Meaning 6

RPNRC 3

The client's journey 7

Context-ualization (zones) 4

Identity construction 8

Interventions 5

Humanization 9

Cristalization 10

Meta-strategy

Fig. 5   The 10 Strategies seen as holomorphic

intuition and spirituality, the study of which Frankl calls "noetics". This view of human reality is based on the belief that human beings are moved by things other than psychological forces and manifestations. Raymond Panikkar speaks of a "cosmo-theo-andric consciousness"[3] to describe this part of human nature that is at once cosmic and spiritual. This perspective takes us beyond the frontier of mind and body, Psyche and Soma, and gives us access to a person's spiritual dimension—beyond the visible, beyond even the senses, but discerned through intuition (Fig. 6).

From this perspective my client, like me, is a pneuma/psycho/somatic personality made up of not only a body (soma) and a mind-soul (psyche) but also of a spirit (pneuma). This view of human nature helps me personally, as a coach, to welcome the whole person, in his multi-dimensional complexity.

The strategic approach developed in this book aims to open the helping relationship to all these possibilities and levels of awareness and self-actualization. Using a mix of the ten strategies, this expanded awareness can enable the coach to intervene at the appropriate levels without reducing the complexity of the client. In some circumstances, the coach may act within a highly

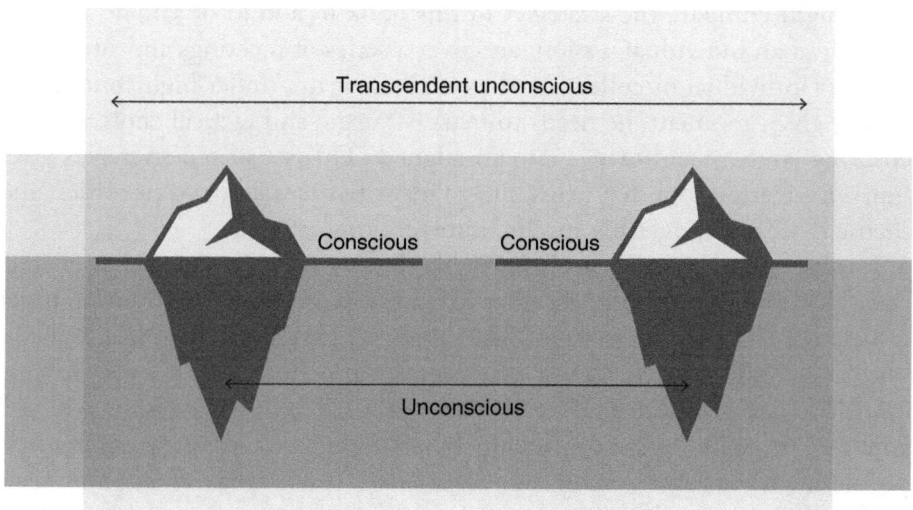

Fig. 6 Conscious, unconscious and the transcendent unconscious

---

[3] Raymond Panikkar, *The Trinity and the Religious Experience of Man: Icon-person-mystery*. Orbis Books, 2009.

mechanical paradigm, like a doctor who prescribes a pill. At other times he may adopt an attitude close to that of a psychoanalyst who places his patient in a position of being able to listen to his unconscious and the primal elements of his own history revealed by the transferential* elements that lie at the heart of the coaching relationship. In yet other situations, the coach will rethink his whole strategy as an existential dimension emerges, where the meaning of a "here and now"' event needs to be redefined in terms of final purpose rather than past causes—that is, in terms of how the client represents his own inevitable death, and what he wants to do (or not do) with the years that remain to him.

Associating coaching and strategy implies a true capacity for integrating multiple paradigms. The coach needs to be able to shift from a "microscopic" view to a "helicopter" perspective, to jump at a moment's notice from one point of view to another as a result of what has meaning and what emerges in his, then in the client's consciousness. The coach is there to support, if not guarantee, the client's awakening and awareness-raising process.

The Satnav Metaphor

One might compare the strategies in this book to a kind of satnav.

Both in an individual session, and over a series of meetings and situations, whether individual or collective, the coach navigates under high complexity. At any given moment, he needs to make strategic and tactical choices, while ensuring strategy and tactics remain aligned. This set of ten strategies gives him a navigation tool that helps him to identify the stakes and priorities, and then choose and target his specific interventions.

Having these strategies to hand is like having a good satnav that enables the coach to process a large number of diverse pieces of information in order to help the client on his journey. The satnav knows some, if not all the roads, but never obliges the driver to take a given direction. When I am driving, even if I take a different route to that proposed by my satnav, it will still continue to guide me by continually adjusting its calculations from my new position, without ever getting angry or sulking. It will speak in its gentle male or female voice and will continue to comment on my progress, whilst pointing me in the right direction.

With the help of the perspective provided by these strategies, the coach will be able to enjoy watching the client make his own way, and be content to help the client discover his route—and maybe even design and build his own road.

Because, of course, it is the client, not the coach or the satnav, who is doing the driving!

Strategies for Helping the Coach Become a True Professional

The coaches I train have told me that beyond the operational concepts and keys for understanding it provides, this ten-strategy model helps them inform their own theory as they live and practice their trade.

Their comment highlights a central element in turning the coach into a true professional: acquiring a set of tools and references and using them so that:

Practice informs theory, just as theory informs practice.

Doing this involves distancing oneself from one's own practice, and then dialoguing with oneself, as one would with a supervisor. This act of distancing enables the coach to metacommunicate* about where he is in his journey, why he is acting the way he is, or why he is choosing one option over another. This can even be done with a client, and can help the client to become more aware of what is happening, both in the relationship and within himself.

Metacommunication

A way of communicating about how one is communicating that enables both parties in a conversation to distance themselves from and understand what is going on between them. It can include "all exchanged cues and propositions about (a) codification and (b) relationship between the communicators".

Nevertheless, consciously using these strategies should never stop the coach from intervening instinctively or intuitively when the situation requires it.

Mastering this set of strategies, discerning the limits of tools and techniques and then being able let go when one comes to the end of one's own competence as a coach. This, in the end, is what make the coach a true professional.

Strategy 1: The Person-centered Approach, or Rogerian Alliance

Am I truly centered on my client's potential?

The Client at Heart

All ten strategies combine to structure the coaching intervention as they interlock and influence each other. The person-centered approach has pride of place in that it permeates all the other strategies, and underpins the whole coaching relationship. It is holomorphic* in that it contains, and is contained by, all the other strategies.

My conviction about the primacy of the person-centered approach stems from a number of radical realizations during my journey over the years.

One of the most significant moments in this journey was my encounter with Carl Rogers' theories of education in the 1970s. In his book "Freedom to Learn",[1] Rogers states, on the basis of his experience as a university teacher, that it is impossible to teach anyone anything; one can only facilitate

---

[1] Prentice Hall, 1969. The approach Carl Rogers invented and developed in the 1960s and 1970s, according to which a person possesses within himself the resources needed to learn about, and better accept himself. The "Rogerian" position taken by the person accompanying either an individual or a group, is deployed through active listening (both the verbal and non-verbal messages of the client) and orients the relationship towards a non-directive process. See also two books by Carl Rogers: *On Becoming a Person*, Constable (new edition) 2004 and *Encounter Groups*, Penguin 1973.

© The Author(s) 2017
V. Lenhardt, *My 10 Strategies for Integrative Coaching*,
DOI 10.1007/978-3-319-54795-4_3

learning. His idea, so simply expressed, turned my beliefs about access to knowledge and about therapy upside down.

Rogers' "person-centered approach" was reinforced in my training as a therapist in humanistic psychology*, in particular Transactional Analysis (TA). It became even more deeply engrained in me as I read Eric Berne and other practitioners of TA[2] who all encouraged its use.

My experience in the Cathexis Institute in San Francisco, where Jacky Schiff was able to free schizophrenic patients from the chemical straightjackets in which previous therapies had bound them, was another revelation for me. Even in someone considered "seriously ill" psychologically, and diagnosed as a danger to himself and society, there remains a healthy part that can understand what is happening, is capable of participating in his own healing, and can become an active player in his own transformation.

During that period the Asklepieion school, founded by Martin Groder, was very active in prisons. Taibi Kahler, my supervisor at the time, joined me in a therapy group in Cummings penitentiary near Little Rock, Arkansas. As a result, several dozen prisoners underwent a transformational process that resulted in more than 60% not reoffending. This reinforced in me the idea that it is possible to trust the person one is helping, as long as this trust is based on activating the radiant, rather than the shadow part of his being.

Other realizations came as I trained in humanistic psychology* and human potential, experiencing them first as client, then as a trainee therapist. One such experience is what John Pierrakos called "Core energetics".[3] One very simple practice of his was to take the patient by the hand, and, addressing him gently and full of kindness, invite him to answer a few direct and clear questions. After only a few minutes the patient, feeling unconditionally accepted and loved, would begin to trust the therapist, trust himself, and little by little take the risk of dropping his defenses.

A few years later, I read the works of Francisco José Varela.[4] Putting Rogers' approach together with Varela's concept of enaction* was a revelation to me, and was foundational in determining the way I developed my approach of helping the client to set himself in motion—or enact his own world—rather than bring him solutions. For me, the ultimate goal of a

---

[2] Especially the Gestalt therapists Bob and Mary Goulding, mentioned in the Introduction.

[3] John Pierrakos, *Core Energetics: Developing the Capacity to Love and Heal*, Life Rhythm Publications, 1990.

[4] *Principles of Biological Autonomy*, Elsevier/North-Holland, New York, 1979; *The Embodied Mind: Cognitive Science and Human Experience* (with Evan Thompson and Eleanor Rosch), MIT Press, Cambridge, 1991; *Ethical Know-How*, Stanford University Press, 1999.

person-centered strategy is to help the client become the creator, or at the very least the co-creator of his solution. This is also the overall goal of coaching.

> **Enaction**
>
> A dynamic process of world-constitution, beautifully summed up by the poet Antonio Machado:
> *Wanderer, the road is your footsteps, nothing else; There is no road, you lay it down in walking.*

Prince(ss) meets Prince(ss)

> **Princes(s)' Alliance**
>
> When the Prince(ss) at the heart of the client meets the Prince(ss) at the heart of the coach, a special, powerful alliance is created that generates solutions for the issues facing the client.

The concept of the Princes(s)' Alliance*—another way of articulating the Rogerian alliance—is the fruit of this journey. It was inspired by the metaphor Eric Berne used for therapy. When in front of his patient, the therapist often sees his client as a "frog", locked up in his limiting beliefs and the difficulties generated by his script*. The therapist is not trapped by this image, since he knows that someone else is hiding behind the mask. With the help of his "magic wand", the "frog" becomes the Princess or the Prince.

This metaphor reflects a belief that lies behind humanism and most faiths: behind our masks and defenses, in the deepest part of ourselves, there lies a positive part—call it what you will—that is just waiting to blossom and flourish. Though I have chosen to use Berne's metaphor, the Princess or Prince is not a fairy-tale figure, but represents all a human being can be when he is truly free—ontologically secure*, kind to others, congruent with his own values, and taking full responsibility for his own transformation and life journey. Since the growth potential of the Princess or Prince is limitless, a free person is always being and becoming.

The view of human nature underpinning integrative coaching is that a person is capable of progressing and changing by activating this positive part of himself. Carl Rogers' theories are perhaps the most radical statement of this view, and they tend towards Rousseau's debatable view that human beings are fundamentally "good". I believe that each and every person is capable of the best, but also of the worst—as borne out by our own personal experiences and by History itself. Though the notion of free will is ambiguous, we subjectively experience it as our capacity, at any given moment, to choose between good and evil. I do not agree with those who say that hell does not exist. I have seen people live through different forms of hell on earth: they may be ill, living in a prison of lies, in a poisonous relationship, or living through a cycle of self-destruction. They also often make hell of others' lives.

What is important here is that the coach has a realistic perspective on the ambiguity that constitutes our fundamental human nature—each of us can make our own lives (and the lives of others) into hell or heaven.

Whether human beings are fundamentally good or not, each of us possesses a certain measure of free will. In all its ambiguity, this free will can be lived out experientially as the ability, at any given moment, to choose between good and evil. Even if we can be tempted to do the worst, through our free will we can also show ourselves *capable of the best*. This is where coaching is intimately linked to Carl Rogers' person-centered approach. The work I do as a coach, with respect to myself and to my client, consists in seeking the best in me and in him, while being aware that we are on a quest—or a conquest—that is always tentative, and never definitively attained.

This reminds me of a story Father Minguet once told me about a very old monk in a desert monastery. Father Anthony, a devout old man, is close to death, and the members of the community are gathered around him. The young monks, sad and confused, are torn between the knowledge that Father Anthony is on his way to heaven after many years of self-denial and kindness, and their feeling of losing a loving father and spiritual guide so full of wisdom. The devil uses this situation to make one last attempt to vanquish him. He disguises himself as a monk, comes close to the half unconscious Father Anthony, wakes him, shakes him, and asks him: "Anthony, do you recognize me?" Of course Anthony recognizes him, having so often fought against him. The devil then pulls out his secret weapon and adds: "I wanted to meet you just before you die, to pay tribute, and to acknowledge that you have vanquished me by your humility." Anthony, having reflected a short while, draws his breath, looks at him and replies: "Hmm, I see I am not yet dead!"

This story illustrates a fundamental principle in coaching: accepting the other unconditionally, seeing the Prince(ss) who lives within, yet realizing that the other's positive side is always fragile. No-one can be reduced to his positive side; at the same time, everyone has a positive side that can be discovered and developed—and this includes psychotics and criminals.

Accepting the other person unconditionally opens the door for him to understand that he is able to change, and leads him on to become an agent of his own transformation.

This is where humanistic psychology* and traditional psychiatry part company. From the perspective of humanistic psychology, people do not heal through pills that put them in a chemical straightjacket, though medication may sometimes be necessary. People heal when they are empowered to take charge of their lives, thereby activating their own positive energy. When people are energized in the context of a trusting relationship, they begin a process of healing, restoration and true fulfilment. As Irvin Yalom, the great American therapist, said throughout his teaching: "the place of healing is the relationship".

From this point of view, coaching may be seen as closely related to alternative medicine. The coach, like the acupuncturist, simply frees up the person's blocked energy through his "needle of intervention". Another metaphor for coaching might be gene therapy, which works on a person's DNA: it is not just about finding renewed energy, but also about discovering and changing the base script* through which the client gives form and meaning to his life.

For Rogers, who asserted that he had "never taught anyone anything", non-directiveness is a consequence of fully accepting the other person. Though non-directiveness is not a sacrosanct principle, it remains fundamental to coaching. Even if the coaching process evolves within a structured relationship, it is not up to the coach set the client's direction. Non-directiveness is an expression of both an absolute respect for the client's freedom, and of the coach's confidence that the client possesses, within himself, the necessary resources and desire to move forward. It goes with active listening—another attitude inspired by Rogers. Active listening can take many forms (silence, reformulation, open or closed questions) but is always centered on the client, and what emerges from the client.

Accepting the other person unconditionally means fully welcoming his frame of reference, without restriction. It also means accepting the fact that there exists an irreducible incommunicability between human beings. Each person is unique, with a "map of the territory" that the coach can only partially access. As François Varillon[5] says, the human person is not an "enigma", but a "mystery": able to be partly understood, but never fully comprehended as a subject. Unconditional acceptance involves unconditionally accepting the mystery of the other person. This leads me to suggest that the coach is not so much a

---

[5] *Joy of Faith, Joy of Life*, Paulines, 1993. page 10.

pedagogue (a teacher) as a mystagogue (an initiator into mystery) who initiates his client into the mystery of relating. By his empathy, the quality of his listening and his kindness, the coach encounters the mystery of his client. Because he never encloses his client in his own frame of reference, he enables his client to open up to the mystery of relating to others.

Relating is central to this view of human nature. If we wish to become who we really are—not an isolated individual or an ego separate from others, but a "social being", even a "being in fellowship"—we can only do this through intersubjective* relationships.

Relating is at the heart of being. The coaching relationship is about developing another "being in the world", a "being who is with others, 'for and through' others". When a coach or a manager opens up to this dimension, the color of the coach-client relationship—or even more, the leadership relationship—takes on a new hue. The intersubjective space of relating becomes the place where the capacity for accepting otherness, and the talent for cooperation and sharing is fostered.

When this happens, the relationship becomes a shared space of construction—of the other by the coach, and of the coach by the other.

To help others move forward and build their lives, the coach—or the manager—needs to be on his own path of personal development. Through his own transformation, he becomes a lever for the transformation of others; in return, the transformation that others go through challenges the coach and helps him open himself anew to the world.

Françoise Dolto[6] once responded to the question: "What do you do when you listen silently to your client?" by saying: "I work on myself".

This intersubjective dynamic is the wellspring from which the processes of co-construction emerge to address the issues and challenges facing the client.

A Matrix of Empathy

The coach's challenge is to free up the potential that lies behind a person's defences, behind the "frogs", behind the masks we wear (and that we need to keep in part, because of social constraints—it is hard to imagine a social life

---

[6] French paediatrician and psychoanalyst, famous for her research on babies and childhood.

where people never wear masks). The coach's role in the helping relationship is to build the trust and openness needed for the Prince(ss) to come to life. It is here that the coach's Prince(ss) meets the client's Prince(ss), and generates the Princes(s)' Alliance*.

It is this small miracle that John Pierrakos, my teacher in bioenergetic therapy, performed again and again as he took a person with him by the hand, and spoke so powerfully from his own Prince that the other person in a few short moments opened himself up to his overflowing love. It is when I experienced this for myself that I deeply understood the extraordinary liberating power of this kind of alliance. From then on I decided to adopt and practice this approach, as best I could, in my personal and professional life.

To generate this Princes(s)' Alliance is to create what the Austrian psychoanalyst Heinz Kohut[7] called a "matrix of empathy". Far from the famed and respectable "neutrality" of the psychoanalyst, therapists—and even more, coaches—who practice humanistic approaches are able to create this matrix of unconditional acceptance of the client, though they do not disregard the issues generated by the neurosis of transference*.

In his book on the global development of empathy, *The Empathic Civilization*,[8] Jeremy Rifkin speaks of how the writings of Melanie Klein, William Fairbairn, Donald Winnicott, John Bowlby and René Spitz all converge on the primacy of a need even more fundamental than the libidinal drive: the need for empathy. Kohut speaks of the mother's role when breast feeding, which is not only to offer her nipple to enable the baby to get the mother's milk, but also—and above all—to create a space of kindness, tenderness and play as the mother joyfully invites the baby to take possession of the tip of her breast. This enables the child to be active in not only nourishing itself, but also in meeting the world through its mother, its primal sensory reality. By taking possession of the mother's breast, the baby develops itself. Its mother opens up a space for initiative that enables the baby not only to nourish itself, but also to apprehend the world in a gesture of self-creation.

---

[7] Heinz Kohut, *The Analysis of the Self: A Systematic Approach to the Psychoanalytic Treatment of Narcissistic Personality Disorders*, University of Chicago Press; Reprint edition, 2009. Kohut's axiom was that the self "arises in a matrix of empathy".

[8] Jeremy Rifkin, *The Empathic Civilization: The Race to Global Consciousness in a World in Crisis*, J. P. Tarcher/Penguin Putnam, 2010.

For me this is a beautiful metaphor for the coach's stance with his client (though of course the coach will never "mother" the client). Through his unconditional acceptance and his capacity to generate a matrix of empathy, he creates the conditions whereby his client becomes the author of his own deeds, life and identity through enaction*.

The coach will never make the client dependent on him. Instead, he helps the client free himself from any dependencies he may have, and develop his own sense of responsibility and autonomy.

The coach watches his client, recognizes his positive part, and trusts him. As he becomes aware of this, the client discovers and frees up within himself the energy needed to break through his defenses and his barriers to change. Educational psychologists call this the "Pygmalion effect", where the student's potential is activated by the teacher's positive outlook. This is not an idealistic approach: the "frog" is neither repressed nor forgotten. Trusting the client does not mean the coach accepts anything and everything; indeed the coach is there to challenge, question and change attitudes, behaviors and beliefs!

Empathy

Listening to one's own emotions involves listening intelligently to those of others. In a helping relationship, the coach resonates with his client.
Empathy is not sympathy. Sympathy, etymologically speaking, means to "suffer with", and can be defined as "sharing" the feelings and emotions of the other.

Empathy, contrary to sympathy, means that I do not confuse my own stance with that of the other person. I enter into contact with what the other is feeling, but remain aware of my own feelings; I do not identify with the other person. In other words, empathy preserves intersubjective distance. This emotional intelligence enables the person in charge of the relationship, whether he is a coach, manager or leader, to have access to the stakes involved in the other person's ecosystem, including meaningful elements that the other person may not yet be fully aware of. When the coach expresses this understanding, the client feels genuinely understood.

Empathy does not require the two parties to agree, nor does it resolve all the issues. It does, however, enable the creation of a bond, which is one of the functions of leadership. Moreover, the difference between the way each party perceives his own emotion and the emotion of the other sheds light on where each party stands in the relationship, and where they are on their respective personal journeys.

The coach who understands this possesses a key to unlock situations and, more generally, to adjust the relationship according to two key factors: how far the client is on his development path, and what is at stake.

From Personal to Organizational Development—Pygmalion at Work

The dynamic of enaction* has its place, not just in personal development, but also at the heart of organizations. Douglas McGregor's pioneering research on management[9] led him distinguish two theories of authority and control used by managers. According theory X, work is not natural to a human being, who is productive only when constrained or threatened. Theory Y says that work is natural for a human being; to become productive all he needs is autonomy for his creativity to be stimulated and "set free".

Each of these views reflects a belief about human beings and a vision of management in organizations. If we consider that work is not natural (theory X), motivation needs to be found from the outside; management is then exercised in the form of external control and positive or negative reward ("the carrot and the stick"). If, on the other hand, we consider that work, and beyond that, the desire to create a better world, are natural (theory Y), then people's key motivation is no longer extrinsic, but intrinsic, and the appropriate management style is to create a dynamic of self-evaluation and self-regulation.

In practice—things are never black and white—coaching and other Organization Development approaches need to continually move the cursor between the two poles of management logic. However, the coach always has theory Y in his mind's eye, and his end goal is enaction*.

Before being a therapist and coach, I was a consultant and trainer in Organization Development (OD). OD looks at the organization, not as a mechanical entity on which to perform an external intervention, but primarily as the dwelling place of a human community. At the time, I noticed that if I offered assistance by education and positive support rather than by giving advice, a community would find within itself the means to build its own solutions and to develop itself autonomously.

I believe that it is not only possible, but highly desirable to cultivate the Pygmalion effect in companies. The change agent can be external or internal, a coach, trainer, or manager-coach. He needs to be in a position of authority and vested with the identity of a resource provider or meaning bearer. Though the role of change agent can be effective at all hierarchical levels

---

[9] Douglas McGregor, *The Human Side of Enterprise*, McGraw-Hill Professional; Annotated edition, 2006.

(team, department, business unit, enterprise) or within a cross-functional project, the impact of change is exponentially increased when it is the Board who initiates and drives it, thereby setting the whole business in motion.

This is not about "management techniques": some leaders know instinctively how to instill a relationship with their people that builds their confidence, reinforces their ontological security*, opens up their range of possibilities, and mobilizes their energy so that they give the best of themselves. It also has nothing to do with manipulation, as long as the rules of the game are made explicit, and accepted by all involved. Though one might speak of charisma or leadership capability, it seems to me that the term "alliance" most adequately describes this mysterious transmission of energy: the manager-coach is "in his or her Prince(ss)", sees the Prince(ss) in others, and helps others to give meaning to what they are doing, in accordance with their deepest motives.

Levels of Change

The same philosophy lies behind personal development and change management in business: people have a desire to change, and to find their Prince or Princess.

Whether it is in the context of individual, team or organizational coaching, it is important to identify to what depth managers and their teams are willing to go, as well as the nature of their request, their degree of resistance to change, their maturity and their openness. This enables the coach to intervene appropriately. (Fig. 7)

There are at least seven levels of change. Each requires a different kind of coaching.

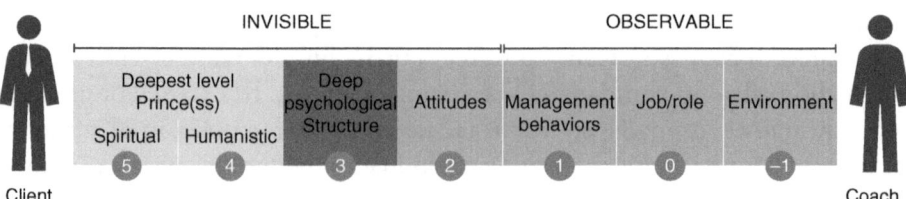

Fig. 7   Levels of change

Level -1 is the most visible. This is about change in the external environment where a person operates. It focuses on company culture, policy and strategy, management systems, competence grids, and collective change initiatives. A new organization may affect the overall functional definitions of the players involved, but will not necessarily change their job description or have an impact on their identity. Change at this level remains largely impersonal.

Change at **level 0** is about a change in people's **job** or role. Here they are more personally involved. It is about their job description, budget, personal scorecard, challenges, responsibilities, resources, or "territory" as they take up a new role (a classic situation for coaching). It may involve helping managers define their teams, draw up a roadmap, or better manage their budget. It also involves addressing certain difficulties inherent in taking up a new position, especially the "impostor's complex" ("I was incompetent, but up until now nobody knew; now everyone will see that I'm not up to it"). By definition, those who take up new responsibilities do not master the domain they are in the process of discovering, and yet they have to demonstrate that they are in charge—one of a number of paradoxical situations they need to learn to cope with.

At **level 1**, we touch on changing people's **behaviors**—without necessarily changing their underlying attitudes. In the first instance, it is about helping people change certain behavioral patterns in order to increase their chances of achieving a specific result (a successful hiring interview or negotiation, a new product launch, persuading an employee not to resign…). At a deeper level, it may aim to help people develop their "management style" by working on listening skills, communication or openness to others. If the coaching involves moving from being an order-giver to "manager as resource-provider", it will be about both. While consolidating his competence in giving orders and ensuring rules are followed and boundaries put in place, he will also learn to be a "resource" by giving them permission to act while providing them with the necessary support and protection, and by creating a collaborative climate that stimulates their energy and creativity—this requires a specific kind of coaching, but remains at level 1.

As we dig deeper, we reach **level 2**, which is not just about changing outward behaviors, but working with clients on their inner **attitudes**—the belief sets, values and world view that condition their actions, decisions and behaviors. Moving a person from an attitude of subordination to delegation, and then on to subsidiarity* is a radical change. It involves transforming the person's view of management, and along with it, their relationship with people in power. Here, behavioral change is not enough: this paradigm change requires working through the client's mindsets, sometimes beyond that of his professional role.

Level 2 corresponds to type 2 change as identified by systems thinkers, where the system itself changes, not just its visible attributes. Whereas the previous levels dealt with the visible part of the iceberg, level 2 begins to go below the waterline, where one meets the deeper layers of identity that are not directly observable, but that are to a certain extent revealed by behaviors.

Level 3 represents the transformation of a person's **deep psychological structure**: his past, family grouping, his psychological wounds and defenses, the unconscious, his primal emotions and bodily tensions. Even though it is sometimes difficult to identify the frontiers beyond which we enter level 3, it is important not to cross them. Even a life coach should not pry into this secret part of a person's life—he is not equipped to do so, and any intervention at this level amounts to amateur therapy. Within organizations, it is even more important not to cross this frontier.

At **Level 4** (existential), we go beyond people's psychology **to the heart of their human dimension, to the Prince(ss)**—what makes a person deeply human. The energy released here breaks through the defences at other levels of change and generates enaction.

Level 5 goes to a person's deepest level, to **the spiritual dimension of the Prince(ss)**. Here too, the energy released breaks through the defences at other levels of change and generates enaction

This raises the question of how deep change can go in an organizational context, since it is at level 3 and beyond that a person finds the resources to live the change fully. How can we manage a transformation at all these levels, if we cannot work beneath the surface?

My experience in coaching has led me to two observations.

- Firstly, it seems possible to live through extraordinary change in one's personal or professional life without necessarily engaging in therapy.
- Secondly, it is the Princes(s)' Alliance that enables this change to happen. When the relationship is sufficiently open and secure, the coach does not need to intervene explicitly beyond level 2 for changes to happen at the deeper levels where the Prince(ss) abides.

During the coaching process, the coach passes through these levels as the client reveals them to him—like the different layers of onion skin—and joins the person in the secret garden of their Prince(ss) (Fig. 8).

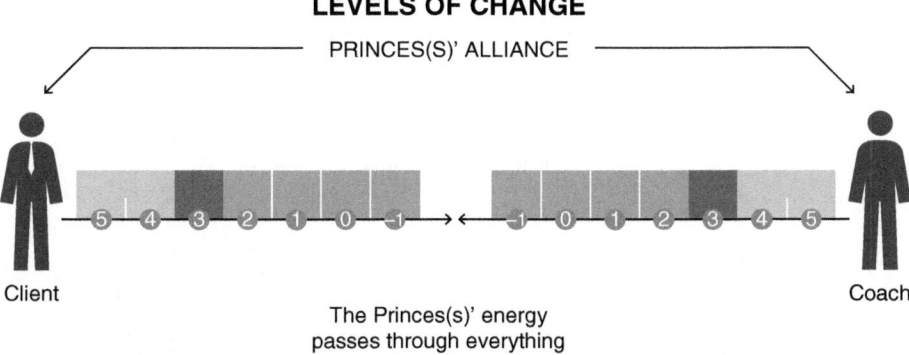

Fig. 8   Levels of change and the Princes(s)' Alliance

The Princes(s)' Alliance

A simple way of representing these levels, which I owe to John Pierrakos, is that of the mask (the outside envelope), the "frog" (the negative self) further within, and the Prince(ss) (the positive self) at the heart of a person (Fig. 9). In my experience, the positive self can expand and radiate, powerfully yet gently within and beyond the person (rather like Yalom's rippling effect[10]).

When a helping relationship becomes a Princes(s)' Alliance, the client experiences something deep, mysterious, beyond the rational: an energy which radiates from the client or client team, breaks through barriers and defenses, and sometimes has an immediate and decisive effect on the issues at stake. This enthusiasm, confidence, or "charisma", carries others along on the crest of its wave with a rippling effect across the organization.

I have experienced this phenomenon a number of times with business leaders (especially the three with whom I co-authored books). These leaders and their teams had not done any special therapeutic work, and yet their personality, the way they had learnt lessons from their past experience, and

---

[10] Yalom describes rippling in the following way: "the fact that each of us creates——often without our conscious intent or knowledge—concentric circles of influence that may affect others for years, even generations. [...] The idea that we leave something of ourselves, even beyond our knowing, is a potent answer to those who claim that meaninglessness inevitably flows from one's finiteness and transiency." *Staring at the Sun*, Piatkus, 2011.

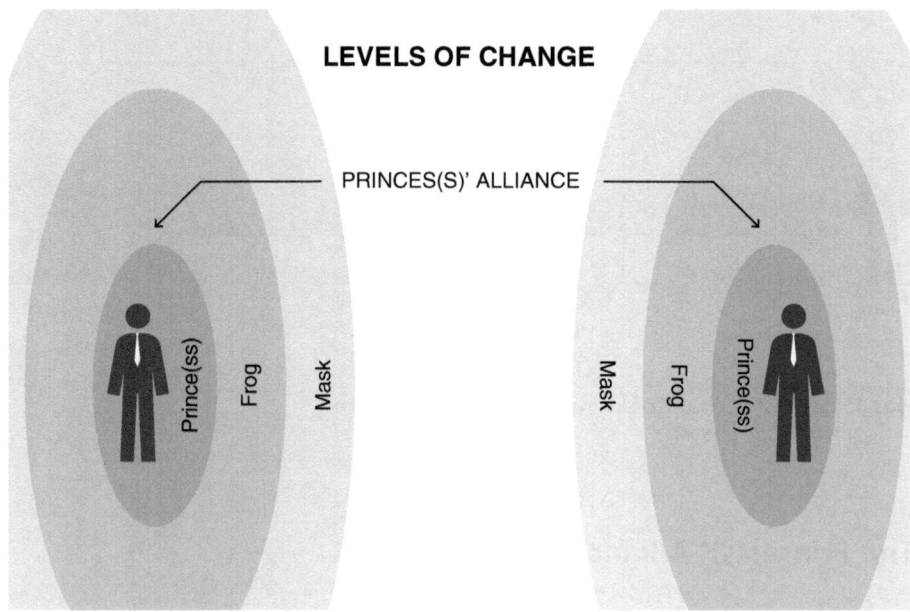

Fig. 9   The Princes(s)' Alliance

their personal commitment generated extraordinary energy, that radiated from their Prince.

Because of the above, the coach can help his client live through seemingly improbable, exemplary and extraordinary transformational experiences, whilst avoiding unduly trespassing into the domain of therapy.

Being Able to See the Prince(ss)

Let us pause to consider how the coach looks at both his client and himself when they bond in an alliance. The coach activates his deep beliefs about the world and mankind, anchors himself in his own ontological security*, deals with the layers of emotions that might shut him in, and connects with his Prince—this deep part of himself full of love, that every human being possesses. It is this special way of being in contact with the most intimate, positive and rich part of himself that enables him to see the other in this unique way, and to create an alliance with the client. The quality of the relationship thus established will generate an energy in the client that has the power to break through his defenses and pass through all the different levels of his identity.

Masculine/Feminine

We are all at the same time both a Prince and a Princess. According to Jung, each human being has an *animus* (the masculine part) and an *anima* (the feminine part). These two dimensions live together within each of us without one ever completely displacing the other. There are two sides of the helping relationship—whether coaching, training, therapy or management coaching—that the custodian of the relationship needs to balance. The feminine part, which consists of listening, empathy and relational openness, and the masculine part: taking a stance, reminding the client of the laws of the land, or exercising a certain authority when putting protections* in place and giving permissions*. Because the coach has opened himself up to this duality and welcomed both masculine and feminine parts in both himself and the client, he implicitly makes the client feel unconditionally accepted in the relationship with the coach.

This in no way implies the coach should ignore a client's pathologies or harmful behaviors. However, the client needs to feel unconditionally accepted and considered with love and kindness.

Third-Order Listening

The Princes(s)' Alliance implies a certain stillness and presence, both of which form part of the matrix of empathy. The coach can use different types of listening, such as the active listening technique of reformulating feelings, or various questioning techniques. But his key competence is in the use of what I call third-order listening: third-order listening involves empathetic listening (in contact with the emotions of the other) rather than sympathetic listening (identifying oneself with the emotions of the other). While remaining attentive to the client's stakes, and all that goes with them—his emotions, his past, his current situation, his sense of social belonging or his ecosystem—the coach stays constantly in contact with his own emotions, including how what is happening resonates with him bodily, emotionally, in his fantasies and in the behaviors he observes in himself.[11]

---

[11] I discuss third-order listening more fully in Strategy 2: *Fish-fishing rod/His frame-my frame.*

From Socrates to Frankl, towards Modes of Generative Questioning

The coach's techniques may include "Socratic questioning*" (or Socratic maieutics) to help the client "give birth" to what he already knows without being conscious of it. The Rogerian alliance takes this further and draws from a number of sources to help clients set themselves in motion, co-construct solutions, and move into enaction*. The coach may use techniques for interpreting the subconscious from psychoanalysis, or draw upon the use of ego states*, scripts* or games from Transactional Analysis. He may also call upon notions of Gestalt therapy or Bioenergetics to accompany the client's emotional and bodily feelings, and help him access his own sensations or emotions. Techniques to help the client create meaning can be found in Logotherapy, developed by Viktor Frankl, whose three constitutive values are: **creation** (what I bring to the world), **experience** (what I get from the world) and **attitudes** (the meaning I give to events that I had not wished for, but which enable me to construct meaning for my life). These techniques not only help a person come to terms with his past, but also help him to face the present and the future, whilst being careful to avoid hyper-reflection.[12]

Socratic questioning

Socratic questioning is used to help uncover the assumptions and evidence that underpin people's thoughts in respect of problems. For example: "Why do you think that?...And why is that?...Are you aware of another explanation?"

Ego State

Transactional Analysis splits the different ways we express different parts of our personality into three main ego states: Parent, Adult and Child (written with capitals to distinguish the states from actual Parents, Adults and Children). The Parent corresponds to that part of the Self that was formed under the influence of one's parents and other close parental figures. The Child corresponds to our spontaneous self, or our obedient self. The Adult corresponds to our rational self.

---

[12] Viktor Frankl speaks of hyper-reflection to describe a person's tendency to go over past scenes again and again, and remain locked up in his past, rather than building his present and future.

My recent encounter with Appreciative Inquiry,[13] which takes Rogers' approach even further, has reinforced my view that coaching should not focus primarily on problems to resolve with the client, but on the stakes involved. Problems need to be taken into account, but in looking for a solution I first focus on the client's imagination to help him tap into his resources, his past successes, and what is needed in order to reignite his enthusiasm and appetite for life.

This approach generates a positive dynamic that activates the potency of the client and elicits a story-telling process. The client constructs himself by telling the story not only of his past but also of his future on the basis of his successes, qualities, competences, and especially the desires and dreams that mobilize and nourish him. This approach goes beyond the Socratic questioning that seeks to deconstruct a person's frame of reference. It also goes beyond the questioning used in active listening, the assessment of ego states in Transactional Analysis, or the analysis of sensations in Gestalt therapy. Appreciative Inquiry seeks to probe into the living experience of a person, his own resources, what deeply motivates him and is the source of his successes. It uses questions that generate stories rather than static responses. For example, instead of asking a person what vision he has of the business where he is working, the coach will ask about what makes him proud to work there, or what motivated him to choose that organization as a place to build a meaningful life project. This questioning can lead the client to realize the meaning of his work, and he may end up saying things like:

Yes, my friend, of course I'm cutting a stone. But can't you see, I'm building a cathedral!

A Code of Ethics for a Princely Alliance

Coaching objectives are many and varied, and may differ in both their nature and what they are trying to achieve. They may range from resolving a short-term issue to the long-term support of a person, a team or an organization in

---

[13] A Diana Whitney, David L Cooperrider, Jacqueline M Stavros. *Appreciative Inquiry Handbook: For Leaders of Change* Berrett-Koehler Publishers; 2nd edition, 2008. In chapter 1 they define Appreciative Inquiry as: "An approach to change management that grows out of constructionist thought and its applications to management and organizational transformation. Through its deliberately positive assumptions about people, organizations and relationships, AI leaves behind deficit-oriented approaches to management and vitally transforms the ways to approach questions of organizational improvement and effectiveness."

a process of deep transformation. Whatever the objectives, the coach uses all the means at his disposal to enable the desired results to be achieved in line with the client's request—but not to the deliver the result itself. His pledge is to put in place the enablers, but not to achieve the result, for several reasons. Firstly, the coach's job is not to force others to change. Secondly, he does not have a "magic change pill" that he administers to his clients. Furthermore, the change delivered at the end rarely coincides with what was requested at the beginning. Of course, the coach does everything he can to help his "champions" to attain the best performance they can, but he is there to help them find within themselves the means to change and to develop themselves. If we use the image of the goose and the golden egg, the coach focusses primarily on goose's fertility so that she can produce her golden eggs, but is not targeted on how many eggs the goose produces. Otherwise he is in danger of being exploited by others—or even exploiting others.

The individual is always more important than the objectives. The foundation of coaching practice is total respect for an individual: the client is unconditionally accepted, just as he is. It is this respect for the other, the clarity of the framework for action (limits, permissions* and protections*) and the strong stimulus that comes from freeing up the client's energy, that provide the operational impetus for success. Coaching is not about using motivational or influencing techniques, let alone using one's position to indulge in any form of abusive influence. The boundaries with respect to seduction, power and money need to be clearly stated, and should in no circumstances be infringed.

The coach needs to guard himself against acting like a "guru", in the bad sense of the word. Those who manipulate others use the intersubjective* relationship and its transferential* elements to take control of their subjects. They know they hold sway over the individual, and take a narcissistic pleasure and perverse joy in seeing the other person regressing, getting completely involved in the relationship and becoming completely dependent. This scenario is in complete contradiction with the coaching approach, whose first and foremost concern is to develop an individual's freedom and autonomy. There are times when the client's request takes the form of a call to look after him and become a rescuer* (in the psychological sense: who does things in the place of the other). When this happens, it is vital for the coach to have gone through the grieving process of any fantasies of omnipotence—one more reason why the coach needs to have been through therapy.

The coach is neither an amateur therapist, nor a therapist in disguise. There is a nonetheless a therapeutic dimension to coaching, as in all helping relationships, since the process itself brings the client into a virtuous cycle of self-confidence, self-esteem, and appeasement in his relationships with others. The coach activates a restorative energy at other deeper levels of the client's identity and relationships—yet without directly touching his psychological structure, which remains "out of bounds", and represents the limits of his intervention compared to therapy. This complex, ambiguous, subtle and intimate dimension of the coach's intervention requires constant watchfulness, coupled with a steadfast refusal to give in to the temptation to respond to the request of the client in domains outside the contract they have agreed. When the request cannot be managed within the framework of the coaching relationship, the coach should refer the client to the competent helping professional.

The coaching process requires a climate of trust, so that the client at all times feels both respected and protected from any kind of manipulation or perverse relationship. It also requires tacit agreement on the level of mutual commitment between coach and client—"how far are we willing to go together?". This "alliance for change" is much more than a simple legal contract; it implies a strong intellectual, psychological and emotional complicity—not only between the parties, but also with those around them. At the same time, this alliance also needs a formal contract that guarantees a protected space-time where the parties can confront each other, refocus, and even shake each other up, as they tread the path of change together.

By putting a formal contract around the relationship, the objectives and the means to achieve them—"Where? When? How? Who recommends? Who pays?"—both coach and client establish their shared responsibility with respect to outcomes.

By putting in place the Princes(s)' Alliance, the coach and client establish the space within which they relate and generate the energy that enables them to achieve that outcome.

Key Points and Pause for Reflection—the Rogerian Alliance

The questions below will help you think through how much the Rogerian Alliance is part of the helping relationships that you manage. They are designed to help you search inside yourself, so it is important to take your time, even if it is only to think through one question, rather than simply going through a "checklist" exercise.

1. "For and through the Other". To what extent am I really focused on developing the potential of the other person?
2. To what extent is it my constant concern to develop the other person's autonomy rather than to increase my own standing?
3. To what extent do I take care to center myself in an attitude of deep openness, and to connect with my Prince(ss)?
4. To what extent am I careful to make myself available, in a state of "inner emptiness" (akin to fasting), of ontological security*, and of deep stillness, so as to receive the other?
5. While paying attention to what the other person is saying (the "content"), to what extent do I pay attention to the relationship, my intuition, my emotional intelligence and third-order listening (the "process"), as well as the final purpose of our conversation (its "meaning")?
6. When I see "Masks" and defensiveness (the "Frog") in the other person, to what extent do I respect them, and then identify and kindly and confidently acknowledge the Prince(ss) behind them?
7. To what extent do I make sure that a Princes(s)' Alliance emerges and is strengthened between us, once I have understood the nature of the stakes involved, and the level of change requested?

Strategy 2: Fish/fishing Rod—His Frame/My Frame

> *Should I propose a solution (give my client a fish)…*
> *or help my client build his own fishing rod?*
> *Am I centered on my client's frame of reference or my*
> *own?*

The Fish/fishing rod—His frame/my frame strategy is all about mobilizing the energy of the coach and client, in synergy with one another.

Fish/Fishing Rod

The Fish/fishing rod metaphor illustrates a central issue for the coach: does he propose a solution, or at least the beginning of a solution ("give the client a fish")? Or does he teach the client to help the client find his own solutions and become autonomous ("fish for himself", or even "build his own fishing rod")?

Throughout the relationship, the coach constantly adjusts the emphasis between these two alternative polarities. In the end, however, the coach's objective—as opposed to that of the consultant or the expert—is always to create the conditions under which the client develops his own solutions, using the co-constructed relationship with the coach to support him.

© The Author(s) 2017

V. Lenhardt, *My 10 Strategies for Integrative Coaching,*
DOI 10.1007/978-3-319-54795-4_4

Giving the Client a Fish

When I give my client a fish, I stand alongside him and look at the situation that is causing the problem, or I work with him through the stakes involved. In a certain way, I take up the issue and help my client resolve it by proposing a diagnosis of the situation, suggesting potential options, and bringing a certain number of things to the table to move things forward—information, thought processes or tools. This is similar to the standard "answer-first" approach of a consultant: he brings the richness of his experience and expertise to the situation, provides the analysis and suggests a solution that not only solves the client's problem, but also enhances his own standing with the client, so as to vindicate his intervention and justify his fees.

This approach has its advantages. The client no longer feels alone facing the situation, and may even have the feeling of being cared for. However, the coach runs the danger of taking the client's place and becoming a "rescuer".[1] When this happens, the solutions the coach proposes never truly become the client's own, and even when they do not work he is never be able to discard them in an autonomous manner. Furthermore, he may simply reject them because he does not feel his own perspective has been taken into account.

Bertrand Martin[2] confirmed this to me when he confided the following, from the fruit of his long experience: "As CEO, I am careful not to express my ideas too soon. Instead I elicit ideas from the person I am with. If I tell him my idea, it will never be his idea: it will be the CEO's idea."

Providing a Fishing Rod

As a coach, I pay attention to the issue at hand, but I refuse to propose ready-made solutions. I focus on my client and my relationship with him, considering him to be fundamentally competent. I nurture a process of empowerment that develops my client's self-confidence and opens his awareness to a range of new possibilities. I work to trigger the resources he needs to become

---

[1] In the sense used in Stephen Karpman's Drama Triangle, which has three roles: the victim, the rescuer and the persecutor. See Karpman, S. *Fairy Tales and Script Drama Analysis*. Transactional *Analysis Bulletin*, 7(26), 39–43, 1968.

[2] Former CEO of New Sulzer Diesel France, with whom I wrote *Dare to Trust* (*Oser la confiance*, INSEP Consulting 1996; not translated into English).

the sole decision maker with respect to any potential solutions we may have developed together. I may even take this to the extreme and let him develop solutions on his own, simply lending him an empathetic ear. By proposing a fishing rod, I give my client a sense of responsibility.

Examples of fishing rods

The coach has a number of fishing rods in his toolbox, in the form of "content" or "process". But he is always careful not to propose a solution (a "fish"). Here are some possible options:

- Information useful to the client such as knowledge of the problem, domain expertise, or standard management practice.
- Feedback. This may include the coach's analysis of the situation, including his feelings and interpretations. It may also include feedback from the coach's Third order listening—his bodily sensations, his emotions or his behaviors.
- Elements based on the coach's experience, which is not yet part of the client's frame of reference.
- The coach's own behavior, attitudes, etc., that the client can then internalize when he moves into action.

This option is not always available, either because my client has not yet reached the degree of autonomy needed (see below on autonomy), because the relationship needs to be refocused, or because his is facing urgent or important issues that need a more directive approach.

Which Approach, When?

In my experience, the coach needs to use both approaches: these two approaches are not contradictory, but complementary. It is not "either... or", but "and": the fish *and* the fishing rod.

The coach helps the client find solutions—not solutions out of the blue, but solutions co-constructed between client and coach in an ongoing process as the client matures, becomes ever more autonomous and develops a deep sense of responsibility for his own solutions.

Fig. 10, Fish/Fishing Rod illustrates how the coach either addresses the coach's problem directly by giving a fish, or works with the client so the client has the means to create his own solution, or fishing rod.

There is no hard and fast rule that defines up front when in the relationship, or in which circumstances, the coach should adopt one stance over another. In some cases, silent listening is all that is needed, though the

FISH OR FISHING ROD

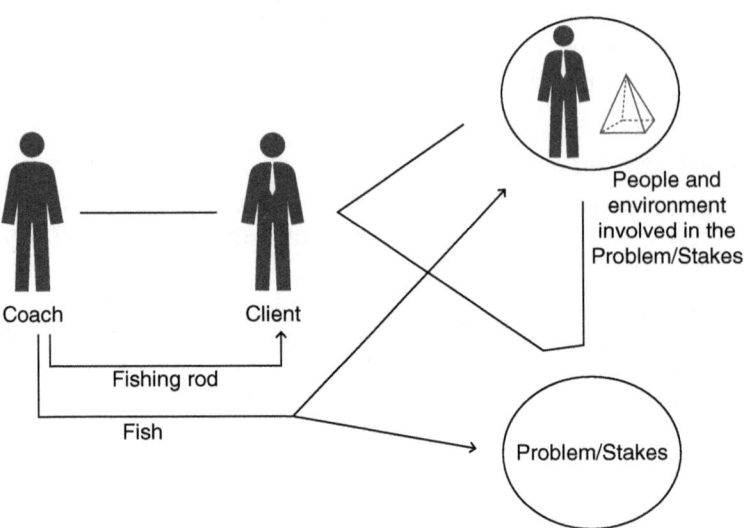

Fig. 10   Fish/fishing rod

coach's non-verbal messages will signal that it is active listening. At other times the coach will express himself and take a more proactive stance: suggesting paths for action, providing feedback, putting in place protections* by pointing out potential dangers, or giving permissions* by encouraging the client's initiatives.

The coach needs to define his own strategy in the context of the ambiguity and ambivalence between these two stances as the coaching process evolves. At any given moment the coach has to decide which stance to take, based on the overall coaching strategy he has defined. The coach's skill lies in his capacity to find the right stance at the right place at the right time, in line with his relationship with the client. This situational intelligence* takes a number of parameters into account, such as:

• interferences that may exist between the coach's and the client's frames of reference;
• how well each is able to listen to the other;
• how well coach and client are able to metacommunicate;
• the client's degree of autonomy.

His Frame/My Frame

Behind the *Fish/fishing rod* strategy lies a more subtle interaction: that between the coach's and the client's frames of reference*. *His frame/my frame* introduces a new perspective: as a coach who wishes to help my client create his own solutions, should I put myself within my client's frame of reference, focusing on his freedom, autonomy, potential and self-fulfillment? Or should I invite my client to "borrow" my frame of reference in order to rebuild his own frame of reference? I may need to do the latter because I know things he does not, I possess certain competences he needs to acquire, or he needs to nourish himself on the strength and energy I can communicate (Fig. 11).

> ### Frame of reference
> The way a person represents the world, including his culture, social groups, values, past history, mental maps, psychological structure, competences and resources.

Here again, ambiguity is ever-present, and the coach constantly adjusts the cursor as he juggles with the two frames, using parameters such as the context, the importance of the problem and the client's attitude. If the client appears lost, confused, overexcited or on the contrary, passive, it is probably appropriate to use the coach's frame of reference. This point of external

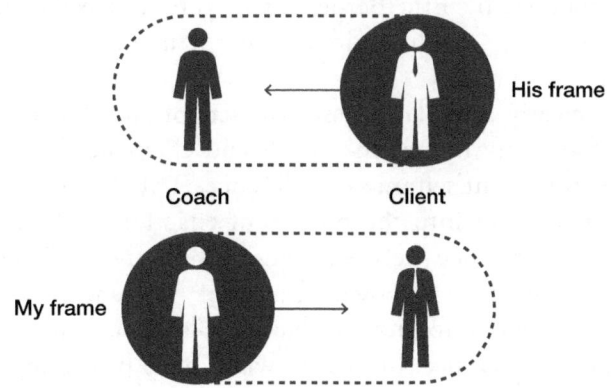

Fig. 11 His frame/my frame

support enables the client to rebuild himself. However, whenever the coach chooses to take up this "dominant" stance, he should be ready to leave it at a moment's notice in order to take into account what is emerging from within the client. The coach then opens up to the client's frame of reference, actively listening to him, providing a kind and welcoming presence and giving him his trust, so that the client can discover within himself the resources he needs to be able to progress. As the coach oscillates between the two, a relationship gradually takes form that enables the client to draw upon his own inner resources in order to progress.

Young—and even experienced—coaches are sometimes under the illusion that they should only take up a listening attitude, and avoid taking a firm stance with respect to their own frame of reference. On the contrary, taking up a clear stance once the client has expressed himself is actually one of the most fruitful attitudes a coach can take, as long as this is done appropriately and intelligently. Here are some examples.

> *I hear you loud and clear...AND I have a different view.*
> *What you are saying does not seem completely right to me...AND there are some issues that you have either not seen, or not taken account of.*
> *The emotions you are expressing don't match the situation.*
> *I see you are angry, yet what you are going through is opening up opportunities for you.*

Taking up a firm stance does not necessarily involve confronting the client head-on. The coach can draw on at the very least the eight "therapeutic operations" proposed by Eric Berne: interrogation, specification, explanation, confrontation, confirmation, interpretation, illustration, and crystallization.[3]

In order to clearly articulate these two sets of alternatives (Fish/fishing rod and His frame/my frame) the coach and client need to establish and work through the client's frame of reference. This is an essential step in helping the client enter into the process of enaction*. The key to success is optimizing the balance between these alternatives. When the coach intervenes from within his own frame of reference, he nonetheless remains on the lookout for non-verbal signals about the client's experience and frame of reference. Similarly, when he is projecting himself into

---

[3] Eric Berne, *Principles of group treatment*. New York: Grove Press, 1966, pp. 233-247.

the client's frame of reference, he never stops listening what is going on inside himself.

The solution emerges from the relationship

It is generally accepted in coaching that the solution lies with the client. This is not always entirely correct. In reality, the solution emerges within the intersubjective* space of the relationship, even though the client normally does most of the work to craft a solution and identify what needs to be done.

In order to allow the client to craft his solution, the coach sometimes needs to take up a directive stance, or even, in certain circumstances, to confront the client. At other times, the coach needs to "let go", or place himself somewhere between the two extremes, or even oscillate between the two frames of reference. The coach needs to know how to operate all along the continuum and, at any given moment, to be able to go back and check the nature of the relationship and its evolution in order to know where to place the cursor. Business leaders that I have coached have often said to me: "When you say 'yes', I know that you would have said no if needed. I rarely get this from my employees or even my life partner."

The coach's stance is different to that of a consultant in that it is fundamentally ambiguous and paradoxical. When he lets go, he needs to retain some control. Conversely, he takes control and brings certain elements to the table in order to be able to let go and for his client to express himself freely. As the coach helps the client through the different stages of autonomy, he at the same time inevitably maintains the client in relative dependence (which must of course remain healthy). Fully displaying one's talent as a coach means knowing how to step aside and to **dissolve one's own competence in the other's competence.**

It is by constantly offering a kind and accepting perspective, an actively listening ear, and the required protections* that the coach enables the client to move forward, and achieves the paradox of **being the helper who ensures that the other no longer needs help to craft his own solutions.**

The way the relationship is managed determines what is achieved (within the context of the formal request documented in the contract). The relationship is not just an "adjustment variable", it is the wellspring of the dynamic of autonomy that the coaching process sets in motion.

Metacommunication: The "Listening Word" and the "Eloquent Ear"

When coaching my client, I am always ready to pause at a moment's notice, and let whatever is surfacing in the other person—a sudden realization, maybe—to express itself. Eliciting what is behind a sigh involves giving free expression to an emerging emotion that may have been suppressed or repressed, but may be deeply significant.

The practice of the "listening word" and the "eloquent ear" is based on a skill that Gregory Bateson discovered in the 1930s, then formalized by the Palo Alto systems thinkers and called metacommunication* (from the Greek *meta*, "beyond or at a higher level") or "communicating about how one is communicating". It also describes a special kind of communication that includes the totality of the messages exchanged between two or more people, including non-verbal messages that either reinforce or contradict what is said.[4]

In the training course I run, we use pictures to help our students become aware of the fundamentally ambiguous nature of our representations of reality. The image of the "two cubes" is the simplest, and perhaps the most striking. In *Fig. 12, One...or two cubes?*, one can see a cube perceived either from below or from above, depending on one's perspective.

Each of us will spontaneously look at the cube in a certain way. At the beginning, we can only see one of the forms (or Gestalts*). We think this is the only way of seeing the whole picture. When we are confronted with a different perspective, either from another observer or when we take the time to explore the image for ourselves, we realize there are other ways of looking at the picture. Both cubes coexist, the only difference is the way we look at them.

Gestalt

In Gestalt psychology, a Gestalt refers to the integrated structures or patterns that make up our experience at a given moment. They cannot be broken down into individual parts, and exist only as a whole "form", or Gestalt of that experience.

When we place ourselves on the edge between these two perspectives, we realize that that both realities are possible simultaneously, yet at any given moment our eyes can only see one or the other, depending on how we, the observer, frame what we see. When two observers' points of view diverge, each needs let go of their own frame of reference in order to adopt that of the other person: in other words, they need to "metacommunicate".

The cubes can be seen as metaphors for our frames of reference. Our cultural reference points (linked for example to the country we grew up in, the language we speak, our social milieu, our education or our jobs) are

---

[4] *Communication: The Social Matrix of Psychiatry*, Gregory Bateson, (Ruesch and Bateson, 2008, p. 209 ff.)

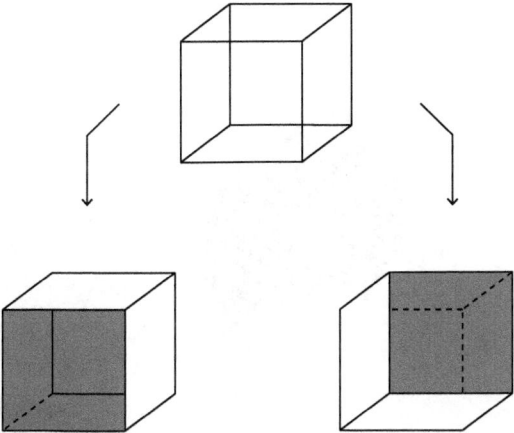

Fig. 12   One...or two cubes?

largely unconscious. They condition both the way we represent reality and the way we communicate about the reality we have constructed. Two people who do not have the same frame of reference need to distance themselves from—or rise above—the way they represent the world. By doing this, they place themselves in a "meta" stance, which gives them a broader perspective that enables them to integrate, or at least to be open to, the other's frame of reference. Those who have been through a significant transcultural experience, such as being immersed in the culture of another country without speaking the language, are often well prepared for this level of communication. Others are likely to need a certain amount of practice!

Metacommunication is an essential part of the basic "gymnastics" of coaching. Practising it is more valuable than attending all the courses in communication you can go to. Resolving conflicts, adjusting frames of reference, clarifying people's assumptions; all this requires a capacity to be at the same time "inside" the communication and the relationship, and at the same "abstracted" from them. The coach is a direct actor in the relationship, and at the same time the analyst of what is going on, both for himself and for his client. This is how he maintains a global vision of the stakes involved for his client, whilst ensuring that the specifics of what he is doing with the client remain relevant.

Other classic exercises such as Boring's figure (Fig. 13) also help us understand this mechanism. The person who sees an elegant young woman from the back left, and the person who sees an old woman with a headscarf

Fig. 13 Boring's figure

from the front left, are both right. But it is impossible to see more than one woman at a time, *because you have to change the way you look to see the other image.*

If John sees the figure in one way, and Mary sees it in another, John needs to "let go" of his own representation in order to see what Mary sees. The German psychologist Wolfgang Köhler calls this moment "insight", when one suddenly moves from one Gestalt* to another. John can only see the new solution when he has completely reorganized the elements he is looking at. An effective way of moving from John's perspective to Mary's or *vice-versa,* is to use metacommunication, whereby both share what they each see and feel. In his work with the client, the coach not only metacommunicates (communicates about how they are communicating—or not communicating), but also plays a role as educator, to help the client realize that there is another, irreducibly different, way of seeing things. As the coach opens up this space for metacommunication, opening up to other perspectives becomes a continuous process in the coach-client relationship. As the coach keeps the space open, both parties come to realize that there will always be a part of the other's frame of reference that remains mysterious and forever inaccessible.

In spite of all our efforts to understand the other, we can never fully see what the other sees from his frame of reference.

Let us come back to Boring's figure. What the two parties observe (an "event" in general semantics*) cannot be seen directly. Reality is accessed through representations, which are themselves the result of a person's mental processes. Both coach and client believe they are directly accessing reality, but in fact they are interpreting the world through the "black box" of their frame of reference. This black box is composed of at least three elements: the person's past (history, education, experience…); the present (the context in which he observes the event, with all its different interactions); and above all, the intention the person has when communicating about his representation (Fig. 14).

General semantics

In general semantics, it is always possible to give a description of empirical facts, but such descriptions remain just that—descriptions—which necessarily leave out many aspects of the objective, microscopic, and submicroscopic events they describe. According to general semantics, language can provide people with a structural 'map' of empirical facts, but there can be no 'identity', only structural similarity, between the language (map) and the empirical facts as experienced and observed by people as humans-in-environments.

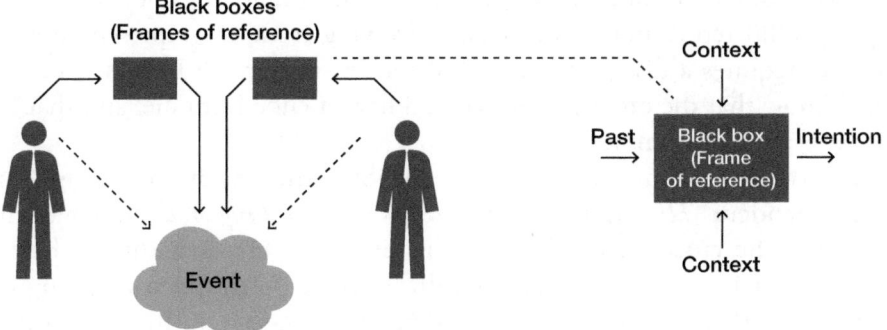

Fig. 14 Metacommunication and black boxes

The only thing we can really communicate about is our subjective experience of reality, in other words our representation of reality, not objective reality itself.

In the end, metacommunication means communicating about the way we see things with our respective frames of reference. Each person speaks from their own experience, history, context and intention—in short, their mental map, by which they represent their world. Again, in the end we cannot fully access the other's frame of reference, only certain elements of their "black box".

The black box: past history, context and intention

We can only access reality by sharing our respective frames of reference. Each "black box" is conditioned by the person's past history, the current context, and the person's intention when communicating.

An irreducible mystery

When I speak out of my black box, I can only communicate certain elements of it. I also only have access to the other person through my and the other's perceptions, not their mystery and unconscious parts.

Meta and Telos

My job as coach, using metacommunication, is to create the conditions whereby we move from a monologic mode (I'm right, you're wrong) to a dialogic mode (I understand your frame of reference, you understand mine). Forging the Princes(s)' Alliance* enables us to go even further and enter a teleologic communications mode (the logic of end purpose). You accept my frame of reference as I accept yours, and together we co-construct and take hold of a common vision and a common frame of reference, focused on the future we wish to build together, imbued with the meaning we have each given to it.

I see a different cube to that seen by my neighbor, yet both images are equally valid representations of reality. Moving from one representation to another requires a discipline that I call the "meta stance": I can see a cube, but I know that the other person sees a different cube from me, and that his vision is as valid as mine.

This ability to metacommunicate enables the coach to manage the interdependent *His frame/my frame* and *Fish/fishing rod* strategies by adjusting the cursor depending on the situation. He does this by listening to what is going on inside himself, what he perceives to be going on inside the other and what he understands to be going on in the relationship (Fig. 15).

Learning this "meta" stance is an essential part of developing the coach's identity. As we have seen, it depends on the coach becoming aware of his own frame of reference, and then exploring and constantly decoding the client's frame of reference. However, the act of sharing representations of reality will never enable us to reduce that mysterious dimension that imbues each and every intersubjective* relationship: we will never be able to communicate with the other in the way we can communicate with ourselves, because of our ever-present unconscious, and of the irreducible uniqueness of our identities.

Activating this "meta" stance is one of the main aims of training in integrative coaching. It helps the coach take into account the whole person in all his complexity. For the coach, this means being fully involved in the relationship, whilst at the same time standing back from it and taking a global perspective that includes himself, his client, and the relationship.

Mastering metacommunication enables the coach to do the following:

- Genuinely share representations with the client, whilst accepting that each frame of reference cannot be reduced to the other.
- Maintain a global vision of the stakes at hand for all parties at all times, so the coach knows where to "insert the acupuncture needle" (see Strategy 3: *RPNRC,* and Strategy 4: *Contextualization*).
- Ensure the relevance of the approaches and intervention modes used in the coaching process, and constantly adjust them using situational intelligence* (see Strategy 5: *Interventions*). No intervention is good in itself: its value depends on a number of factors, such as context, timing, the level of autonomy of the client, the level of development of the relationship, or the nature of the problems encountered and their urgency and importance.

So What is Third-order Listening?

Over the course of a series of coaching sessions, the relationship constantly oscillates between the coach's frame of reference and that of the client. The key factor here is the ability of the coach to move, at a moment's notice, from operating within his own frame of reference—perceiving what he himself is doing—to focusing on the client's frame of reference—understanding what is going on for the client. This metacommunication assumes that the coach is constantly checking his attention and his intuition for optimal focus. As he does this, the coach uses three orders of listening.

- **First-order listening** is when the coach concentrates on the words the client is saying, and the way the client is saying it.
- While noting what the client is saying, the coach pays attention to the client's non-verbal communication. **Second-order listening** is centered on the other's speech rhythm, intonation, physical posture, body language, mimics and gestures. These are often more eloquent than the words being said.
- **Third-order listening** is directed towards the coach himself, as he notices what is happening inside himself at a number of levels. Firstly, he listens to what his body, his emotions, his mind and his behavior are saying. Depending on the situation, and what the other person is saying (explicitly or not), the coach will feel certain bodily sensations: he may feel cold, or hot; he may feel tense or relaxed; or he may breathe with more or less difficulty. Secondly, he may feel a wide range of emotions—joy and anger, love and boredom, tenderness and irritation. Thirdly, his mind may sometimes be flooded with unexpected thoughts—fantasies, projections, or things harking back to his own past. Finally, when the coach becomes fidgety, constantly shifts in his seat, stutters or sighs, it is an expression of something that needs to be understood. It is up to the coach to embrace these phenomena and the information they bring, since they can enlighten him on what is being played out in himself and in the client through their relationship.

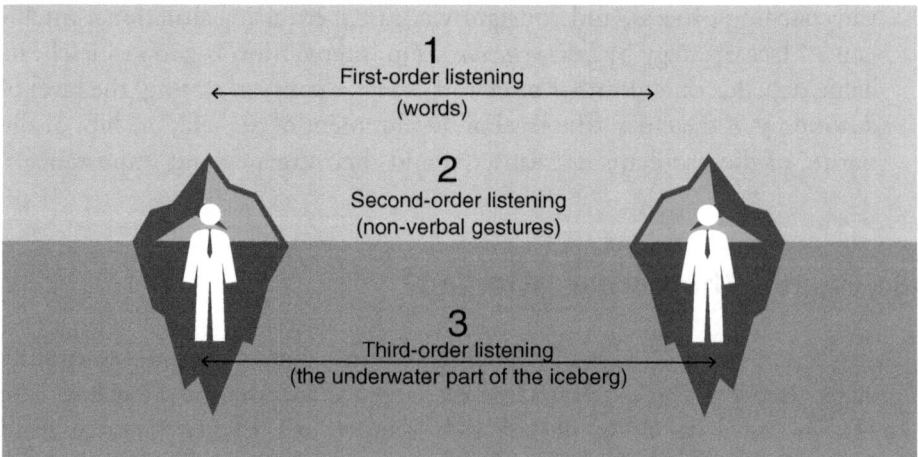

Fig. 15 The iceberg and third-order listening

At the level of unconscious fantasy, the client's transference* onto the coach may reactivate some of the coach's ancient, partly-resolved conflicts. His bodily, emotional and behavioral reactions are all involved in any counter-transference that may occur. They provide him with important information about what the client is activating more or less consciously in the coach. Paying attention to these manifestations of the unconscious encounter between the two parties helps the coach to understand what is happening as he takes into account the external context, the client's subjectivity, the coach's own subjectivity, and the intersubjective relationship itself, along with all its processes. This awareness enables the coach to distinguish between issues relating to the "here and now", and those resulting from transference or parallel processes*, where "there and then" issues are crystallized in the "here and now" client-coach relationship.

A prerequisite for the use of third-order listening is the coach's previous deep therapeutic work on himself. If he has done this, the counter-transference that occurs during his coaching practice can provide invaluable information as to what is happening below the waterline of the iceberg. This helps him establish an appropriate diagnosis and carry out the right kind of interventions (questioning, reformulating, feedback...) as he takes the client through an awareness-raising process. The purpose of metacommunication through third-order listening is to help the client center himself so he can become fully conscious of the issues involved, free himself from his chains, and move to enaction*.

Autonomy and the Paradox of Education

Helping the other to do away with my help: this is how I summarized the coach's educational paradox in my previous books. To do this, the coach needs to continually oscillate between the two extremes of the "Fish/fishing rod" alternative. At any given moment he may switch between intervening and listening, and he needs to know how to move one way or the other depending on the situation, or on new elements in the relationship. Even when he is listening, he is on the verge of intervention—and, as we have seen, in a certain sense he is in fact intervening when he listens. In order to help the client do without his help, the coach is an agile gymnast who takes up a stance that corresponds to the level of autonomy he has diagnosed in the client.

The notion of autonomy has a special place in an integrative coaching culture: it is central, cross-functional and holomorphic*.

- It is **central** because it is at the heart of the growth of the client's identity that the helping relationship aims to generate. The end goal of an integrative, constructivist* helping relationship is to develop the client's autonomy by developing his capacity to accept otherness.
- It is **cross-functional** because it affects all the different domains of coaching. The notion of autonomy applies to individual coaching, to team coaching, and to the wider domain of organizational coaching using Collective Intelligence*. Above and beyond solving immediate problems, the coaching relationship aims to free clients from a state of dependence so that they can move to interdependence and share common meaning with others: in other words, build peer-based relationships between free and responsible individuals.
- It is **holomorphic** in that understanding most of the other key concepts and tools used in coaching is a prerequisite for understanding autonomy, and *vice versa*.

A few references

Transactional Analysis (TA) and the work of its founder Eric Berne[5] represent one of the main reference points for my approach to autonomy, and why I consider it to be central to coaching. In TA, autonomy is defined as the ability to become an active agent in one's own life. It develops through three fundamental capabilities:

- awareness (or responsibility), that is being in contact with reality in the "here and now", aware of one's needs, and of the consequences of one's choices;
- spontaneity (or freedom), that is being able to interact with one's environment without being a prisoner of preprogramed personal scripts*;
- intimacy (or authenticity), the quality of one who can share in an authentic relationship with another person, without manipulation or inhibitions—very much like the concept of openness developed by Will Schutz.[6]

In her reflections on "The Dependency Cycle"[7] Nola-Katherine Symor has proposed a helpful model to define autonomy as a loop with four stages: dependence, counter-dependence, independence and interdependence.

Based on her work with dying people, Elisabeth Kübler-Ross[8] highlighted the phases of the bereavement process that occurs in all change. Being aware of the five phases of bereavement—denial, anger, bargaining, depression and acceptance—helps the coach to understand what occurs as the client moves from one stage of autonomy to another.

---

[5] Eric Berne, *What Do You Say After You Say Hello?*, Corgi, 1975.

[6] Will Schutz, *The Human Element*, Jossey Bass; 1994.

[7] Nola-Katherine Symor, *Actualités en Analyse Transactionnelle (Transactional Analysis News)*, AAT vol.7, n°27, July 1983 (available only in French).

[8] Elisabeth Kübler-Ross, *To Live until We Say Goodbye*, Simon & Schuster, 1997.

Degrees of Autonomy

The concept of autonomy is fundamentally ambiguous. Its etymology (from the Greek *autos* "self"" and *nomos* "law") suggests self-governance, or being the creator of one's own laws. It is the state of self-determination of an individual or a group who have the right to govern themselves according to their own internal laws. Yet it has a symbiotic relationship with its antonym, heteronomy* (from the Greek *heteros*, "other") where one's law is prescribed from the outside.

> **Heteronomy**
>
> Subordination or subjection to the law of another or action that is influenced by a force outside the individual. For Kant, it represents laws which are imposed on us from without.

Let me explain. Even though the term is often used to express the capacity to live one's life independently of others, autonomy is not independence. Paradoxically, achieving autonomy requires a person to experience heteronomy: it requires a person to have introjected* preexisting laws. I become autonomous as a driver when I have integrated the physical laws of movement, the Highway Code, and the presence of other people on the road—all of which are outside and beyond me as an individual. In the same way, it is when I accept society's laws that I become an autonomous citizen: I introject a law which is outside and beyond my control, and I make it mine. Autonomy plays out in processes such as delegation, obedience, initiative and decision making. The objective of coaching is to build the client's autonomy by relating to others. A person learns, little by little, to manage on their own through and in an intersubjective* relationship—by accepting the help of another person in finding the right stance in the complex dance of human relationships orchestrated between heteronomy and autonomy.

> **Introjection**
>
> The unconscious internalization of another person's behaviors, ideas, values, or points of view. A person who picks up traits from their friends (e.g., a person who begins frequently exclaiming "Ridiculous!" as a result of hearing a friend of theirs repeatedly doing the same) is introjecting.

Autonomy is never acquired once and for all; it is a never-ending journey. One can think of it as a spiral with multiple loops that represent a continual, open, and in theory limitless, process: that of our potential for growth. In the same way that a child grows through different stages from infancy to childhood to adolescence before reaching adulthood, realizing one's potential for autonomy leads a person to live through different degrees of autonomy, each of which involve specific needs.

Degree 1: Dependence (Deviant Form: The "Doormat")

This is the "yes" stage, where a person identifies himself with a relationship—the infant with the mother, or each person in a passionately symbiotic couple. In the business context, a person in a completely new job discovers a new profession and a new organizational environment; as he is unable to make decisions or fix objectives by himself, he depends entirely on someone in authority.

More generally, dependence is a relationship where an individual finds in someone else something which "completes" him by providing what he lacks. The individual needs information, protection and permissions from a guide. This is normal, inevitable and perfectly healthy to begin with. It becomes unhealthy for the individual and for the relationship when it lasts longer than it should. When an individual drifts into passive dependence, he becomes a "yes-man", or a "doormat". The danger of remaining too long in dependence is ever-present, and the coach needs to be constantly on the watch to prevent the client stagnating here.

Degree 2: Counter-dependence (Deviant Form: The "Hedgehog")

This is the "no" stage of the adolescent in revolt, that enables him to assert himself and to begin to test out reality. At this stage, the individual is in search of his identity through opposition to someone else or some other external reality. This can be done in a healthy, appropriate manner, or by locking oneself into deviant or exaggerated forms of rebellion. In business, the employee who has moved to counter-dependence stills needs to be managed, but will begin to mark out his identity by (rightly or wrongly) opposing authority or refusing to do things.

This stage is particularly ambiguous since the counter-dependent person remains in a position of submission, and yet has gone beyond it. As he builds his identity through a process of separation, he realizes that he cannot do it on his own. Here again there is a risk of settling down permanently in this stage. We see this in many adults who, like eternal adolescents, are unable to take responsibility for their lives and spend their whole lives accusing others. If they have problems, it is "the others' fault". If they are unable to move beyond counter-dependence in their quest of autonomy, it is because of the others. In counter-dependence, we learn to say "no" to authority: the issue is to learn to do this in a healthy and constructive manner, without permanently turning the "doormat" of the previous stage into a "hedgehog", tucked in on itself and locked into sterile opposition.

Degree 3: Independence (Deviant Form: The "Rascal")

In this "me" stage, an individual builds his own identity by confronting it with reality. Whether in his private, social or professional life, he is no longer conditioned by those who trained him and his reaction to them, but by the new way he relates to others. Having seen the limits of counter-dependence, he seeks to free himself of all control and wants to decide for himself when it comes to setting objectives and managing his schedule.

Moving to independence represents an extremely important discontinuity in terms of identity. We are no longer in opposition whilst remaining in a relationship, but we dare to break off a relationship, with the risk of having to cope on our own, choosing to live at our own rhythm and define our own values. This means experiencing life for oneself and establishing oneself as an individual in one's own right, in the fullest sense of the word. The downside of this stage lies in the danger of an excessive preoccupation with oneself and one's own "law". This can lead to selfishness or exacerbated narcissism, along with the refusal in one's social life to take account of the views of others, or even negating their existence. The "Rascal" does not want to depend on anyone and stubbornly works on his own. In business this is a counter-productive attitude, since employees are expected to able to function independently, but also to work in a manner consistent with the rest of the organization.

Degree 4: Interdependence (Working in "Unison")

Once fully lived out, independence enables an individual to move on to interdependence. He now has access to "we", and is able to freely choose to submit to authority, to manage on his own, or to help others on the journey, without putting his own identity at risk. He is able to fully live out relationships with others without losing himself in the other's identity, or falling into a dominant relationship. In business, the individual takes on responsibility and knows how to say "no" and set limits. At the same time, he knows how to obey when circumstances dictate, how to work with others in the knowledge they may sometimes know more than he does, and how to interact as equals when necessary. The Rascal has now learnt to work in Unison.

A minor drawback of this stage is that the person may sometimes have difficulty working well with others who not have achieved the same level of autonomy. He may wish to only live and work with those at the same level, and not with those who are more or less advanced. The next stage for him is to be able to work with those who have not yet reached his stage in the journey.

Degree 5: Alter-Dependence (The "Alter Ego")

In this "Alter Ego" stage, a person accepts relationships that are not necessarily among equals. The individual enters another dimension, that of open growth that integrates and goes beyond all the previous stages. He is now able to fully live out relationships with others, whether they are at the same level of autonomy or not. He may lose the comfort of a relationship between equals, but gains in being able to live out different kinds of relationships: whether in a helping relationship (professionally or otherwise) or in a hierarchical relationship that contributes to the growth of all the parties.

The client has moved from dependence to counter-dependence, from counter-dependence to independence, and from independence to interdependence. As he enters alter-dependence, he moves from inter-dependence to living out all the previous stages in a different way, informed by the experience of having passed through them already (Fig. 16).

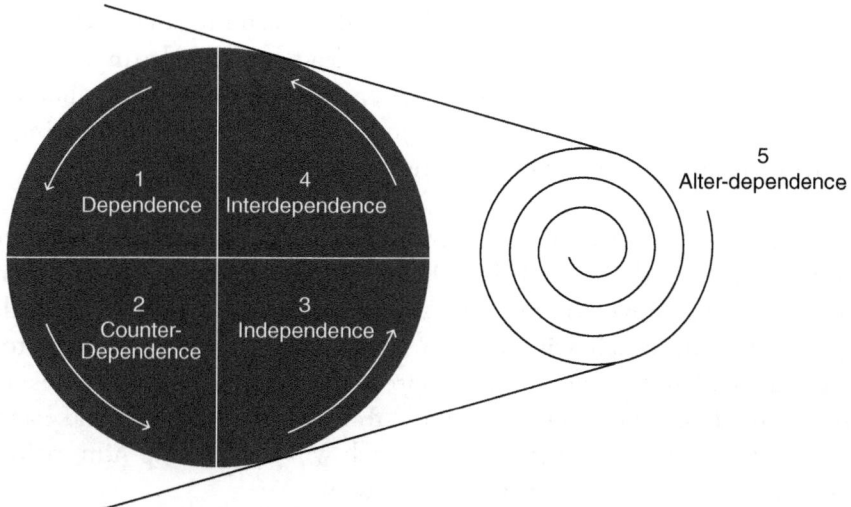

Fig. 16   Alter-dependence

Spiraling Growth—the Coach's Stance

Depending on his level of maturity, the client will go through situations of dependence, counter-dependence, independence, interdependence and alter-dependence in his relationship with the coach—sometimes in succession, sometimes simultaneously. The coach needs to adopt the appropriate stance for each level of autonomy.

- If the client is in the dependence stage, the coach will need to take charge, and provide information. In terms of the Fish/fishing rod metaphor, he will be giving him fish while preparing him for the task of building a fishing rod.
- When the client moves to counter-dependence, the coach patiently bears with the challenges, protests and rebellions of the client with unconditional acceptance, and remains on his guard against any reactions of rejection he may feel towards the client.
- When the client declares his independence, the coach needs to manage his own frustration as the client distances himself and stops communicating. It is up to the coach to re-establish the relationship, whilst again being on his guard against any reactions of rejection he may feel towards the client.

• As the client moves to interdependence, the coach nurtures a relationship of equals by letting the client take the lead, or even letting the client lecture him on what needs to be done. The key thing is to validate the client's choices (if they lead to a just solution) whilst reinforcing the client's feeling that he is shouldering his own responsibility.

Depending on the situation, the coach will adopt a stance that is either in line with, or slightly beyond the client's degree of autonomy, in order to help the client move to the next stage. When the client is in healthy dependence, the coach will adopt a stance that is complementary to it. When dependence is no longer appropriate for the client—he is in a position to choose solutions in response to his own questions or take action on his own but is not doing so—the coach will aim to help him make his own choices and take responsibility for them.

The coach also needs to take into account the ambiguous and multi-facetted nature of autonomy. In one and the same relationship, a person may be dependent in one area, counter-dependent in another, independent in a third, and interdependent in a fourth. In a married couple, for example, the husband may be financially dependent on his wife, blame her for not giving him enough freedom, and manage on his own when she is not around, yet consult with her for important decisions.

In the same way, an employee in a company will adopt behaviors with varying levels of autonomy depending on the tasks he accomplishes, where he stands hierarchically with respect to those he interacts with, and the specific situations he encounters.

This ambiguity is part of all institutional systems: each manager reports to someone else who may or may not have the same level of personal development, and is engaged in many and varied relationships with other employees. One of the key qualities of a successful management style is to be able to smoothly integrate and manage this complexity. It is also a key quality of the coach who needs to be able to respond appropriately for each level of autonomy, and to be comfortable with the attitude required at that level.

The path round the cycle of autonomy may be travelled quickly or slowly, easily or with difficulty, but one cannot skip a stage. Business leaders will often say to me: "Let's run a workshop, so you can make my managers responsible and interdependent." I respond that it is impossible to get people to move directly from dependence to interdependence, unless they have spent at least some time in counter-dependence and independence. Each stage is essential, requires time to proceed at its own pace, and has its own needs and constraints which, if they go unheeded, will prevent full access to the next stage. When a stage has been skipped or neglected, and its needs remained unsatisfied, a person will always come back to it like a broken record, like many mature men and women who remain in counter-dependence because they have not resolved their adolescent issues.

A change in one's level of autonomy implies a certain amount of identity transformation, along with the disruptions and bereavements that accompany all change. As an individual moves from one degree of autonomy to another, he needs to discard behaviors, representational systems and ties that are no longer appropriate, in order to reinvest his energy in new relationships. Each transformation is the result of a crisis or of questioning (though change is not always painful), followed by renunciation and reconfiguration. It is here that people often need support.

Support for moving to the next stage can often be found in a parental figure in a person's family system, or an authority figure in an educational or professional context. When people are involved in mirror play and the paradoxes of interpersonal relationships (like teenagers and parents during an adolescent crisis), it is often wise, and sometime necessary to call upon a third party, who may, or may not, be a professional of the helping relationship. Autonomy development occurs within a relational dynamic, where the entity—be it a person, team or organization—is part of a wider ecosystem including the client, the helper and the relationship between the two. The parameters change at each stage: needs, problems, relational issues, pitfalls and obstacles, along with people's positioning and posturing. I have described this ecosystem in some detail in previous books,[9] from the perspective of the relationship, the client and the helper—be he parent, teacher, manager, therapist or coach.

The coach's strategy depends on the time and context of the intervention, the client's level of maturity and how the coach decides to help the client on the journey through autonomy. It will always aim to ensure that, at the end of the day, the client stands on his own two feet. The way the coach implements the strategy will not be linear or circular. Rather, the client's development will often proceed by "learning loops" where progress is followed by retreats that serve to prepare further progress. This is why the spiral is such an appropriate representation of autonomy development: at each loop, the coaching relationship adjusts to the rhythm and needs of the client (Fig. 17).

---

[9] In particular *Coaching for Meaning*, Palgrave, 2004, pp 49–68.

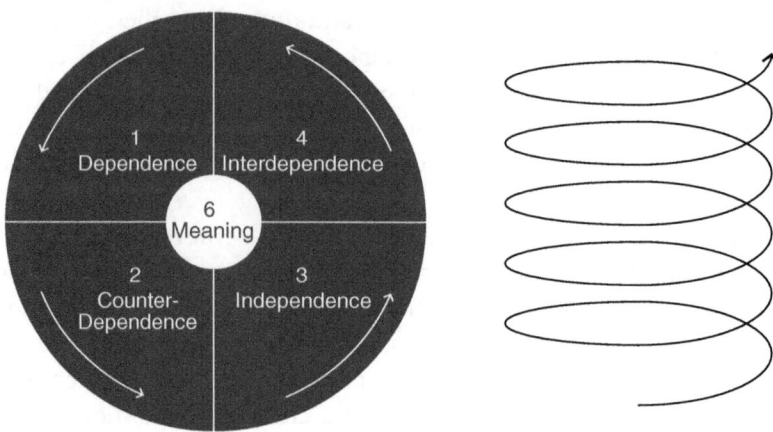

Fig. 17   The autonomy spiral

During the client's journey, the coach will always be careful to place the cursor so the client can move beyond the frustrations of a given stage and reach the next stage. This requires the coach to have a certain level of relational competency, be well-accustomed to changing his stance, and be able to live with a certain amount of personal frustration. This is not always easy!

If the client is in the stage of dependence, the coach will help him move from the ignorance and confusion of an unhealthy dependence to a state of sound and healthy dependence. The coaching contract provides a framework that both prevents the coach from becoming all-powerful, and the client from refusing all and any interventions. This framework also avoids the danger of a fusional relationship that would hinder the emergence of the client's freedom and responsibility. It also enables coach and client to put in place a set of indicators from the outset that ensure the relationship evolves satisfactorily (see the section *The Fifteen Parameters* in Strategy 3: *RNPRC*). Above all, it creates the conditions for free and sincere expression, since the client will feel secure as he is welcomed unconditionally.

Degree 6: The Dimension of Meaning at the Heart of the Spiral

Above and beyond the stages I have mentioned, autonomy is linked to access to meaning. There is, at the heart of the spiral, a sixth degree of autonomy, of a different order to all the others. It represents a "meta" stance of meaning that gives an individual a degree of autonomy of a higher order, whatever their level of relational maturity.

Even when I am in a state of dependence, the moment I connect with the meaning of what I am doing, or of the situation I am in, I am able to experience a different kind of freedom. This form of relating is calmer, and much more satisfying, than if I was progressing through independence and interdependence without seeing the end purpose of this growth for me and the others.

In this way, an individual can be in a state of dependence and nevertheless be freer than someone who has a highly-developed relational capacity, because what he is living is full of meaning for him, and he is living it out in harmony with his values—be they human, social, professional, existential or spiritual. He does not identify himself with the relationship he is in, but imbues it with a dimension that transcends it. In my book *Coaching for Meaning* I give the example of the mother who is willing to forgo her nights of sleep to look after her child: the existential meaning she attributes to that relationship enables her to live out this dependence in a positive manner that would be inconceivable for an "autonomous" single adult.

I discuss the notion of meaning in greater depth in Strategy 6: *Access to Meaning*, where I distinguish a number of levels of meaning that make up a person's identity backbone*. There, I discuss in detail the three different ways of finding meaning according to Viktor Frankl: by creating a work or doing a deed; by experiencing something or encountering someone; and by facing a fate one cannot change, thereby rising above and growing beyond oneself.[10] This dimension gives people a form of freedom as they face their fate (what they cannot change) and their destiny (what they do with their lives). At this level each person's autonomy depends more on where they stand with respect to meaning than on their relational maturity (Fig. 18).

Access to meaning transcends, and is a significant enabler for, the autonomy cycle. It helps the client and the coach avoid rivalry or

---

[10] Viktor Frankl, *Man's Search for Meaning*, Beacon Press, 2006, pp 144–146.

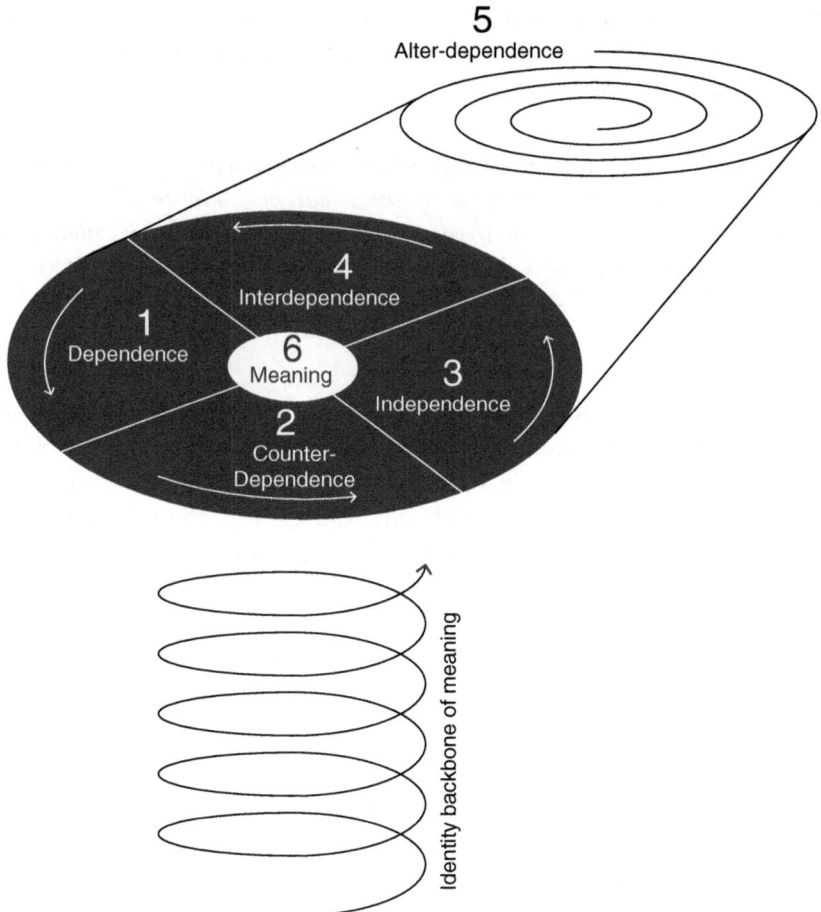

Fig. 18 Meaning at the heart of, and passing through autonomy

hostility which would make the relationship unproductive or stunt the client's growth. Access to meaning enables the parties to accept the inevitable frustrations in the relationship, and gives another dimension to the *Fish/fishing rod* strategy. The helping relationship is there to broaden the client's possible choices, in line with the coach's diagnosis of the client's degree of autonomy and as a function of the meaning the client is creating. From this wider perspective, the coach will constantly be focused on helping the client build his own rationale and creating his own meaning in order to take his own decisions. It is here that the culminating meta-strategy of *Crystallization* comes into play, as we will see in the final chapter.

From coach to meaning-bearer

Within the human community that we call a business, developing a common sense of meaning creates a core element at the heart of the development of each person's autonomy. This sense of meaning transcends the differences between those going through various stages of autonomy. Over and above these differences, the fact that a shared sense of meaning exists between different people at different stages of autonomy enables them to engage in a shared project in view of a common final purpose.

Shared meaning is a decisive factor for the leader of a team or an organization. Whatever the situation, and whatever his hierarchical status or his specific competences, the leader is the person who gains the most by taking up and maintaining a "meta" stance and a focus on meaning. This is how he brings together players at different stages of development and with different levels of responsibility, as they agree to take the same path and work interdependently, because they share the same vision.

In leadership, as in coaching, focusing on meaning helps a person move more effectively through the different stages of growth. The leader, like the coach, metacommunicates on values and objectives that lie beyond the relationship. By clarifying the causes (the "Why?") and the end purpose (the "What for?") he helps those with him overcome the frustrations and fear of change that are part and parcel of every transformation.

Autonomy in Summary

- Autonomy development can apply to individuals, to a group or team, and to an institution or organization.
- Autonomy should not be confused with independence.
- Autonomy is never acquired once and for all. It is a complex, ambiguous process, always in the process of becoming.
- The process of autonomy contains both disruptions and unavoidable stages, which each have their specific characteristics (needs, pitfalls, bereavements, attitudes), along with potential upsides and downsides.
- Once he has diagnosed the client's level of autonomy, the coach needs to adopt a specific stance that varies according to each stage.
- Autonomy does not exist in isolation, but should always be evaluated with respect to a given context and growth dynamic.

Key Points and Pause for Reflection—Fish/Fishing Rod and His Frame/My Frame

The questions below will help you think through how much the Fish/fishing rod—His frame/my frame strategy is part of the helping relationships that you manage. They are designed to help you search inside yourself, so it is important to take your time. Even if you only deal with one question, take the time to reflect fully on it, rather than simply going through a "checklist" exercise.

1. To what extent am I able to I incorporate the role of consultant, and keep it in my back pocket to use when needed?
2. As a coach, to what extent do I position myself first and foremost as the owner of the relationship and of the framework supporting my client's development?
3. To what extent am I seeking to "look intelligent", or is my intent to make my client "look intelligent" by the things I say and do?
4. To what extent am I seeking to generate and co-construct with my client a domain of shared experience and intelligence?
5. Even though I am always ready to propose a solution (provide a fish), how far is my attention constantly focused on listening, and enabling the other to move into enaction*?
6. *What, how, why, what for, who?* Am I going beyond the "What?" (the content), and focusing on the "How?" (the process), the "Why?" (the causes), the "What for?" (the final purpose) and the "Who?" (what the other is actually living through, along with his identity issues)?

Strategy 3: RPNRC (Reality-Problem-Need-Request-Contract)

> *What problems is my client facing? What are the stakes?*
> *What is he really asking for? What does he want from this session?*
> *What does he want from me?*
> *Do we have a clear contract? Over and above the contract, are we "in alliance"?*

My coaching practice has led me to observe that, rather than rushing head-long into a person's problem and trying to resolve it, it is better first to understand the context of the intervention, and define how we are going to work with the client. This means:

* assessing the nature of the problem, the underlying issues, and the context;
* identifying the individual's needs, and at what level;
* understanding what he is really looking for;
* agreeing on what we are going to do together, and how we will relate.

The RPNRC strategy enables the coach to do just this. Each element describes one aspect of the issues that the coach needs to explore with the

© The Author(s) 2017
V. Lenhardt, *My 10 Strategies for Integrative Coaching*,
DOI 10.1007/978-3-319-54795-4_5

client. R for Reality (the situation), P for Problem (or stakes), N for Need, R for Request and C for Contract.

Building a Relational Ecosystem

I designed RPNRC after hearing therapists and consultants questioning themselves again and again about their approach to clients who came to tell them about their problems. They were asking questions like "Where's the problem?", "What's the issue?", "Why is it a problem?", "Why is he coming to see *me* with this issue?" When a client finds a listening ear, he can spend hours speaking about himself, without ever clarifying the nature of his problem. Even when the problem is clearly stated, the root cause is rarely obvious. One needs to understand the context, clarify the issues, bring to light the client's needs and underlying requests, check if the client is in a position to act, that it is the right time to act, and also make sure that the client really does want to change.

If this is not done, the whole coaching relationship can be distorted. RPNRC is not a "technical tool" external to the coaching relationship, but is the means of setting up an implementation framework within which the coaching process is deployed.

- R, P and N—bringing the reality of the situation to light, getting to grips with the problem and the stakes involved for the client, understanding the client's need—these are needed to establish a diagnosis based on the client's situation in his ecosystem.
- R and C—making the client's request and the ensuing contract explicit— these define the relationship between the coach and the client.

The coach will avoid any significant intervention until these five points are sufficiently clear. Only then will he be able to intervene appropriately—with the right stance, in the right place, at the right time.

Even though they occur at the beginning, these "status checks" are never definitive. All through the coaching relationship, and at least at the beginning of each session, the coach will confirm or reassess them using RPNRC. It is like a scarlet thread running through the whole coaching process that checks the priorities at any given moment. It is in this sense that RPNRC is an operational strategy (Fig. 19).

RPNRC FRAMEWORK

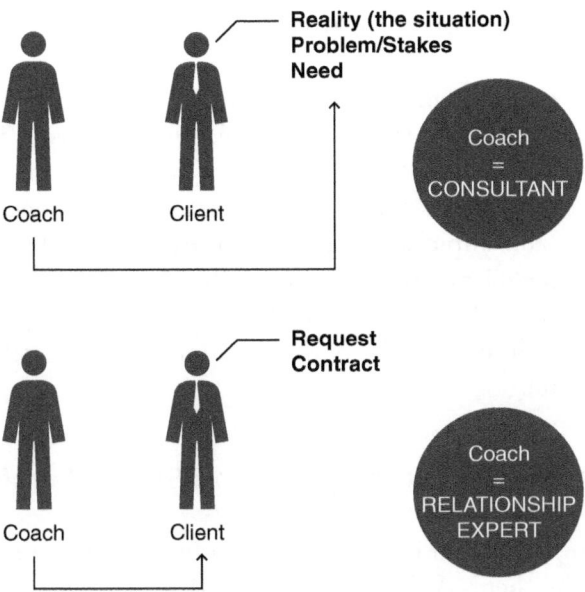

Fig. 19 The coach as "relationship expert"

The essential difference between coach and consultant: the Request and the (relational) Contract

When dealing with the first three parameters, R, P, and N, the coach operates very much like a consultant, to establish a diagnosis of the situation, the problem and the client's need.

But the coach does not stop there: he checks the kind of relationship that needs to be built with his client before making any attempt to solve the problem. This is where the two other parameters, Request and Contract, play a decisive role. The coach only acts when he has validated what the client is really asking for, and is sure he has established a relational (not just a legal) contract in line with the client's request(s).

This places the coach in a very different position to that of a consultant—he becomes a **"relationship expert"**. Though he remains attentive to the other parameters, the coach relies on the client's request and the contract to position the cursor throughout the coaching relationship at the right point between directive intervention and non-directive listening. He does this as a function of the client's level of autonomy and the issues as they evolve.

Five Facets of the Same Issue

Identifying the Client's Reality

Identifying the client's reality is about getting to grips with the complex and multiform reality of the situation as perceived by the client. The coach asks questions like: "Who is telling the story of what happened? What really happened, when and where? What is the status now?" He gets to know the client's context, and unpicks the situation as experienced by the client. The more confused the client's presentation of the situation, the more details he gives, the more he will have trouble clearly expressing why he came to be coached. The coach seeks to clarify the situation through careful questioning and reformulation.

Identifying the Problems, Issues and Stakes Involved

Once the client's situation is clear, the coach focuses on understanding what is at stake for the client. As he listens to the client outlining his problem, the coach asks questions like: "In what sense is the issue you describe a problem for you? Where exactly is the gap between your current reality and what you want to happen?"

The issue is always more complex than it appears at first sight. Behind the initial problem statement, other hidden, unconscious, emergent or underlying issues and agendas quickly appear.

In my current practice, I often speak more of the stakes involved rather than "problems". As we saw in Strategy 1: *The Person-centered Approach, or Rogerian alliance*, the practice of Appreciative Inquiry encourages us to take a step back from problem-centered approaches focused on the negative aspects of situations (with their share of guilt and denial). It invites us to focus on what works, on existing resources, on past successes that others have recognized—everything that is "alive" in the client and represents a strength that can be galvanized into action.

Jack Dusay, who invented the egogram[1] in Transactional Analysis, was already encouraging practitioners to focus on positive ego states* back in the 1970s. In terms of the integrative approach to coaching described in this book, the coach speaks more to the "Prince(ss)" than to the "Frog", and is

---

[1] Jack Dusay, Egograms and the "Constancy Hypothesis". *Transactional Analysis Journal*, 2, 37–41 (1972).

more interested in the client's potential than in his current performance. This is why I focus more and more on the stakes involved, including the client's dreams, wishes and desires that imbue his acts with meaning and purpose.

Identifying the Need

Once the problem or stakes involved have been made explicit, the coach performs an initial diagnosis of the situation, and forms hypotheses as to the client's needs. The coach may sometimes inform the client of this diagnosis, but I do not normally recommend this, since the client may not be sufficiently mature to recognize his needs in this explicit way. Clients who come for coaching are often not clear in their own minds: they may confuse their situation with the problem they have in that situation, and they may mix up objective events with the impact of those events on them, with more or less deep psychological repercussions.

Later in this chapter, we will see how examining the client's needs and requests requires certain precautions, which need to be meticulously observed by the coach.

Clarifying the Request

Clarifying the request is absolutely central to the whole coaching process. It is vital that the coach not only checks that the client has a request, but also gauges the gap between the client's request and the need the coach has identified. People often come to coaching with a huge need (the underwater part of the iceberg) and a tiny request (the tip of the iceberg). In other words, they are unaware of how serious their problems are. When making a request, the client may also express a number of different expectations that the coach needs to detect if he is to avoid being trapped in relational games.

My experience has taught me that **four types of request** always coexist:

- a request for results (the content): what the client expects from the session or from the overall coaching process;
- a request with respect to process and the relationship: what the client expects the coach to do in his role as coach (provide feedback, listen, help diagnose the situation, help find options), and what he himself hopes to achieve when the coach is there with him;
- an explicit request made by the client;
- an implicit request, hidden behind the client's explicit request.

Throughout the coaching relationship, the coach needs to make adjustments at all four levels as the request evolves. This is why the coach needs to establish, before the start of the intervention *per se*, a contract and work plan that takes these four levels into account and gives him permission to make adjustments along the way. The objective is to define a request with respect to the results to achieve, the process to use, and the kind of relationship to develop, whilst letting implicit or latent requests emerge from behind the explicit request.

Developing the Contract

It is vital to make the distinction between Request and Contract. Once the request has been clarified, the contract specifies and validates the content, the conditions and the limits of the coaching intervention. The coach is free to accept certain parts of the request and refuse others, if he believes he is not competent, or does not have the time to fulfill a request, or considers a request to be unclear or unethical. He may also propose changes to the contract with respect to content or process. He also needs to ensure that the contract corresponds in some way to the client's implicit demand. I make a distinction between three overall kinds of contract[2]:

- the **legal contract**, written and signed by both parties, which defines the material, financial and other conditions;
- the often unwritten, more or less explicit, **relational contract** that defines elements outside the legal framework such as the context and purpose of the intervention, informal arrangements, how to deal with unforeseen events and constraints, and how the parties will manage their frustrations; it also sets the boundaries of the relationship between coach and client;
- the **secret contract**: a totally implicit agreement between the unconscious parts of the coach and the client; the unconscious, hidden concerns of each party strongly influence the mutual consent and

---

[2] Based on distinctions proposed by Jut Meinniger, *Success Through Transactional Analysis*, Mass Market Paperback, 1974.

trust between the parties, even if a trusting relationship is explicitly acknowledged (Fig. 20).

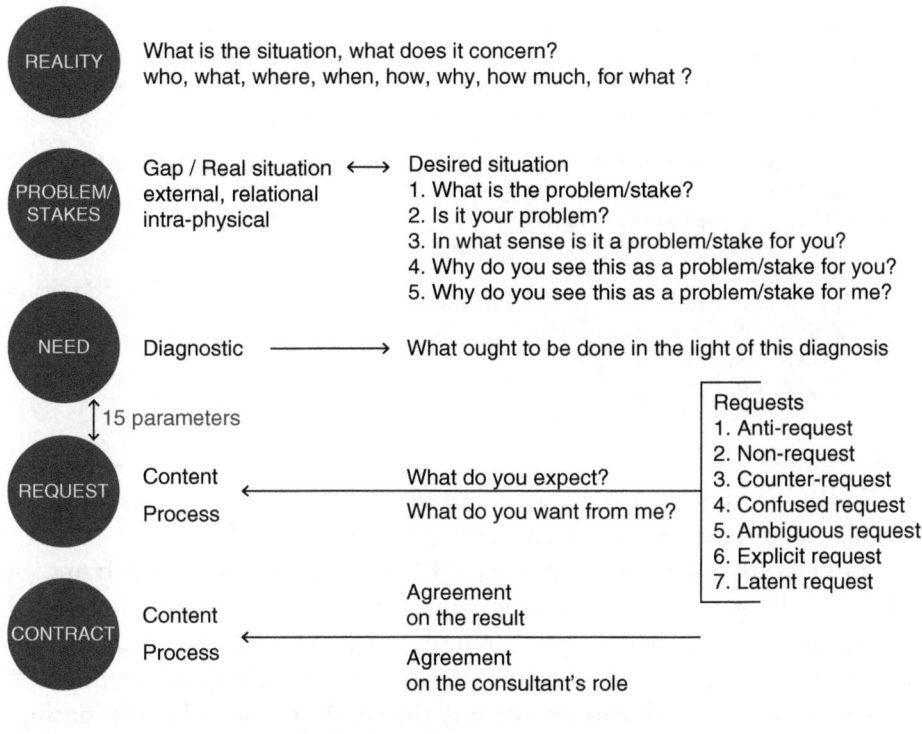

Fig. 20 RPNRC in summary

A Comprehensive Approach to the Relationship and its Ecosystem

RPNRC is an essential part of the coach's dashboard, and also one of the main tools in his toolbox, since it a synthesis of all the other the tools. A plumber or car mechanic who is called out for a repair job will not bring out all the tools in his workshop, just the vital few. In the same way, RPNRC is the coach's "emergency kit" that enables him not only to establish a relationship with the client, but also to know when to give the hammer blow (see box) or, to use the metaphor of the acupuncturist, "place the needle in the right place".

A metaphor: "one blow of the hammer"

I often quote the Eric Berne's "boiler repair" story[3] to highlight the importance of RPNRC.

A specialist engineer is called out to repair a boiler. He arrives with his tool-box, and slowly walks round the boiler three times. He then opens his toolbox, takes out a hammer, and hits a pipe at a precise point. As if by a miracle, the boiler starts working again. The client, surprised and delighted, says:

– *That's wonderful, you've repaired my boiler with a single blow of your hammer. Do I owe you anything?*
– *100 dollars, replies the engineer.*
– *What? 100 dollars for a single blow of a hammer? I'm not sure I've heard you correctly.*
– *The engineer proceeds to write out the bill:*
– *Hitting boiler with hammer: $1*
– *Knowing where to hit: $99*
– *Total: $100*

RPNRC encapsulates the core culture that a coach needs to incorporate, whether he does individual, team, or organizational coaching.

Through its apparent simplicity, RPNRC provides a broad frame of reference. To get to the "profound simplicity"[4] of these five parameters, I had to go on a journey through complexity. This simple, yet comprehensive approach takes into account all the domains of a coaching intervention. It integrates the client's dynamics, the way the coach manages the relationship, the ins and outs of investigating the client's needs, finding out what the client really wants, and the way this is formalized in a contract. Keeping RPNRC constantly in mind enables the coach to remain centered on the client, to check the nature and quality of the relationship, and to make adjustments as needed (Fig. 21).

The RPNRC Radar

Though I normally present the RPNRC parameters sequentially for the sake of clarity, this does not mean that they should be rolled out in strict order; it is not a linear process, even though each parameter needs to be validated one

[3] Eric Berne, *The Structure and Dynamics of Organizations and Groups,* Ballantine Books, 1984.
[4] In Will Schutz's sense of discovering deep simplicity by going through complexity. See Schutz *Profound Simplicity,* Thorsons, 1979.

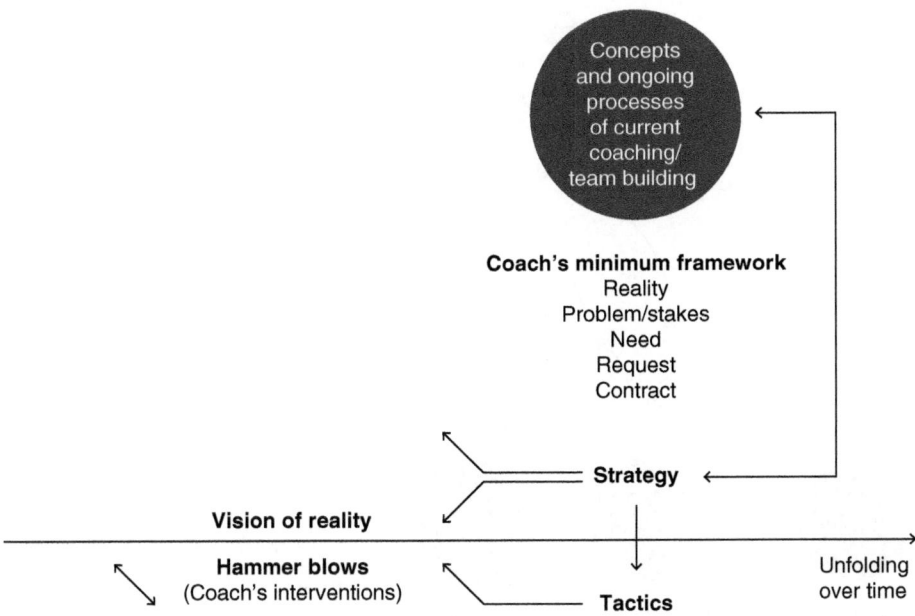

Fig. 21   RPNRC in context

by one. In a real-life situation the coach explores the "complex landscape" of RPNRC in continuous loops, as the client's issues constantly evolve along with the relationship—sometimes even within the course of a single session. As the coaching intervention progresses, the coach constantly revisits, reconfirms and sometimes readjusts the way he intervenes. New elements emerge which shed new light on the situation, or influence the client's perception of the problem. When the coach focuses on a particular issue, this may highlight a new need, which will shed a different light on the client's request.

The reality of the situation is constantly changing, and obliges the coach to constantly readjust his interventions. He uses RPNRC as a kind of radar, constantly scanning the environment, enabling him to check his leverage with the client, to verify whether the relationship is at the right level, or is at least evolving towards it, to question the client's request, and to reconfirm the contract (Fig. 22).

The five "screens" of the RPNRC radar are at different logical levels. Describing the reality of the situation for the client can take forever without the client's problem ever being clearly identified. Focusing only on the problem presents a risk that coach and client lock themselves into the issue when it is only a symptom, or a manifestation of the client's deeper,

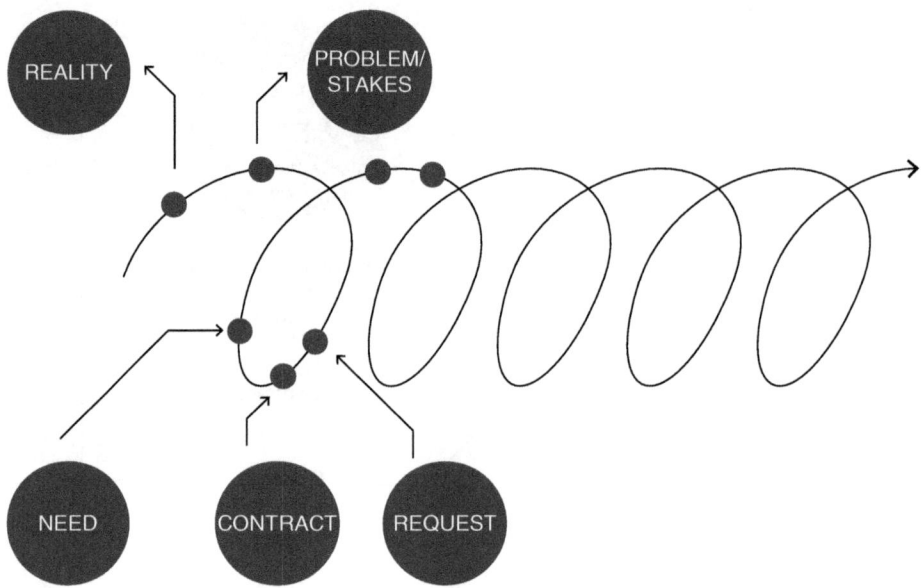

Fig. 22 The RPNRC radar and its five screens

unsatisfied need. We sometimes see clients talking indefinitely about their need, but never getting round to expressing the request that is an essential lever for the client's development. Then again, the request may sometimes be disproportionate to the situation, or correspond to a deep need that the coach cannot satisfy, and needs to be excluded from the contract.

The contract, unlike the unilateral request made by the client, represents a bilateral or mutual commitment. The contract—be it legal, relational or secret—provides the framework for crystallizing the client's request based on the perspectives provided by the relationship.

Though the coach is deeply concerned with the relationship and the client's request, he never lets himself be taken hostage by a request. The process for confirming a request and formalizing it in a contract aims to (re)establish parity between the client and the coach. It is important to bear in mind that the coach is not a supplier, but a partner, and that he is accountable for the means he puts in place to achieve an outcome, not the outcome itself. He is not obliged to respond to a request made by the client, though he is responsible for framing it in terms of the contract that enables him to weigh up its depth and potential implications.

Helping the client to become aware of his needs

Whatever the request (for content or process, explicit or implicit), a major part of the coach's job is to clarify the client's position with regards to his request. This may be tricky for the client, who may be struggling to identify his own needs. Some people do not make a request because they are unaware of their needs, or are unwilling to recognize and deal with them. Even when a need is acknowledged, the way it is expressed often hides other underlying and implicit needs of which the client may not even be aware.

To enable the client to access his needs and express his request, the coach takes the client through a six-step protocol that the coach links to the overall coaching strategy.

- Accepting the principle that everyone has needs.
- Being OK with the idea of having needs oneself.
- Identifying one's own needs and giving oneself permission to have them.
- Understanding which of one's needs can really be satisfied.
- Expressing a request for satisfying the needs, inasmuch as they are reasonable and can be satisfied appropriately.
- Experiencing satisfaction of those needs, even partially.

It may take several months before the client becomes clearly aware of the above.

Beyond RPNRC: The Coach's Fifteen-Parameter Dashboard

The RPNRC strategy is based on a dynamic between coach and client which makes it far more than just one of the tools in the coach's toolbox. At the same time, it is also very operational (helping the coach to know exactly where to "place the acupuncture needle"). The "15 parameters" described in this section unpack the core of RPNRC.

In Transactional Analysis, where there is a contract for each session, the rule is to always check if the parties are OK with a few key items in the contract before the session: What is the subject? How will we work? What means shall we use? For how long? My experience as therapist, coach and teacher has convinced me that the helping relationship requires attention to many more parameters than that. In Zen archery, the "right gesture" depends on 147 parameters, such as the way one places one's foot, breathes, takes hold of the bow, or gazes at the target. If there are 147 parameters for an apparently simple exercise, we should not be surprised that there are at least fifteen key "indicators" for managing the complexity of the coaching relationship. There many more than these, but the coach will normally get by with the fifteen I describe below, and in an emergency he can get by with RPNRC which represents the five essential elements to watch out for.

While RPNRC helps the coach know where to "place the needle", these 15 parameters help him know where *not* to place it. They are like dials on the dashboard: when one of them flashes red, the coach knows he needs to stop everything else and focus on the flashing dial. Each and every parameter conditions the success of the coaching relationship; ignoring it may even compromise the coach's ability to pursue the coaching intervention. These 15 parameters, which complement RPNRC, are particularly useful when working on the gap between Need and Request. They also help the coach to intervene appropriately and intelligently, both with respect to short-term tactics with their specific interventions, and also with regards to the long term strategy and the overall relationship.

The 15 parameters are made up of:

- a number of factors that determine the quality of the relationship and the ability of each party to deal with issues that may arise;
- a set of indicators to steer the intervention in the form of a dashboard that the coach keeps constantly in mind throughout the relationship;
- a subset of specific items that distinguish the way the coach behaves from that of the consultant, and that enables the coach to adjust the relationship in all its complexity, ambiguity and paradox.

The Fifteen Parameters

Though I present the 15 parameters sequentially, together they make up a holomorphic* set: each parameter interacts with the others, and partially includes the others.

1. Being OK. OKness implies that the coach has worked on himself, and also on how he relates to others. His own personal work involves acquiring ontological security*, giving up the illusion of omnipotence, knowing how to challenge himself, and fully accepting both his freedom and his responsibility. His work on relating to others includes fully assuming the limits of a relationship, accepting the irreducible complexity of the other person, seeing the potential for growth in the other, and acknowledging another person's capacity, both to change and to take responsibility for that change.

2. Diagnosis. The diagnosis positions the problem or stakes with respect to the client and his environment. It is based not only on the analysis of the client's needs and challenges, but also on the coach's intuition and empathy. To establish a diagnosis, the coach needs both a conceptual frame of reference (acquired and developed through training) and also hands-on experience (of coaching, or of working in business). He also needs to be continually "cleaning his own spectacles" through therapy.

3. Level of development. Here the coach assesses the level of development of the individual, the team or the organization. This determines the nature and extent of what can be done. The coach will ask himself questions like: "What is their experience of change? What level of autonomy? What ability to challenge and call themselves into question?"

4. Protections*. There is no question of moving forward into a coaching intervention without having first created a safe environment for the client. Putting protections in place means taking precautions, giving information, guaranteeing confidentiality and defining clear rules of engagement so as to move forward without taking unnecessary risks. It also involves saying "no" to the client when necessary. Putting in place protections is a precondition for giving permissions* (saying "go ahead, take the initiative, or dare to change..."). The coach who gives permissions without putting in place the necessary protections is in danger of playing the sorcerer's apprentice.

5. Errors. Remember Eric Berne's aphorism: "the difference between professionals and amateurs in any game [is that] the professional knows when to stop".[5] The maturity of the coach can be measured by the number of potential errors he spots and avoids. In order to be alert to this, he will never lose sight of the complexity and paradoxical dimension of the change process he is facilitating.

6. Relationship Structure. This parameter conditions how the whole intervention unfolds. Beyond the coaching contract (parameter 15, below) the two parties need to agree how they will meet, both formally and informally. The way they meet will structure the relationship, create openness and trust, and enable them to function in harmony. The coach also needs to know if the client is involved in another helping relationship at the same time, whether it be mentoring, coaching or therapy. The client may either use another relationship to "sabotage" the coaching relationship, or use it as an invaluable complement.

7. Alliance for change. This reflects the mutual commitment of coach and client to maintain the relationship in spite of the setbacks, misunderstandings and disagreements that are bound to occur. Sometimes the client will find

---

[5] Eric Berne, *Games People Play.*, Ballantine Books, 1964

the coach's challenges hard to deal with, since they will require him to put himself in question. The coach will also sometimes make mistakes, and the client will need to set him straight. There is an alliance between the two when mutual trust, along with the agreement on the objectives and approach, enables both parties to overcome the frustrations along the way without calling the relationship into question. This occurs when the relationship is lived out, not in dependence, counter-dependence or independence, but in interdependence or even alter-dependence.

8. Transferential* elements. The client will often bring past unresolved situations into the present coaching relationship. For example, he may project figures he has introjected* from his own past onto the coach. If the client projects the "ideal parent" onto the coach, the client will expect him to play the part of rescuer*, and expect him to provide magic solutions (positive transference). The client may also project a "bad parent" onto the coach (negative transference). The coach will need to identify and deal with this, and also be aware of his own potential projections onto the client, either of transference or of countertransference (in reaction to the client's projections).

9. Request. As discussed in the section on RPNRC, requests can be made at several levels, and there are many types of request: explicit requests, latent requests, anti-requests (the client does not want to be coached either because he was forced to or he reluctantly took advice to be coached), non-requests (the client is there, but is not motivated to do anything), counter-requests (the client opposes the coach in order to affirm something else), confused or ambiguous requests, to name but a few.[6] The coach will always need to clarify what the request actually means in terms of content (the subject and the results) and process (the roles of client and coach, along with the type of relationship).

10. The will to change. This parameter has two poles: on the one hand, the coach needs to assess the extent to which the client is willing to change; on the other, he needs to be careful that his own will for the client to change is not greater than that of the client (this means he needs to accept the client's relative reluctance to change). Even if all the other indicators are green, if the will to change flashes red the coach is fully justified in suspending the coaching relationship to check the client's OKness and degree of resistance.

11. Intervention plan. This parameter is about defining the length of the coaching intervention, the frequency and number of sessions, the overall

---

[6] My book *Coaching for Meaning* pp. 107–109 provides a more detailed discussion of different types of request.

strategy (the means used by the coach, and the steps he will take the client through), as well as alternative strategies and tactics. The more well-prepared the plan, the more the coach will feel free to operate, moment by moment, in full situational intelligence*, without losing his bearings with regards to the overall purpose of the intervention.

12. Here and now. There are sometimes unexpected events that crop up in the here and now of the coaching relationship, and change it, such as an urgent phone call right in the middle of the session that heralds bad news for the client. The coach needs to be able to prioritize these unforeseen incidents, and if needed change the agenda or even interrupt the session.

13. Space and time. The coach's role is to ensure the relationship and the duration of the intervention are well-managed. This involves first of all ensuring that the meeting space is both calm and guarantees confidentiality. It then involves allotting sufficient time: one cannot do the same amount of work in ten minutes as one does in a two-hour session. When unforeseen circumstances upset the best-laid plans and agendas, the coach needs to be able manage the consequent adjustments.

14. Power. The coaching relationship cannot exist without a high degree of mutual trust. It is the absence of a power relationship between the two parties that gives the coaching relationship its power, as it frees up the energies of client and coach in a positive manner. This parameter is inseparable from OKness and the issue of identity that I deal with in Strategy 8: *Identity Construction.* If a relationship is polluted by power plays, this may mean point to lack of clarity in the contract, unresolved issues of transference*, or even feelings of being threatened in their identity in the client and/or coach.

15. Contract. When I described RPNRC, I emphasized that the contract between the parties involved at least three levels of agreement that needed to be validated (the legal contract, the relational contract and the "secret" contract). In an institutional setting, the contract may include a third party, the institution (the trilateral contract) and sometimes multiple players (the multilateral contract). It is not helpful to turn the contract into a straightjacket, but it is important to validate the overall terms of engagement as a reference point, and a tool to clarify and reinforce the relationship (Fig. 23).

A Shared Change Agenda

Each of the 15 parameters involves specific intervention zones that need to be scanned, as we will see in Strategy 4: *Contextualization.* The coach does not deal with them all at the same time, and I have placed them in a specific

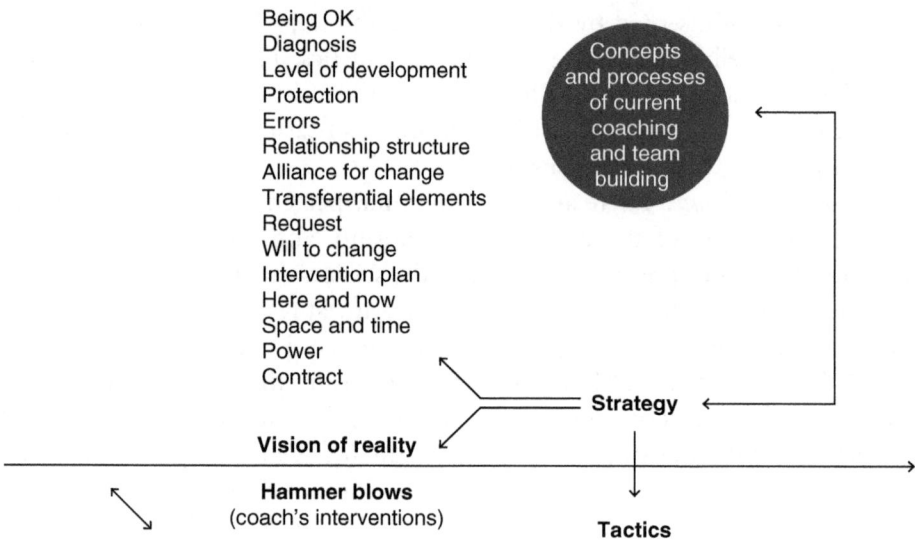

Being OK
Diagnosis
Level of development
Protection
Errors
Relationship structure
Alliance for change
Transferential elements
Request
Will to change
Intervention plan
Here and now
Space and time
Power
Contract

Concepts
and processes
of current
coaching
and team
building

Strategy

Vision of reality

Hammer blows
(coach's interventions)

Tactics

Fig. 23   The coach's 15-parameter dashboard

order. The first thing to do is to establish or restore OKness, without which the whole relationship will be distorted; the diagnosis follows hard on its heels, and involves evaluating the situation and degree of development of the client. Putting in place protections*, avoiding errors, and the other parameters then follow naturally.

By working through these 15 parameters, the coach gradually builds the framework for a successful intervention. Having built it, he continually checks it as the relationship evolves, like the radar mentioned in the section on RPNRC, or the constantly spinning top which falls over if it stops (Fig. 24). The coach keeps them constantly in mind in order to:

- regularly revalidate the context of his intervention;
- optimize his strategy as he adjusts the cursor between the fish and the fishing rod;
- suspend work in progress as often as is needed when an indicator flashes red in order to focus, not on the content of the coaching intervention, but on the item that is causing the problem;
- refer the person to other bodies, such as a therapist if the gap between the need and the client's request is too wide, or if the problem being dealt with is too serious for the "here and now" approach of coaching.

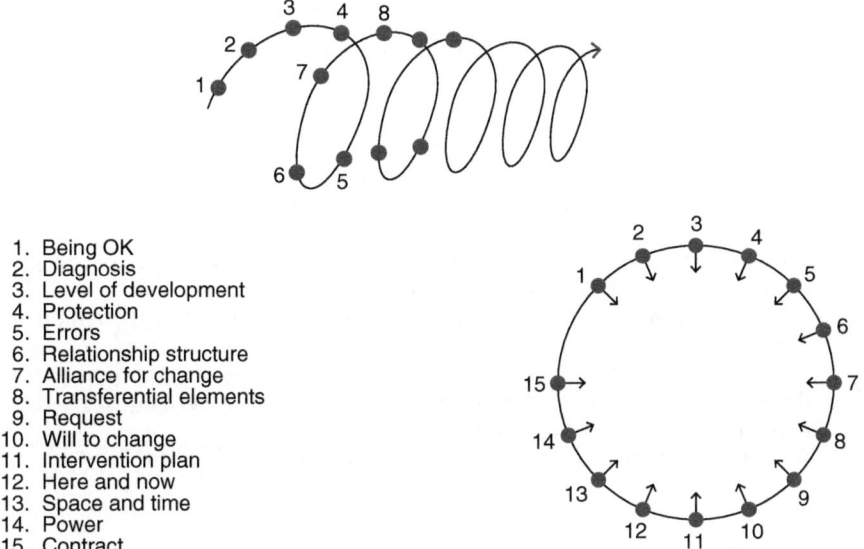

1. Being OK
2. Diagnosis
3. Level of development
4. Protection
5. Errors
6. Relationship structure
7. Alliance for change
8. Transferential elements
9. Request
10. Will to change
11. Intervention plan
12. Here and now
13. Space and time
14. Power
15. Contract

Fig. 24   The 15 parameters over time (the spinning top)

The end game of these indicators is not only to check that the job is feasible, but also to validate that it corresponds to a shared change agenda. They create the conditions for the client to progress to ever-greater autonomy.

A sixteenth parameter?

The phenomenon of parallel processes* (discussed in Strategy 4: *Contextualization*) can be seen as a "meta" parameter, since it encompasses and conditions all the others. It forms the backdrop to the rest of the dashboard that the coach is constantly surveying so as to intervene with situational intelligence* and build the most appropriate relationship with his client.

Key Points and Pause for Reflection—RPNRC and the 15 Parameters

The questions below will help you think through how much RPNRC and the 15 Parameters are part of the helping relationships that you manage. They are designed to help you search inside yourself, so it is important to take your time. Even if you only deal with one question, take the time to reflect fully on it, rather than simply going through a "checklist" exercise.

- To what extent do I seek to understand the "reality" of the client's situation and context?
- To what extent do I identify all the stakes involved and the problems to be solved?
- How do I pinpoint what is "alive" in my client (strengths, resources, past successes) before diagnosing what is impeding his progress?
- To what extent am I able to I discern implicit needs that may lie behind my client's explicit request?
- In what way do I navigate as an "expert in relationships", act appropriately to the situation and adjust myself moment by moment according to how the client's requests and needs evolve?
- Am I at ease with "content and process", "explicit and implicit"?

Strategy 4: Contextualization and the Intervention Zones

> *Where do the problems and stakes really lie in my client's ecosystem?*
> *In which "zones"? Where should I focus?*
> *How might I plan the intervention as a result?*
> *What is being played out in my relationship with the client?*

We often distinguish three main zones in the coaching relationship: the coach, the client—each with their own issues and stakes—and the intersubjective* space between coach and client, or the "interdividual*" relationship.

Whilst this is true, the client (individual, team or organization) is never completely separate from the surrounding environment. The coach always needs to bear in mind that the client carries within him different kinds of identity. In business coaching, this may be the identity of the team that the client manages, the organization he works for, and the socio-professional sector he represents, as well as the client's own multiple personal identities.

Whatever the context, the coaching relationship evolves within the wider relationship that the coach builds with his client's ecosystem. Seeing the client as an agent in an environment with which he interacts in multiple ways avoids falling into a simplistic analysis of what is happening in the coaching relationship.

© The Author(s) 2017   **101**
V. Lenhardt, *My 10 Strategies for Integrative Coaching*,
DOI 10.1007/978-3-319-54795-4_6

Putting the Problem and the Stakes into Perspective

In a coaching situation, all the interactions between coach and client are conditioned by the client's ecosystem. As well as looking at the coach-client relationship, the coach may also consider what the client is going through—his discomforts, request and identity issues—as symptoms of the reality in which he operates.

When a coach acts on certain aspects of the client's reality, this may not only reveal the client's interactions with his environment, but may also generate deep change the whole of the ecosystem around him. This takes the coach from a relatively mechanistic view of the relationship with his client—"just work on the client, change the relationship with him, work on one's identity, share emotions and representations"—to a more systemic, even holomorphic* perspective.

The coaching relationship is about more than just coach and client. It affects, and is part of the whole ecosystem, which, in turn is ever-present in the coaching relationship. In other words, when the coach receives a client with his problem, he receives not only an individual but also…

…a person with and within a whole relational ecosystem.

How can the coach put all this into context? What kind of work plan should he develop? The contextualization (or intervention zones) strategy aims to answer these questions. It is part and parcel of the RPNRC strategy, and is embedded mainly in the "P" (analysis of the problem or stakes), since probing the intervention zones enables the coach to "unfold" the client's issues. A client never has a single challenge or a simple, isolated problem: he always operates within a complex relational system with multiple interfaces that include not only the coach, but also all the other parties involved in the problem or situation. As the coach faces a tangled mesh of knotted problems, the contextualization strategy provides a vital roadmap and compass to navigate this complex landscape.

The coach deploys the contextualization strategy over at least eight zones, and in six, not necessarily chronological, steps (Fig. 25).

Contextualization provides an integrative approach, and is also a useful tool in itself, but it is important not to use it as a prescriptive framework. The coach will use it without letting himself be boxed in by it. Below is an illustrative example, based on a real-life case.

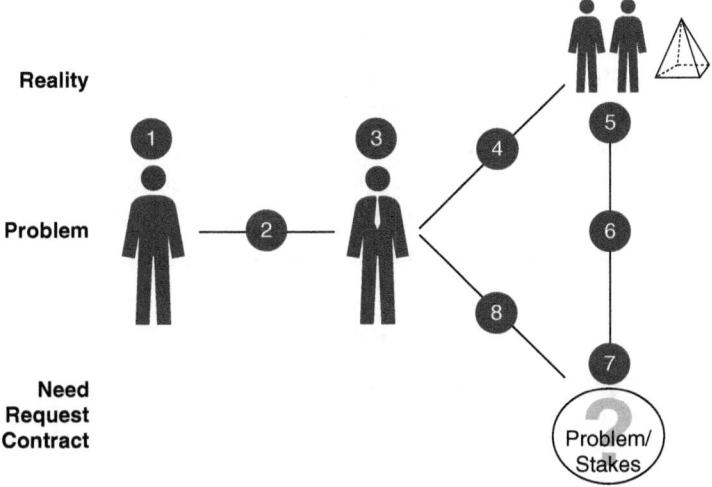

Fig. 25   RPNRC with the intervention zones

Jane, CEO of a major corporation, calls on me to help resolve a series of problems she is having with her board. In particular, she would like to talk to me about her fraught relationship with Ben, her production MD, who is not meeting his production deadlines.

My first job is to identify which zones to focus on:

- *Zone 1*: Me, the coach.
- *Zone 2*: My relationship as coach with Jane.
- *Zone 3*: Jane's personality as CEO.
- *Zone 4*: Jane's relationship with Ben as her production MD.
- *Zone 5*: Ben's personality, as production MD.
- *Zone 6*: Ben's relationship with the problem, and how he sees it.
- *Zone 7*: The problem of missed production deadlines.
- *Zone 8*: How Jane reacts to the problem of missed production deadlines.

One could imagine a ninth zone[1] that links the contextualization strategy to the *Fish/fishing rod* strategy, and distinguishes the role of

---

[1] Suggested by my friend Todd Senturia, partner at Bain.

"coach-as-consultant" who directly advises the client on his problem from the point of view of his greater expertise.

Things are often far more complex: in the multiple realities of coaching situations, contextualization enables clients to mention any number of internal and external interfaces and varying numbers of problems, depending on the complexity of the organization and its interactions with the outside world. There will often be at least 10 to 25 zones to cover! In our example, we will stick to the eight zones outlined below (Fig. 26).

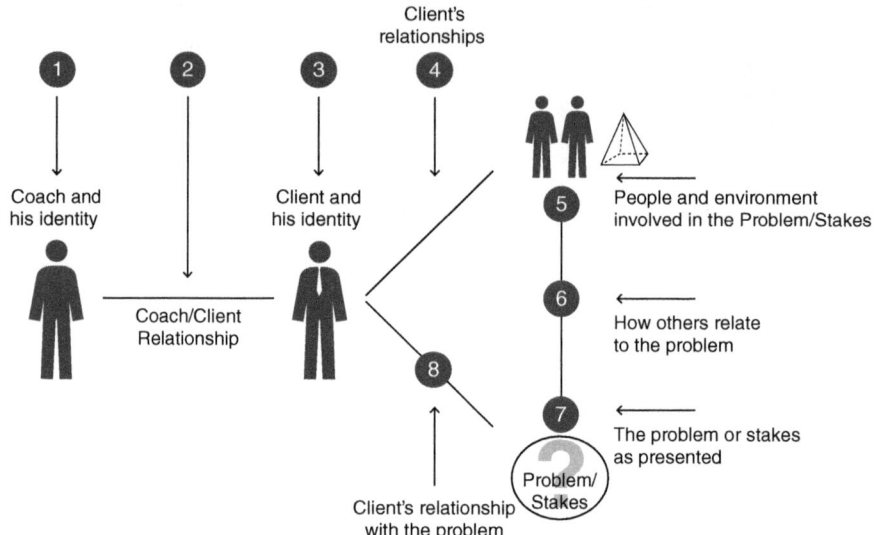

Fig. 26   The eight main intervention zones

Zone 1 concerns me directly as a coach, as I think through the stakes of this coaching situation for me. I take into account my own different levels of identity (see Strategy 8: *Identity Construction*), my emotions, my feelings, my mood and my physical health, including how tired I am. I also take into account my fantasies with respect to my client, especially if he represents an authority figure, is a business leader, or operates in a sector unfamiliar to me. In short, I need to be aware of everything I bring to the table, as a person, when I meet with the client.

If I am new to the coaching profession, I am unlikely to have the confidence and security that comes with experience, and may have doubts about my own competence. Organizationally, I may represent the consulting business that has hired me, and if my boss has already been in contact with the client's organization, I need to manage the pressure that the stakes associated with that client represent for the consulting business I work for. Here again, the stakes involved may affect my self-esteem and sense of ontological security*. If I am troubled by the coaching situation I face, I may, consciously or unconsciously, react inappropriately.

Zone 2 represents the relationship with my client, and entails a different set of stakes. As a coach, I need to question myself about the nature of my relationship with my client, the contract and the context. Is this *pro bono* coaching, is it happening before formal negotiations with the client, or before the invoice has been sent? Am I being paid a reasonable fee, or is it too low, possibly because I do not have the self-confidence to ask for more? Or on the contrary, are my fees too high, because I want to compensate my lack of confidence and my doubts about myself through money? Were the fees negotiated with the client organization by my consulting business, without my involvement? Am I clear with myself about my fees? All these factors will impact my relationship with the client in one way or another.

The RPNRC strategy is particularly useful in this zone. Using the RPNRC radar enables me as coach to check that the relationship, in its different dimensions, is in phase with the problem and the client's request. Have we come to a clear relational contract based on the client's explicit request and the resulting legal contract? Am I able to manage the gap between the client's explicit and implicit requests? Even more importantly, what are the transferential* elements or power plays at work, and should I as coach put in place specific protections* or be on my guard against certain mistakes to ensure that I manage the relationship correctly? If the coaching is being paid for by my client's organization, does he have his own private requests, independent of the formal requests made by the organization he works for? Does he really want to change the way he relates to his colleagues and the wider organization?

If this zone is not taken into account, the coaching intervention will fail. The coach will become hostage to the client's dysfunctions and to the more or less opaque and conflict-laden relationships the client has with the surrounding ecosystem. As the owner of the relationship, the coach needs to structure it in such a way as to avoid the relationship becoming either fusional or, conversely, being the excuse for a drawing-room discussion. He will need to watch out for parasitic elements linked to the problem, the people involved, or the wider ecosystem (I will come back to this when I discuss parallel processes later in this chapter). The objective in this zone is to creating the Princes(s)' Alliance* through a stable, trusting relationship, and to ensure significant energy is spent in nurturing this relationship.

Zone 3 is about the client. The coach assesses the different issues at the different levels of the client's identity and may use the identity backbone* with its nine levels of meaning (described in Strategy 6: *Access to Meaning*). In business coaching, three of these levels take precedence: professional (in the sense of the client's expertise in his domain), managerial (linked to his management responsibilities) and organizational (linked to the ecosystem in which he is embedded). Coaching often affects all three levels, each of which have specific issues and stakes, and which are not necessarily consistent with one another. For example, a manager may have been given new responsibilities in an area not linked to his domain of expertise, or may think he is not sufficiently prepared to take them on. Or a highly-qualified engineer has been thrust into leading a team or a project without the experience or management competence he believes to be essential to be able to take on this responsibility.

Zone 3 is also often the place where the client raises issues outside the strictly professional, managerial and organizational dimensions. A problem at work will generally echo across the personal, family, psychological or existential levels of a person's identity. Gaps or conflicts will often occur between a client's deep existential aspirations, his personal life, and the function he is asked to fulfill at work. These inconsistencies are particularly visible with people in their forties and fifties going through their mid-life crisis. Someone who has until now devoted his life to his work will suddenly realize that he has neglected his marriage, has not seen his children grow up or has foregone certain dreams or projects that would have seen him achieve fulfilment in a different way.

These overriding identity issues will positively or negatively condition the client's relationship with his ecosystem, or with the professional issues for which he is responsible. Issues around a client's ontological security* make up an extremely important part of coaching. Those taking up new responsibilities may have the "impostor's complex"; they may hide their insecurity by over-investing in acquiring new competences, or by playing power games. The coach will need to differentiate between the client's objective situation and the way the client experiences it subjectively. To do this, he needs to be able to appreciate the stakes involved for the client, and the client's sense of meaning at different levels, at the same time as avoiding the plunge into amateur therapy.

Zone 4 represents the interfaces that the client needs to manage with the other parts and players in his ecosystem. Among the client's many potential interfaces, the coach needs to focus on the vital few that relate to the client's issues. As he explores the different interfaces, he takes account of the stakes, the items to encourage (actions or future projects) and the items that need resolution (problems or obstacles to remove). It is in zone 4 that the latent, unconscious and mysterious complexity of organizations and human interactions comes to light. The coach fulfils his role by helping his client to become conscious of the appropriateness (or otherwise) of the relationships he cultivates in this complex space. The coach takes the client's multiple interfaces into account, and focuses him on those which need to take priority in order to deal with his problem.

Zone 5 corresponds to the parties with whom the client interacts and the communities to which he belongs (teams, divisions, production units or commercial organizations). The coach seeks answers to questions like: "Who are the key players? Are they in the right place? Are they competent? What are their individual and collective stakes?" Looking at this zone helps the client better understand the issues that face those around him, so that he can better position himself.

Zone 6 deals with the relationship that others have with the problem. Looking at this zone enables both coach and client to think through how the parties in zone 5 might be perceiving the problem as defined in zone 7, and how the client might influence their attitudes to the problem.

Zone 7 focuses attention on the problem or stakes as defined within the client's explicit request. Here, the coach's questioning may reveal the apparent problem to be a symptom of a deeper issue. The coach may focus on the reasons why the client needed help on this particular problem in this particular situation with these particular stakes, rather than focusing on the problem itself. This is where the coach will help the client to surface his implicit request, and get a better idea of the client's real need. To do this, the coach needs to be able to understand the gap between the client's explicit request and its latent content.

In my example, Jane, the CEO, perceives the production delays as symptomatic of an organizational failure in her company. As she explores zone 7, she realizes that these failures may themselves be symptoms of the different teams' inability to work together, or of the company's weak relationship with its suppliers. She is now able to undertake a more complex and more appropriate systemic analysis. The parties in zone 5 who perceived zone 7 as being secondary, and blamed others by suggesting that certain orders received from "on high" were not followed, were underestimating the complexity of the latent issues beneath the problem.

Zone 8 is about the client's relationship with the problem. The issues here may be completely different from those identified in zone 7.

The differences in points of view concerning one and the same issue will enable the client (zone 3), to do two things. Firstly, to have a better grasp of the extent to which the situation in zone 7 is an objective problem (production delays, for example). Secondly, to change her attitude to the problem. Instead of reprimanding the employees in zone 5, she will be more aware of the need to improve the recruitment or nomination processes, or may realize that she urgently needs to put a coaching initiative in place for key players in zone 5 in order to start to resolve the issues.

If the production MD believes that he did not have the resources to meet his deadlines, by exploring zone 8 the CEO (zone 3) may detect a level of incompetence in the production MD (zone 5), because he was not capable of putting in place a proactive strategy to avoid delays.

I would add a **zone 3a**, just above zone 3 (the client). It is of a different order to the others, since it is normally used in coaching supervisions. The issue raised in an operational coaching situation, like the coaching relationship itself, can lead to a kind of supervision. This involves identifying and articulating information or knowledge that the client needs in order to deal differently and more effectively with the situation, thus widening and enriching the client's frame of reference. The coach may share his own experience of similar situations, and the way he solved them. This gives the client examples of how to call upon extra resources in order to resolve an issue. The coach (zone 1) takes a supervisor's stance and provides levers so that his client can better understand the complexity of the stakes involved. He does not tell her what to do, but takes her through an awareness-raising process so that she is more keenly aware of the issues she needs to address.

A Work Plan to Enable Step-by-Step Contextualization

Once the coach has contextualized the situation and identified the intervention zones, he needs to think through his execution strategy. I propose the following six-step approach (Fig. 27).

1. List the key stakes involved. It is important to move from the notion of problem to that of the stakes involved. Each zone does not necessarily contain a problem, but does contain parameters that the coach needs to take into account. His first task is therefore to run through all the zones so as to identify the stakes, where they lie in each zone, and their relative importance. As he questions his

1. List key stakes

2. Develop work plan

3. Establish priorities

4. Checkup on identity

5. Check immediate stakes

6. Deal with parallel processes

Fig. 27 Key steps in the intervention zones strategy

client, the coach may wish to draw up a table with a list of the different players, parameters and stakes in each zone. This helps the client clarify what is at stake for him and enables him to find his way out of the confusion he may be experiencing.

This moment is also the opportunity for an invaluable exchange that reinforces the climate of trust and cooperation between coach and client.

This step may only take a few minutes, and does not necessarily need in-depth treatment, yet it enables coach and client to build an overall common vision of the context and stakes involved that is needed to prepare the work plan.

2. Develop the initial work plan. In step 1, the coach gauges the priority and urgency of the different stakes involved. Once the client has decided which are the first items to address, coach and client can create a roadmap with objectives, phases, quick wins and key longer-term issues to address. Building the work plan together strengthens the alliance between coach and client and reinforces the overall dynamic of co-construction that is the distinctive characteristic of coaching.

3. Establish the priorities. All the stakes cannot be addressed in one go. The overall vision of the different zones and stakes enables coach and client to define the key priorities. In response to the question: "What will we address in this session?" coach and client will focus on what they agree is most important and urgent.

If we take the example of Jane, our CEO who highlighted the deadlines missed by her production MD, the first three steps will have helped her better identify the stakes involved in zone 7 (the problem). She will focus on zone 5 (the competence of Ben, her production MD), whilst being aware that the relational contract between her and Ben (zone 4) needs to be better specified: production tracking may be inadequate due to a lack of shared strategic logic between them. As the session draws to a close, our CEO takes the decision to meet up with her Production MD and knows better how to broach the issue and tackle the problem. This is an example of the interaction between the overall work plan and the stakes that emerge in a particular session.

4. *Checkup on identity (zone 3).* If the client has come for coaching, it is because, at least at the beginning, she feels unable to deal with the problems on her own. The coach's role is to help her "get back in the saddle", in other words to regain a certain sense of ease and security. To do this, the coach will identify areas where the client feels fragile in her identity, either with regards to her competence or to her self-esteem. For example, if Jane as CEO tends to trust her team to get on with things without checking that they deserve that trust, her coach will work to help her become conscious of the fact that she also has her share of responsibility in the problems she encounters: maybe she has not fully assumed her role in checking that the right structures are in place. Inasmuch as she is partly responsible for the problem, she also has the means to resolve it.

If a business leader has only recently taken up the role, she may be having difficulty in taking the full measure of everything the new role implies. If this is the case, the coach should not relegate himself to the role of someone who encourages and motivates a client by recognizing her qualities. He needs to take the more subtle attitude of the person who gets the client to activate her own resources. Whatever the problem, the coach ensures that, at the end of the session, the client is more secure, more self-confident and freer in her choices when she leaves, because she has repaired, rebuilt or reconfigured part of her identity.

5. *Check immediate stakes to address.* During each and every session, it is essential that the coach identifies with his client the next bridges to cross. What does the client need to do as a result of the session? What is the next immediate decision or action? As the coach invites his client to embark on this personal reflection, she begins to develop ideas as to what she might wish to deal with in the next session. Coaching cannot be reduced to a series of occasional interventions: on the contrary, it is about maintaining a continuous and progressive dynamic of onward problem resolution and development.

6. *Deal with parallel processes*.* I will discuss parallel processes later in this chapter, but I can never insist enough on the need to identify this phenomenon that so easily fouls up the whole coaching relationship. More than a

sixth step, this should be a matter for the coach's constant attention. Before and after each session, and throughout the duration of the coaching process, the coach needs to ask himself the following question:

In what way is the client reproducing in her relationship with me the discomfort she is experiencing in her ecosystem?

Once a parallel process has been identified, the coach does not seek to eliminate it. Instead, he uses it as a springboard to help restore the conditions that will favor the client taking full responsibility, and moving to enaction*. If the coach neglects or underestimates parallel processes, he risks keeping his client's system in *status quo*, thus reinforcing her resistance and inability to change.

Behind the Problem, a Complex Interplay of Identity Stakes, and the "Seeding Effect"

As we have seen, the intervention zones link contextualization to the RPNRC strategy. Contextualization extends the notion of "problem" to that of "stakes" in the face of the client's experience of a complex reality. It also enriches RPNRC by reinforcing the constructivist* and enactive* dimension of the coaching process. The problem as expressed becomes part of an evolving ecosystem determined by both the intersubjective* relationships between the players, and their respective relationships with the problem. Contextualization also underpins an approach that deals with the personal and professional identities of the players, not just their relational interplay. What is called a "problem" is in fact simply a representation—or symptom—of a complex, tightly knotted system of interactions and levels of meaning.

Contextualization untangles the knots by doing three things.

- It engages the client in a co-constructed project, with the coach and other people, through a constructivist approach. As the coach questions the client to obtain further clarification, the client becomes aware of the systemic—even holomorphic*—dimension of the stakes involved. He moves forward in awareness of this dimension, and also in alliance with the coach. As a result, the priorities they have defined mobilize the joint energies of both coach and client.

- At the same time, it establishes the relationship in a dynamic over time. Though a single session can sometimes trigger a change, it is best to avoid a "one-shot" approach that does not evolve over time. Contextualization helps the client realize that any true resolution of problems stems from a necessary journey, especially when dealing with complex situations. This is what determines the work plan that is then deployed over time, session by session.
- Finally, the very act of defining a set of stakes, and creating a resulting work plan over time is a strong stimulus for the client to "get back in the saddle". He begins to emerge from his initial confusion, or find his way out of his "bag of bones". He looks at the situation differently: more confidently, more autonomously and more responsibly. Contextualization contributes to re-establishing the client's capacity to resolve his own problems. It sets in motion what I call a "seeding effect": we sow a seed, and time will turn it into a powerful force for resolving problems.

On a strictly operational level, exploring the different intervention zones helps the coach to avoid "getting his hands dirty" too soon with the client. Intervention zones can be used as an complementary emergency kit along with RPNRC, at the beginning of a coaching relationship, and in an ongoing manner, session after session.

Parallel Processes—When an Uneasy Relationship Reveals an Uneasy Client

Few coaches really master the contextualization strategy, even though it has a significant structuring effect in coaching practice. This is because mastering contextualization means dealing with parallel processes. A parallel process occurs when the client's unease or issues in relation to his ecosystem are reproduced in his relationship with the coach. The client "relives" the problems he has in his own relational system by projecting them onto the intersubjective* system he shares with the coach—their helping relationship. A parallel process always occurs in the coaching relationship, though it is generally implicit. It manifests itself in a variety of sometimes paradoxical ways, but in two ways in particular:

- *Transmission.* The client tries to put the coach into the same role or situation that others have put him into. For example, if he feels others have made him feel powerless with regards to an issue, he will set things up, unconsciously and with all the good will in the world, so the coach experiences a similar feeling of powerlessness. If he succeeds in this strategy, the coaching intervention is bound to fail in advance.

* *Reproduction.* The client tries to repeat what he does with others in the context of his relationship with the coach. Even if he has a strong desire to change, he will structure the relationship with the coach according to the way he habitually operates with others. For example, if he habitually plays the victim* role and expects others to rescue him, he will reproduce this in the relationship with his "rescuer*-coach" and refuse to enter into enaction*. Here again, if he succeeds, the coaching fails (Fig. 28).

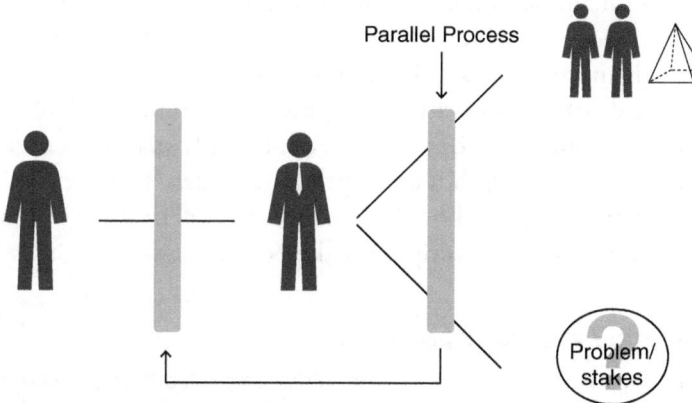

Fig. 28 The parallel process

In a previous book[2] I describe this process in detail; it is a variation of a process that is well-known to those who have studied systemics. It corresponds to what is known in Transactional Analysis as the "hot potato", where a person (generally the patient) transfers his own unease or his problem to someone else (generally the coach or therapist). This unease that passes from one to the other reveals the "pathology" of the client's entire ecosystem.

In coaching, the concept of "hot potato" describes the situation where the client tries to "get rid of" the problem by transferring it to the coach. If he is confused or stressed, he will try to transfer his confusion and anxiety to the coach. If he is unable to make a decision, he will unconsciously generate a climate of confusion

---

[2] *Au Coeur de la Relation d'Aide (At the Heart of the Helping Relationship).* Interéditions Dunod, 2008. Available only in French.

and contradictions in the relationship, that risks locking the coach into decision paralysis.

Beginner coaches are particularly vulnerable to this phenomenon. They see their client trying to pass them a "hot potato" that is too hot to hold, and their first reaction is to refuse this "poisoned gift". They try to avoid feeling uneasy instead of analyzing what is being played out through this unease. My experience has helped me to understand that this "hot potato" is not something the coach can simply set aside, then carry on working with the client as if nothing had happened. It is the expression of an ongoing process that runs through the whole relationship—hence the name "parallel process" (some authors speak of "systemic reflection"). The coach recognizes, names and deals with this phenomenon, not in order to get rid of it, but to identify what may be polluting the coaching relationship. It is an external expression of a problem that is internal to the client and his ecosystem.

When I speak of unease, this presupposes a certain level of awareness. Often the unease remains under the surface and only manifests itself through a particular stance, or through inappropriate attitudes. The client is unable to name what is happening, and he deals with it by reactivating it, more or less unconsciously, in his relationship with the coach.

Common forms of parallel processes

Confusion. The client feels lost in a multitude of entangled issues, relational interfaces, paradoxical situations, and mix-ups. He quickly tries to transmit this confusion to the coach. Firstly, the coach will identify the confusion that he in turn is beginning to feel. Then he will challenge his client, as gently as possible, for example by asking him to prioritize his problems, or focusing in on what he is requesting.

Stress. The client is under pressure, in an agitated state, and again attempts to transmit his stress to the coach, even if this means undermining the coach's OKness. Here the coach will take a "meta" stance with respect to the situation. He will counter the parallel process by adopting a calm, serene stance and thereby bring his client back to a calmer, more stable state.

Overwhelming. The client needs to talk about himself, either because he is alone in life, or because he in a position of responsibility, isolated in his "ivory tower". The coach feels overwhelmed by the client's fast and incessant flow of words that is hard to stop or slow down, and he feels uncomfortable and irritated. Here the coach needs to prevent himself from being swept away by a negative projection. By doing this, he progressively restores a relationship of balanced exchange that enables the client to come out of his imaginary solitude.

Decision making. Decisions often need to be made in a coaching session, and sometimes the client's problems stem from his difficulty in making decisions. If the client asks the coach to take decisions for him, the coach will not help him take the decisions, because deciding for the client will not resolve the client's core issue. Behind the difficulty in making decisions may lie the client's fears about his identity: he identifies with, and cannot disengage from, a fantasy Ideal Self. He will, often unconsciously, place this Ideal Self as a key stake in his relationship with the problem: "If I take a decision, I will be responsible for a choice that commits my whole being. If it fails, my entire defense system will fail, and I will find myself helpless in the face of my fear of death." The client transmits this fear to the coach in what Transactional Analysis calls the "Corner" game[3]: the client who feels cornered will desperately try to corner the coach, by making the achievement of this Ideal Self one of the stakes in the success or failure of the coaching assignment. It is the coach's job to identify this game and to extract himself as quickly as possible and thereby calm the client's anxiety in the coaching relationship. The coach does this by changing logical levels, and showing the client that the issue is not the decision in hand, but his fear of the disintegration and death of his Ideal Self (everything that his Parent ego state* says he ought to be). Once the coach has shown the client that his essential self, based on a clear understanding of his reference points and values, can survive the death of his Ideal Self, his anguish lessens and he is able to make his choice in the full knowledge that he will survive even if his image of the Ideal Self disintegrates.

Drivers.[4] According to Taibi Kahler's Process Communication model,[5] there are five drivers: "Be perfect", "Be strong", "Please you", "Try harder" and "Hurry up". These burdensome and coercive messages come from the client's Parent ego state and archaic parental injunctions. Drivers also reveal an identity problem. "If I am not perfect, I am not OK, and if I am not OK...." The coach needs to identify contagious drivers so as to be able to counter them.

Episcript. The episcript is a specific part of a person's script* that he "implants" or maintains in another person, so as not to have to deal with it himself. The episcript has both positive and negative aspects. For example, in Alcoholic Anonymous meetings, hearing and seeing that another person has stopped drinking can help me stop drinking too. By helping someone who has the same pathology as I have, I help cure myself. The negative aspect of an episcript is when I adopt the pathology of the other person: for example, I become an alcoholic because of my alcoholic friend. The client will often try to "infect" the coach rather than face up to his own problems.

Why Worry About Parallel Processes?

When the coach takes parallel processes into account and uses them effectively, they are, in my view, one the most powerful levers available to resolve conflicts and break out of the deadlocks that can bog down the coaching relationship.

---

[3] Eric Berne, *Games People Play*, p. 39ff.

[4] Drivers are behaviors that repeat consistently, lasting only a few seconds, and function like doorways to further distress. Different personality types display different kinds of drivers.

[5] Taibi Kahler, *The Process Therapy Model: The Six Personality Types with Adaptations*. Taibi Kahler Associates, 2008.

A parallel process is like the "alien in the spaceship": as long as it has not been identified, the relationship is in danger. If the coach misses it, or lets himself be carried away by it, he will not only be unable to help his client, but will also be in danger of reinforcing the client's dependency and difficulties. The relationship will be polluted or badly managed, and the coach runs a significant risk of being absorbed by the *status quo* of the client's ecosystem. Even if there are apparent changes in behavior, the "pathology" of the client's system will only be strengthened, and any intervention by the coach will only reinforce the problem. By contaminating the alliance on which the success of the coaching depends, a parallel process can curb and even paralyze the change dynamic that the client has begun.

On the other hand, by going on the alert as soon as he senses a parallel process, the coach can help his client even if he has not yet recognized exactly what process he is dealing with. If the coach realizes that there is something not right in the "here and now" relationship with the client, it is highly likely that something is not quite right in the client's relationship with his ecosystem. "There is something wrong in my management relationship with my team, so there will surely be something wrong in my relationship with my coach!" Some will say: "the parallel process is just one more problem". Exactly, and that is why it is so important! The coach's job is to identify the "something wrong" in the relationship, and then use it as a lever to help his client extricate himself from the system which shut him in and thus free himself from his discomfort and dead ends.

By using the tools we have already seen—third-order listening, RPNRC and the eight intervention zones—the coach can consciously steer the parallel process towards resolving his client's issues—like finding the thread of wool that unravels the whole pullover when pulled. Bringing up his difficulties in the coaching relationship becomes an enabler to help the client reposition himself with respect to both himself and to all his interfaces (both the problem itself and the actors involved). Over and above his own immediate problem, the client becomes aware of his customary way of functioning in this kind of situation, along with its implications. The client also distances himself from his own representation of reality, and this enables him to reorganize or change it. As a result, he positions himself more appropriately with respect to his own stakes, and those of his ecosystem.

The Coach Who Uses the Parallel Process is in Fact Resorting to a Powerful Transformational Lever

The coach does not turn the parallel process into a transformation lever by fighting against it, but by using its power and dynamics. To use the words of sensei Morihei Ueshiba, found of the Aikido martial art: "No-one can take away my strength because I don't use it. I use my opponent's strength and turn it against him."

Parallel process or transference?

The parallel process is a concept rooted in integrative therapy. It is different from transference, which comes from psychoanalysis. Their mechanisms and the stakes involved are also slightly different.

Transference is "a process by which the feelings that you had for someone (such as a parent) when you were a child become directed to someone else (such as a psychoanalyst)."[6] More generally, in all helping relationships the term designates the way a client projects what happened to him "there and then" into the heart of the relationship with, and principally onto, the helping professional. Countertransference describes the way in which the client's transference generates a number of unconscious manifestations and emotions in the coach. In psychoanalytic transference, the "there and then" is relived in the "here and now" in the relationship with the therapist or coach.

A parallel process, on the other hand, occurs when the "there and now" is reproduced in the relationship with the coach. The client reproduces, in the helping relationship, a situation that he is currently living through in his ecosystem.

Both phenomena often coexist, and can sometimes partially merge when a parallel process reawakens transferential elements or deeper issues with a client's scripts*. A parallel process, like transference, can be positive or negative. The French psychoanalyst Jacques Lacan had these simple, humorous words about the two facets of the transferential phenomenon, which also apply to parallel processes: "Positive transference is when the coach is in favor; negative transference is when the coach falls out of favor".

In a similar manner, dealing with a parallel process means defusing or transforming it so that it becomes a lever for progress in the coaching intervention.

Eight Steps to Manage and Guide the Parallel Process

Once the presence of a parallel process has been brought to light, dealing with it is a priority.

---

[6] Merriam-Webster dictionary.

1. As my client shares his problem with me, I see that something is not quite right in the relationship. My client is uneasy and is unconsciously trying to pass me a "hot potato". It is not for me to mistrust the person, but to make sure he does not drag me into his pathology. If I feel destabilized, the first thing to do is to recover my own OKness and ontological security*.

2. The parallel process is often masked, but it is always there: otherwise my client would not be coming to me. If I am not aware of it, I run the risk of running headlong into a host of relational traps. So how can I recognize it? It can reveal itself indirectly, through the unease or confusion I may feel as coach. I will often need to let the games start: firstly because there may be several parallel processes, and secondly because this will help me better recognize and counter the phenomenon. RPNRC is an essential tool for recognizing a parallel process before it overruns the whole relationship.

3. I am pleased that I have been able to identify a parallel process, because this means I have found a root cause of the problem, and that I will be able to use the parallel process to help my client move forward.

4. Now I have identified it, I need to make some choices: will I challenge my client, make things explicit, metacommunicate*, give advice? Or will I simply take up an appropriate attitude, on which my client can model himself, without explicitly naming what is going on? For example, by refusing to play the role of rescuer*, I will defuse the parallel process, thereby implicitly challenging my client.

5. Above and beyond this, I work on finding a "counter parallel process" on which my client can model himself. I offer my client alternative ways of behaving that he can use to deal with the problems that overwhelm him. By doing this, I help him realize that there is something not quite right in the way he is approaching his problems. For example, if my client is operating under the injunction "work hard", and is transferring this injunction to me, I will refuse to work hard, in order to show him that he has another option. By countering my client's behavior in this way, I reestablish a healthy, appropriate relationship and enable my client to go back to his situation and deal with the challenges in his ecosystem in the same way.

6. I use third-order listening to understand at what level in my own identity the client's parallel process resonates with me.

7. Using contextualization and the eight intervention zones, I identify the relational interface where my client feels uneasy with regards to his ecosystem.

8. I give the right hammer blow at the right moment so as to trigger the insight in my client ("Ah, of course!") that helps him move on to crystallization* (Strategy 10).

Access to Meaning and Restoration: The Path of Humanization

The parallel process is the key to decoding what is happening and to revealing the pathology of the client's ecosystem. It also gives the measure of what needs to be done; identifying it helps the coach to avoid being carried away and preserves the relationship from being perverted. But parallel processes are even more critical than this: if the coach is not aware of the phenomenon, he will be trapped in his own defense mechanisms and may become blind and deaf to what is going on, or give advice that will only exacerbate the client's problems.

Identifying a parallel process does not automatically resolve it. Sometimes the coach can be tempted to suppress the symptom without addressing the underlying need. It is not enough to name the problem (or dis-ease): the coach needs to ensure that the relationship with the client becomes the space for healing, through the mutual trust, ontological security* and empathetic listening that characterize it. Let us give Freud his due for his extraordinary discovery: what is the analytic cure, unless it is this intersubjective* space that enables the client to express himself, free up his discourse or even create a new discourse? As Irvin Yalom so aptly says: "It is the relationship that heals."[7]

Fundamentally, a parallel process is a lever for the coach to make the relationship an entry point for the dynamic of reconstruction for his client. It is not a thorn in the foot that needs to be removed, but the abode of symptom and recovery, the place of hurt and the place of healing. Once the meaning embodied by the parallel process has been identified, the relationship can be restored in a healthy manner, and can become a place where the client can work through what is happening and overcome his resistance to change, instead of repeating previous behaviors or remaining a slave to his compulsions.

Working on parallel processes helps the coach and client detect the inappropriateness of certain attitudes and relationships, and thereby adjust

---

[7] Irvin Yalom, *Existential Psychotherapy*, Basic Books, 1980 (Chapter 1).

them. Through the information, actions and example the coach brings to the party, he helps his client restore consistency to his ecosystem and, above all, take up an appropriate stance. He thus helps his client "get back in the saddle". Furthermore, the coach helps his client—individual, group or organization—to develop, in the sense that they better accept their own humanity in at least two ways.

- On the one hand, the parallel process enables the players to learn to accept their own limits and their own wounds, open up to themselves, reinforce their ontological security*, and relinquish their illusion of omnipotence—all means of becoming more human.
- On the other hand, taking the parallel process into account enables the coach to move from a purely technical analysis of family, professional or other problems, external to the client and brought by him into the relationship, to an analysis intimately related to his identity, and therefore more "human".

No-one is a stranger to these issues, and it is the stance that a person takes that conditions the access he has to the solution. The coach should not neglect the more technical aspects of an intervention, but the most important thing in the end is that the client enters the realm of self-transformation: as the coach works on the "objective reality" with the client, he helps him to revisit his "subjective reality", or the way he represents "objective reality", thereby helping the client to rebuild his identity as a human being with a grip on his own life and his environment.

Working on parallel processes means that the energy "bound up" in the parallel process is "freed up" to move towards the objective of freedom and responsibility for the client's own acts. Through the interplay of the inter-subjective relationship, the client develops his capacity for social bonding, and thus his potential to build a more human world. In this sense, under-standing the parallel process is a remarkable lever for humanization.

Key Points and Pause for Reflection— Contextualization

The questions below will help you think through how much contextualiza-tion, the eight intervention zones and the use of parallel processes are part of the helping relationships that you manage. These questions are designed to help you search inside yourself, so it is important to take your time. Even if you only deal with one question, take the time to reflect fully on it, rather than simply going through a "checklist" exercise.

1. To what extent am I on the lookout for a parallel process, both at the outset, and at all times in the relationship? In other words, to what extent am I aware of how the unease of the client with respect to himself and his ecosystem is—or risks being—reproduced in his relationship with me?
2. How much am I able to remain in contact with a specific issue whilst at the same time being aware of the overall context and the work plan that we have drawn up together?
3. Do I always take the time and spend the energy to ensure that the other's identity, ontological security* and potential riches (as well as those of his environment) are developed? In other words, *making sure the Golden Goose remains fertile as much as focusing on her egg production.*
4. How do I ensure that priorities are balanced between all the different aspects of the coaching intervention, such as practical coaching arrangements, the organization of schedules and venues, time for reflection, actions, relationships or identities?
5. To what extent am I aware that every exchange, every project, every action or time to step back, are moments where I can "sow" in the minds of the players involved, through the insights I can help bring to the people I coach? Insights to enrich them, and increase their awareness of the complexity and depth of their growth.

Strategy 5: Interventions: Categories and Options

In practical terms, what should I do when I am with my client?
What mistakes should I avoid?

The coach's own stance is certainly the most complex parameter in the coaching relationship, both in theory and in practice.

The coach is constantly adapting his stance, depending on his client, the client's structural identity, the nature of the problem, the client's development, the coach's relationship with the client and the context. During a coaching intervention, the coach may radically need to change his stance at a moment's notice as he takes account of these different elements.

The Coach, an Acupuncturist?

A client will rarely make a request about the process used in coaching: most of the time, he will express his request (or non-request) in terms of the results he wishes to obtain—often in an unclear manner. When someone comes with his tangled ball of problems with the request to help him extricate himself from a tricky situation, or at least move forward on some key issues, it is up to the coach to help him articulate more precisely what he is expecting.

© The Author(s) 2017
V. Lenhardt, *My 10 Strategies for Integrative Coaching*,
DOI 10.1007/978-3-319-54795-4_7

Simply reformulating and playing back the client's request (or non-request) helps reestablish a relationship of equals and opens up the possibility of working together: the client will no longer be "rowing alone" but neither will the coach be rowing in his place. Beyond that, establishing what the client actually wants is not a straightforward exercise, since the client is rarely able to clearly articulate his request. The coach has a number of options to get the ball rolling. He draws on this pool of resources throughout the coaching process, whenever he needs to bring in a certain directivity to support or revive the coaching intervention.

The field of possible interventions in coaching is wide, and potentially infinite. In this chapter I will only mention the most important intervention options, which are also the most common. I do this, because the coach should always seek to reduce his interventions to the strict minimum. As a professional of the helping relationship, I often see myself as a kind of acupuncturist, who seeks the greatest economy of means and uses the least possible number of needles when treating a patient. The needles he inserts do not bring energy in from the outside: if they are inserted at the right places, they free up the energy that the client already has within himself.

Among the many different possible interventions, the coach needs to choose those that are in line with the objectives and end purpose of the coaching. He should do this whilst remaining focused on helping his client move into enaction* as much as possible, in the most efficient and effective manner possible—in short, a crisp intervention with the right tools at the right time with the greatest economy of means. This was something I learned very early on as I trained with some of the major American and European therapists. A single, sometimes very short, intervention, can give a patient a major insight, or can help him reconnect to his emotional intelligence and enable him to recover his physical and intellectual energy.

I have already emphasized that it is as important for the coach to know what **not** to do, as it is for him to know what to do. Silence and silent listening are among the most powerful interventions, in term of both efficiency and effectiveness. Silence is not just "free floating attention*" as used in psychoanalysis, and managing a patient's subsequent frustration. Silence in coaching is far more structured, and is part and parcel of the relational space the coach creates, where the client spars with the coach as he works out his own solutions. Trainee coaches are always surprised when they discover for the first time how an appropriate use, and quality of silence enables them to alternate directive and non-directive interventions. This is a real step to freedom in the coach's development. Active listening is one kind of non-directive intervention: the coach shows that he is attentive to, and understands what the client is saying, by his non-verbal reactions: nods, signs of encouragement, or eloquent facial expressions.

> **Free floating attention**
>
> The coach does not try to comprehend every detail as his client tells it. Instead, he relies on his own subconscious and inner thought processes to handle the data. Later on, this enables him to pull together a composite, intuitive picture of what is really going on.

In 1994, during a meeting with the director of business unit of a major corporation, I learned with great surprise what Alain Godard[1] had told them when he had recommended me to them. "Given your situation, I suggest you work with Vincent Lenhardt. He the only consultant I know who is able to attend a board meeting for a whole day and not say a word!" Over and beyond the anecdotal nature of this incident, I am convinced that the coach's stance can resemble a spinning top that spins at great speed, yet appears not to move: full of energy, but not necessarily spending energy on direct interventions in the situation around him.

A counter example is the experiment done by a natural scientist on the metamorphosis of caterpillars into butterflies. He tried to ease the insect's intense and laborious metamorphosis by using different chemical and physical techniques. His interventions shortened the creature's labor and apparent "suffering", but the result was catastrophic: the butterfly did not have the strength to use its wings to fly! By trying to help the caterpillar and doing what the caterpillar needed to do, the well-meaning scientist had prevented it from mobilizing its own transformational energy, a prerequisite for it to be able to fly.

This is why the coach always needs to be careful to choose intervention modes and tools that develop the client's autonomy and help him take control of his own destiny. From the coach's point of view, it is essential always to have four or five intervention modes that help a client break out of his initial confusion and create the leverage for a co-constructed relationship between equals. Among other things, the coach may propose:

---

[1] Alain Godard, a member of Rhone Poulenc's, then Aventis' executive committee and a key player in the creation of Aventis out of the merger between Rhone Poulenc and Hoechst, with whom I co-authored *Engagements, Espoirs Rêves (Commitments, Hopes and Dreams)*, Pearson, 2005. Available only in French.

- searching out different options together;
- refining the diagnosis together;
- a time set aside for listening, and developing feedback;
- a time to reflect in order to enable the client to recover a certain ease in his identity and stance.

Three Main Intervention Categories

The coach has a broad range of interventions that fall into three main categories:

- interventions centered on the coach himself, and his own stance;
- interventions directed to mobilizing and freeing up the client's energy;
- Interventions focused on the coach-client relationship, that aim to change, enrich, stabilize or reframe this interdividual* space.

Coach-Centered Interventions

In terms of the contextualization model (see Strategy 4: *Contextualization*), the coach-centered interventions below relate to zone 1.

Silence

The first form of intervention, as we have just seen, is to **remain silent.** The coach may refuse to answer a question or respond to a request made by the client. He may decide not to fill what appears to be an empty space created by his own silence or that of his client, because being silent is one manner of empowering the client. In choosing to say nothing, I am telling my client non-verbally that it is he who is competent to resolve his problem, that he has the solution, and that he is the author of his own life.

This is not just a behavioral choice: unless the coach has deeply worked on himself, his silences will not trigger empowerment in the client. In this sense, the coach is the result of his own work, where he has learnt to manage his own anxiety and questions of identity (am I important, competent, loveable...?). The coach has identified his propensity for certain compulsions, worked on his unconscious desires and their manifestations and developed a solid sense of ontological security*. He will also have identified any transferential* or counter-transferential elements, and any "hooks" that the client might be attempting to use to bring him into a symbiotic relationship.

With respect to his identity, the coach has resolved the "competence paradox": he is able to ensure the other recognizes his competence, whilst at the same time recognizing its limits, and thereby make his competence—or lack thereof—the means whereby the client can assert his own competence, since one of the main stakes of coaching is opening up a space for the other to deploy his competence. The coach should focus all his energy and attention on achieving this objective. For the coach, this means banning all forms of competitive behavior, and accepting his own limits.

On an existential or spiritual level, it is by accepting unconditionally one's own vulnerability and existential hang-ups that the coach becomes more human—not being a "knowing person" under the illusion of his own omnipotence, or with the foolish hope of being seen by the other as all-powerful.

When the client sees the coach let go and accept his limits, he receives strong permission to accept his own weaknesses, fragilities and limits. It is in this way that silence can be the bearer of a humanizing dynamic, and a stimulus for the client's empowerment.

Over and beyond the inner work needed to achieve this quality of silence, the calm, friendly and soothing presence of the coach produces a rippling effect (described in Strategy 1: *The Rogerian Approach*) that is in itself a source for transformation, and offers the client a secure base for building his own identity. If the bond that is formed through this appeased relationship is to provide the springboard for the client to develop his own Prince, just being silent is not enough. The coach's silence needs to be imbued with the essence of his whole being, otherwise it loses its quality and its power. The quality of the coach's silence is a measure of the quality of his listening.

Swami Satchidananda, a grand master of Vedanta yoga that I had the privilege of meeting, summarizes the attitude of an "enlightened being", or *Jivan Mukta*:

When you are easeful, you are peaceful, and then you can be sure to be useful.

It is by being in contact with his inner being, his Prince (the "Self" of Vedanta yoga) that the coach adds value to his silence, as well as to his words.

The Coach's Stance

Other coach-centered interventions relate to the coach's stance, whether it is verbal or non-verbal. The coach makes explicit what he is experiencing if this enlightens his client. Depending on the time and situation, he may

- express his emotions;
- provide feedback on what he thinks of the situation;
- talk about the emotions, sensations and conscious or unconscious processes that he observes in the client;
- interpret or articulate the reactions that the client's remarks engender in him.

Coaching often has the image of a practice tinted with neutrality, where active listening and reformulation is enough to change things for the client. I am convinced that, even though the coach should remain neutral and refrain from making judgements, he also needs to take a clear stand with regards to the client's words and deeds, and share what he feels with his client. Giving up the illusion of always being right does not mean waiving the right to give one's opinion; it simply means accepting the limits of one's power to influence the other.

The coach may take a stand in many different ways, including feedback on what the other says or does not say, does or does not do. Each time that he speaks of what he is experiencing without denying either his limits or his difficulties, the coach brings the relationship back to one between equals, a necessary condition for the smooth functioning of the coaching process. To help his client to develop a level of awareness hitherto unknown to him, the coach may use explanations, illustrations, or other means of putting things in perspective (inspiring stories, testimonies from other people, metaphors…) that shed a different light on the situation and help the client change the way he looks at the situation.

The coach also takes a stand when his stance embodies certain values and reminds his client that they exist. He does this to stimulate the client's thinking, and also to activate different ego states* that the client may have put on standby. In this context, I have often mobilized certain emotions in myself—such as sadness, joy, anger or enthusiasm—that my client was unable to express, in order to invite him to rediscover that part of himself that had been suppressed or repressed, along with its associated values.

Client-Centered Interventions

There are a large number of interventions that relate to zone 3 (the client). Below are those that I consider to be the most important.

Questioning

The coach can draw on a wide range of question, depending on the situation and the needs of the moment: open or closed questions, clarification questions, questions about specifics, Socratic questioning* that seeks to deconstruct the client's frame of reference in order to give him access to a higher truth, or again questions that aim to activate a given ego state* (for example: "What are you feeling" may help trigger a Child ego state). An extremely rich aspect of a coach's work is to reactivate unrecognized or underused dimensions of a client's identity through various questioning methods. He may question the client with his "head", but also with his "heart" and his "guts". When he does this, he will be careful to encourage flexibility between the client's different identities—in other words, the client's capacity to change his stance according to the context.

Endorsements

Endorsements are used in 30% to 80% of coaching situations. When the coach takes the Rogerian stance of deep belief in the competence of the client, and considers that his client has found the right solution, he keeps to himself any other options he might have proposed, since endorsement is in this case the most appropriate and powerful intervention. The coach has listened long and hard to the client, who has formed hypotheses, worked through his options and expressed his doubts. The client is clear in his mind about his priorities, the decision he needs to take, and now only needs someone to endorse the fact that his plan is sound. The coach has listened to him, heard him loud and clear, and shows him that he has been understood. Through his feedback, the coach strengthens the client's resolve and frees up his potential by endorsing the stand he has taken.

Even though it often occurs in coaching, endorsing the client is not the most gratifying intervention for the coach, who neither brings a new solution, nor shows himself to be creative or proactive—in short, there is nothing here to feed his narcissism. Endorsement is nonetheless an essential role for the coach. When a person has doubts about whether he has made the right choices, or does not give himself permission to shoulder his own decisions, the support of an experienced counterpart, who understands him without playing the courtier, is often enough for him to move forward again. When this happens, the person in question is infinitely grateful for having been respected and considered as competent, because he knows that the coach could also have challenged him if necessary.

Challenging—Where and When to Challenge?

The coach challenges his client when he provides information on an inconsistency or an unease resulting from something that the client has done, said, or triggered in him. "You said you were going to work on this, but I can see no evidence that you are doing so." "You assert that you want to take up your rightful place in the group, but we are near the end of the session, and you have not yet spoken."

The coach needs to take significant precautions when challenging his client, to make sure that the challenge is not taken as a criticism. Furthermore, the possibility of challenging the client should always be explicitly stated in the coaching contract. Challenging a client needs to be done in a caring manner, and with the intention of developing the client: if this is done, challenging the client becomes a powerful lever for his growth.

The person who receives the challenge, and is able to accept it—even be glad about it and thank the person who makes it even though it is not easy to hear—takes a major step forward in relating to others: he is able to receive and take into account the word of another person.

Diagnosis

Performing a diagnosis is another major client-centered intervention. The coach, in agreement with his client, may propose a diagnosis in order to help the client break out of his confusion, or may identify a certain number of critical issues or key stakes. This intervention, based on the client's own words, enriches his view of the issue, and may radically change it. For example, a client's request may be excessive when compared to his real needs, or on the contrary his needs may far exceed his request. The diagnosis helps the client to become aware of this discrepancy, and to reestablish consistency between needs and requests. As we saw when outlining the 15 Parameters (Strategy 3: *RPNRC*), the coach bases his analysis on the client's needs and stakes within his ecosystem when he brings these issues to light. The coach also relies on his intuition and empathy, which means he needs first to have "cleaned his own spectacles".

Options, Protections and Permissions

During his different interventions, the coach often needs to propose different **options**—scenarios, actions, strategies, attitudes—that his client may choose to adopt (or not) in order to resolve his problem. Whatever the case, the coach needs to reflect with his client about how his client functions, before he can open the range of possibilities and explore that range of solutions available.

Putting **protections*** in place means warning the client of dangers, setting the framework for action and putting in place protective barriers to avoid him taking ill-considered risks. It may sometimes mean saying "no", especially in emergency situations. It may involve reminding the client of the laws of the land when he is tempted to break the law, reminding him of potential consequences when he appears to show little restraint, or warning him of potential dangers when he engages in arbitrary or fusional relationships.

Permissions* are the corollary to protections. They are ways of saying "yes": "Yes, go ahead, dare to take the initiative, dare to believe in yourself, dare to change…". Here the coach gives information, feedback, encouragement and trust, which help the client feel competent and authorized to forge ahead without taking unwarranted risks.

Combining protections and permissions

If I invite my client to express himself publicly and freely, this is a permission, which may also constitute a protection against his timidity. I also need to ensure that this permission is without danger for him, and to offer him the necessary protections for this new situation. A protection needs to be commensurate with the risks the client is taking.

The notion of escape hatch* in Transactional Analysis (mainly used in therapy) illustrates the deep reach of this combination of protections and permissions. Suicide, murder, going crazy and sometimes illness are forms of escape hatch: faced with different possible outcomes, the person chooses the most dramatic script*. In a business situation, the equivalent of suicide might be resigning: rather than confronting the conflict-laden situation, breaking away offers a dramatic outcome which is often undesirable, but which in certain circumstances might be attractive. Murder might correspond to firing an employee. The brutal decision to "terminate an employee" is generally a traumatic experience for the employee in question; and yet, this same employee can change his perspective and see it as an opportunity to go for a new job or profession that better suits him. Destroying equipment, sabotaging important negotiations, or even an indefinite strike can be seen as escape hatches in an organization; they may also sometimes be ways of trying to escape from gridlocked situations.

Escape hatch

Term in Transactional Analysis that describes extreme behavior that is activated when our essential needs are not being met. People access extreme choices from their script which are archaic decisions, not reflective of the here-and-now situation.

When the client is in a situation or context when he might expose himself to danger (such as resignation, redundancy, situational paralysis or psychosomatic illness), it is the coach's responsibility to put in place the protections that will enable his client to exercise his freedom, whilst ensuring his safety.

Decisions and Re-decisions

Finally, the coach enables his client to break out of situations where he feels cornered, by helping him with his **decisions**. In almost every coaching session there is a decision moment, whether it be to adopt a new behavior, to set a priority or to dare to challenge another person. The client may sometimes feel cornered by a range of choices that he feels is too limited, or that he believes are unfeasible options. "If I take this option, it won't work, but if I take the other option, it won't work either." "If I choose this path, I will have to forsake too many things that I hold dear, but the other solution also entails impossible renunciations." "If I am assertive with my boss, I expose myself, but if I don't, he will discredit me." What is really happening is that the person feels cornered because he is trapped in his own identity. The coach's role is to show him that his feeling of being cornered stems from a dynamic due to a particular phobia: that of losing his identity, or of being inconsistent with his Ideal Self. The coach's objective is then to identify the Ideal Self that has caught his client, to unhook it from him, and then discard it, just as one unhooks and discards a jacket one no longer needs from one's wardrobe.

The coach helps his client recover the freedom to take the right decisions, by helping him to identify the (often largely unconscious) fear that lurks behind his inability to take a decision. The coach's intervention enables his client to see if there is another viable option, often a "third way" that enables the client to break out his of binary "black or white" choices. The coach's decision aid is often a **re-decision** aid: the client believes he is unable to face up to the current situation, but in fact he is boxed in by a decision he made in the past that is inappropriate or obsolete in the current situation—a choice made five years ago is probably not appropriate today. By pointing out his capacity to re-decide and change his mind, the coach helps his client to break free from his unfounded feeling of powerlessness.

Relationship-Centered Interventions

Parallel Processes

Ah, this *damned...*—no, this *precious*—parallel process*! All the interventions around this process (see Strategy 4: *Contextualization*) deal with what is being played out at the heart of the relationship in intervention zone 2. This is without doubt the most important part of the coaching process: it aims to defuse the discomfort that is expressed in the relationship with the coach, which is simply a replica, or a "model" of the discomfort the client is experiencing in his relationships with his ecosystem.

Chairwork

The **"empty chair" technique,** or **"Chairwork"** is often used in Gestalt therapy, founded by Fritz Perls. It offers a form of intervention focused on relationships. Its aim is to separate the problem area from the transferential* relationship the client has with the coach. When the client speaks about his problem to the coach, he speaks as if to a figure in authority—the imago* of his mother, father or other person having played a significant role in his life history and personal development. If the chair opposite is empty, the transfer with the coach can no longer occur: by speaking to a fictitious person who is supposed to be in the other chair, the client is actually speaking to himself. The solution that emerges from this exercise will be his own, and not one that the client has presupposed that the coach, as a projected authority figure, would wish him to adopt. This process enables the person to break free from the confusion between different ego states*, or internal dichotomies that paralyze him. By speaking to himself, the client assumes responsibility for his own life, becomes aware of the confusion and contradictions within his own identity, and thereby frees himself from them. The coach of course needs to be at ease in working with a client in this way, and have a certain amount of know-how for this intervention to be successful.

> **Imago**
>
> An imago is an unconscious idealized mental image of someone, especially a parent, which influences a person's behavior

The list of other possible interventions is almost infinite, and attempting to list them all here would serve little purpose. My aim is not to write a technical user manual, but to draw the reader's attention to the options which are the most common, and have the greatest effect on structuring the coaching process.

Key Points and Pause for Reflection—Intervention Categories and Options

The questions below will help you think through how you use your interventions in the helping relationships that you manage. These questions are designed to help you search inside yourself, so it is important to take your time. Even if you only deal with one question, take the time to reflect fully on it, rather than simply going through a "checklist" exercise.

> 1. How committed am I to the fact that my interventions should be profitable for my client? How aware am I that I am at the same time not responsible for what my client does?
> 2. To what extent am I constantly aiming to develop my client's autonomy rather than making myself look good?
> 3. To what extent am I able to discern the Prince(ss) in my client behind the mask or the "Frog", whilst respecting my client's defense system?
> 4. How much am I centered on my own Prince(ss), deeply open to the other, though I may remain reserved and partly hidden?

5. Beyond the attention I pay to what I am sharing with my client, how mindful am I about what is being played out in the relationship: parallel processes, third-order listening, intuition and, of course, the end purpose of our exchanges?
6. How often do I check that I am in a state of internal calm and emptiness, in touch with my secure base?
7. To what extent am I ensuring the emergence of a co-constructed Princes(s)' Alliance between me and my client, whilst taking the stakes into consideration, as well as the amount and depth of change my client desires?

*

* *

The five strategies we have covered so far speak of what the coach can do, and how, in a coaching relationship with a client. I call them "operational" strategies.

The next five strategies are based on the stance the coach chooses to take up, and the angle from which he decides to operate, as he aims to help his client develop, become more himself, more "unified", more "human". I call them "identity strategies".

Strategy 6: *Access to Meaning* helps the client become more coherent and find more meaning in his life and his actions.

In Strategy 7: *The Client's Path,* the coach helps his client find his own path.

With Strategy 8: *Identity Construction,* the focus moves on to (re)constructing the client's identity.

When he uses Strategy 9: *Humanization,* the coach's priority is to help the client to discover his own humanity.

I have called the tenth and final strategy *Crystallization*—again borrowing a term from Eric Berne. It is a strategy in its own right, yet it also underpins all the other strategies. Whilst navigating one or more of the other nine strategies, the coach never departs from the stance of refusing to substitute himself for the client. By positioning himself in this way, he creates the conditions for the creation of the (often complex and paradoxical) space where his client becomes freer and more responsible for what he decides, what he does, and what he becomes. In this sense, the tenth strategy is a meta-strategy.

To paraphrase Spinoza, the client owes it to himself to progress and to "persevere in being". The coach gives the client greater access to what he has a right to be. The coach, like the sculptor who senses the statue already present within the rough stone before him, helps his client "carve the block of stone from within himself" so that the statue within, that "being" who is there in all its potential, can appear fully formed and accomplished.

Strategy 6: Access to Meaning

> *What is the meaning of the work I am doing?*
> *At what level of meaning are my issues and my stakes?*

In my previous books, in particular *Coaching for Meaning,* I have spoken in depth about meaning, and described the different meanings of the word "meaning". Working with clients on meaning involves covering a number of different aspects of meaning[1] as applied to their lives.

The Meanings of Meaning

We commonly speak of the *sense* of a word, depending on the meaning we attribute to it. In the same way, when we look at a person, a situation or an event, we can have several potential viewpoints, a number of different ways of interpreting reality, and different levels of understanding. Relating to others and the world around, involves sensing things and people (with our five, or six senses) and then attributing meaning.

---

[1] See the seminal work on meaning by Ogden and Richards: *The Meaning of Meaning* Harcourt Brace, 1989.

© The Author(s) 2017
V. Lenhardt, *My 10 Strategies for Integrative Coaching,*
DOI 10.1007/978-3-319-54795-4_8

The coach will focus on the different meanings of meaning, from the way we sense things and others (through listening, emotional intelligence, empathy or our own quality of being), to what we signify (different logical levels, meaning-building, work on values), to the meaning, or final purpose, of our existence and the goals we set as a result.

Above and beyond these definitions, I have come to the conclusion that meaning-making (or sense-making[2]) can be either a slow *process of construction* like the picture that gradually emerges when one works on a jigsaw puzzle, or a sudden *emergence of coherence in consciousness*—Archimedes' "Eureka!", Fritz Perls' "Aha" moments, or, more trivially, the moments when everything suddenly becomes clear for Sherlock Holmes, as he realizes what actually happened.

Creating Meaning in Complexity

In an organization, the actions often refer to the "*What?*", the sense in which people work together is the "*How?*"; and the final purpose is the "*Why?*". When an executive team puts in place a series of actions, it does so in a certain manner, and because of certain values. Objectives provide a sense of direction for action, the plan details how it will be done, and values represent the end purpose: the Star that ever guides us, but that we never reach.

Within organizations, an essential focus of both management and leadership is the emergence of the shared meaning that team members give to the actions they take. This enables leaders to share a common vision as to the purpose of their actions, whilst meeting, as far as possible, the aspirations of their employees for consistency and wholeness. The reader may be familiar with the well-known story of the stone mason who responds to the question: "what are you doing" by saying: "Can't you see, I'm cutting a stone!" In response to further questioning he gradually becomes aware of different levels of meaning of what he is doing: "I'm earning a living to feed my family...I work in a team where I feel I belong...I feel recognized for the quality of my work..." until he gets the final revelation: "Can't you see, I'm building a cathedral!" The coach's job is to help this awareness emerge, so that the actions of his client are consciously aligned with his values.

The question of meaning is a major challenge for 21st-century organizations, confronted with the chaos and complexity* of a post-modern society,

---

[2] As described by Karl Weick in *Sensemaking in Organizations* Sage, 1995.

where traditional management methods that worked in a complicated* but controllable world are no longer valid. It is vital that those who lead organizations give meaning to work in general, and to people's actions in particular. They manage knowledge workers who, paradoxically, as Peter Drucker says: "have to manage themselves. They have to have autonomy… You can't manage knowledge. Knowledge is between two ears and only between two ears."[3] Complexity lies not only in the environment, but also within the organization, where change has become the only constant, and agility has become the main quality needed to adapt to the continual transformation of the world around. In this context, where "the best way to predict the future is to create it" (Drucker's words again), businesses need free and responsible players. To be free and responsible, people need to be able to create the meaning they give to how they act, how they belong, and how they choose their identities. Jeremy Rifkin, in his analysis of the Third Industrial Revolution* and the transition to a zero marginal-cost society,[4] suggests that we are in a transition phase characterized by a hybrid form of management that mixes the vertical, hierarchical command and control logic of the Second Industrial Revolution with an ever-increasingly flat "project" logic of the Third Industrial Revolution, where cross-functional peer-to-peer relationships are the norm.

These are major issues, which go far beyond the scope of this book. Nevertheless, the coach needs to keep them in mind, because they form the backdrop to coaching in today's world. Coaching today is more about helping clients to relate in a complex environment than teaching them how to act. In Norman Wolfe's[5] terms, the coach stands alongside the "Doers", but he does not "do" in their place, nor does he tell them what or how to "do". He helps them so that their actions contribute to a fruitful dynamic of Collective Intelligence* formed through multiple relationships, as they enact* their lives into a systemic, holomorphic* reality. The coach seeks to bring his clients to a vivid awareness of the complex reality they live in, when they are normally "heads down", pedalling away furiously as they focus on their immediate actions, having lost sight of the meaning of what they are doing.

---

[3] Peter Drucker *The Post-Capitalist Society*, Routledge; 1994.
[4] Jeremy Rifkin, *The Zero Marginal Cost Society: The Internet of Things, the Collaborative Commons, and the Eclipse of Capitalism*, Palgrave Macmillan, 2014.
[5] Norman Wolfe *The Living Organization: Transforming Business to Create Extraordinary Results*, Quantum Leaders Publishing, 2011.

What is essential, and what is important?

Coaching can help reinstate what is essential at the heart of what is important. Whether in our coaching practice or when we exercise any form of responsibility, it is vital not to confuse the two.

What is essential is everything that gives intrinsic value and meaning to human life, what contributes to a person's growth and what stimulates his awakening to the world around him.

What is important—as distinct from what is urgent—is about a person's professional or social life.

Distinguishing between the two does not mean separating or partitioning them. On the contrary, what is essential influences what is important. As Bertrand Martin said when we met[6]:

We should live out what is essential at the heart of what is important.

Today it makes no sense to speak of the economy or business without attending to the human dimension that enables organizations to grow sustainably. I believe that enabling values and meaning to flourish at the heart of an organization is one of the primary tasks of each and every leader and manager, for both are called to become meaning-bearers.

The Secret of the Golden Goose

I often remind my clients that my stated intent and endeavor as a coach is not to "pull the eggs out of the golden goose", but to make sure that it becomes, and remains fertile.

Coaching as I see it, practice it and teach it, focuses as much on the development of the individual and identity building, as it does on operational results. More specifically, the reason that the coach never loses sight of the results—the golden eggs—is that *they are a means to the final end of the development of the individual, team or organization in question*—the fertility of the goose. For me, this perspective represents a potent and foundational value of the coaching profession itself. Here again we are not talking in terms of "either or"—results OR developing the client's identity, operational performance OR meaning. The coach has a different kind of logic, that of AND. From this perspective, taking both of these "opposites" into account is an essential part of the development of the individual.

The coach creates a certain quality in the relationship, respects the client's freedom, and takes into account his level of autonomy and the rhythm at

---

[6] It is through this phrase that Bertrand Martin and I met deeply with each other. He said this to me, just after I had written exactly the same phrase in the preface to my book "Coaching for Meaning". After a brief exchange, we fell into each other's arms!

which he develops best. Over and above respecting the client himself, the coach also has a strict code of ethics with respect to the client's environment. He remains constantly on the alert with respect to the permanent risk he runs of being hijacked for other purposes by the person he is coaching, by the person's hierarchy, or by the organization that funds the coaching.

The ambiguity that constitutes the coaching profession also permeates every management relationship. When we coach a person who has a team under him, the way we consider our client is a model for the way we invite him, and coach him, to consider those in his team. Within a work environment, each and every player has a paradoxical identity: he is an "object of production", in other words, a component that can be replaced and controlled, in a system with performance targets and constraints that has been built and organized to produce results. At the same time, and in no less a sense, he is also a "growing subject", a unique human individual, responsible for the choices in his personal and professional life, and a relatively free being in spite of his constraints, problems and contradictions. Whatever his profession or level of responsibility in a team, organization or project, each and every player oscillates between these two poles, and tries to avoid being reduced to one or the other. An organization that focuses only on production objectives without ever taking into account the meaning its employees give to those objectives, will see its ambitions for development or change fail in the more or less short term. At the same time, ignoring the aspect of "object of production" is out of question. For me, the art of management is about creating, in the work place, the conditions that enable individuals to build, or rebuild, a certain coherence between these two dimensions of their identity; in other words, between their desire for self-actualization and their status as players in a production value chain. In an era where individuals are confronted with ever-increasing lawlessness at the same time as a dizzying openness to others and to the world, access to meaning is a core issue for organizations, and indeed society as a whole. Man's search for meaning goes hand in hand with his aspiration for a certain unity of being, and one way of achieving this is through better integration of one's personal and professional life.

The management stance, and more generally, the relational stance I attempt to cultivate through coaching, permanently integrates this dual polarity. It begins by seeing each player as a free and responsible individual before seeing his function as an "object of production". The manager who has benefitted from the coach seeing him in this way will internalize it, and then seek to generalize it by sowing and promoting it in his team or organization.

The client may not be able to accept this ambiguity. To do so, he needs a secure base with respect to his identity and a minimum level of ontological security*; building these is the end purpose of the coaching relationship. For the client, this means accepting challenges, calling himself into question, and a gradual transformation of his overall identity—behaviors, psychological structure, frames of reference and relationships. We are not in the business of painting over rusty structures; our ambition is the organic transformation of the caterpillar into a butterfly.

The lobster complex

During the decades over which I have coached clients, I cannot recollect a single business leader who was not susceptible, to a greater or lesser degree, to the "lobster complex". The lobster does not need a backbone because its shell serves as a substitute, and this suffices for it to remain stable. Take away the external shell, and it has no structure left and collapses.

The leader's shell, or armor, is his status and power. They protect and confine him at the same time, by trapping him in his own defense mechanisms. Since he is cloaked in his managerial identity like the lobster in its shell, he is not predisposed to invest in his own personal development. Sadly, in a complex world, a business leader locked into his rigid identity of order-giver and unable to call himself into question becomes a hindrance to his entire organization.

Conversely, if he is able to give up hiding behind his illusory armor and work on consolidating his own backbone, (which includes accepting his own limits), he will no longer feel compelled to make a show of his power or to protect his status. He will dedicate all his energy to putting his competence to the service of others, and to generating a dynamic of Collective Intelligence in his organization. As he brings what is essential into the heart of what is important, he becomes a leader who is both a resource for others and a meaning-bearer, and this reinforces his authority. Others will admire his charisma and humility, and the organization will take on new life as he radiates around him.

The Identity Backbone

I propose two complementary models that the coach can use to help the client through this process of access to meaning: the identity backbone and the meaning molecule. When travelling in an unknown land, we need a map to avoid getting lost. I share these models with the individuals and teams that I coach to help them navigate the land of meaning, with which they may be unfamiliar. Using these models helps them to become aware of the path they are treading, the inevitable difficulties on the way, and the inevitable inner work they need to do.

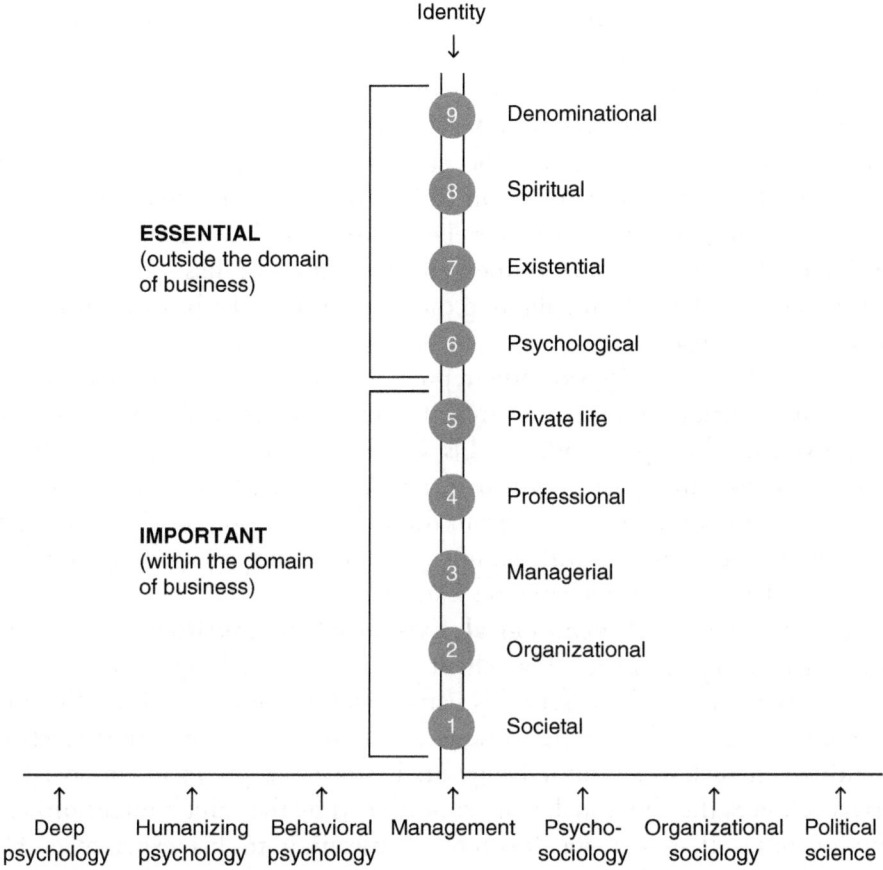

Fig. 29   The identity backbone

The identity backbone, which I first described in my book *Coaching for Meaning*, distinguishes nine levels in a person's identity construction (Fig. 29).

Each level has its place, its coherence and its own logic. No level can be ignored, or reduced to another. At the same time, each level is connected to the others, like the vertebrae in the human backbone, without which we could not stand upright—hence the name of the model. In the "here and now" of a coaching session, the question of meaning can be asked at the level of each of the different vertebrae. Earlier, I compared the coach to an acupuncturist. Here, I will use the metaphor is of an "osteopath of meaning".

Level 1—the first vertebra—represents the client's **Societal** environment. A sense of belonging to an institutional entity (such as a country), a culture or an ideology may be foundational to a person's identity. Some, like soldiers who go to war, or members of the French resistance in the Second World War, are ready to sacrifice their lives in the name of this allegiance.

Levels 2, 3 and 4 correspond to the most common areas in business coaching. Level 2, **Organizational**, deals with how the client belongs to a specific organization, with all the stakes and issues involved. Level 3, **Managerial**, represents his function (this is where clients often need coaching when taking up a new post). Level 4, **Professional**, represents the client's profession for which he has trained and for which he has specific competences. The coach works on aligning these vertebrae as he brings consistency between these areas.

Level 5, the client's **Private life**, represents his identity with respect to his family, his marriage or his social circle. For many, their professional activities have overrun this space. When this happens, it is important to set up protections for this space, nourish it, and restore balance. This "vertebra" gives the client space to recover from difficulties at work, and to experience constructive attachment (with family, partner, leisure or sporting activities with friends) so he can recharge his batteries.

Levels 6, 7 and 8—**Psychological, Existential** and **Spiritual**—are directly concerned with meaning. The client comes to coaching with his own unconscious, his family history, his hang-ups, his emotions, his sentimental or marital issues, all of which resonate within each of his other levels of identity. These levels cannot be ignored, since the professional, social or private choices the client makes are conditioned by the values, intentions and end purposes that give an "existential" meaning to his experience. His spiritual identity nourishes itself with the intimate conviction that the meaning of his existence is larger than that of his individual, finite life.

Working on levels 6 to 8 involves working on the "Why?"—the intrinsic causality within a person's life, linked to his past history. It also, and possibly above all, involves working on the "What for?"—the end purpose—as the coach questions him about what he wants to happen from now on. Here I refer the reader to the different approaches of existential psychotherapy, from Ludwig Binswanger to Irvin Yalom and to the essential contribution of Viktor Frankl. Their position might be summarized as follows: I do not wipe out the past, but I choose to find meaning in my life based on what I wish to accomplish in the space and time that separates me from my death. I will therefore interpret the current event in this perspective. In doing so, I answer the questions: "Where am I going?", "Why?", and "For whom am I working?"

One can inquire about the past and probe the future. A third way of asking about meaning is to ask "What does this mean for action in the here and now?" The purpose of this question is to help the client become aware of the unconscious conflicts between different parts of his personality. For example, the "Empty Chair" exercise mentioned in Strategy 5: *Interventions*, helps the client put a certain distance between two parts of himself that are in conflict, and create meaning by moving beyond this dichotomy. The client speaks to the empty chair, imagining that another part of himself is seated there. Then he sits in that chair, and answers himself. This enables him to unravel the different "internal voices" within himself, and gradually come out of his confusion and deadlock.

The "osteopath of meaning" can even call upon a fourth way of asking about meaning, based on the eighth vertebra, representing the client's spirituality. This questioning goes beyond the visible and the rational—even beyond the emotional. This intuition-based opening, that Eric Berne was so fond of,[7] enables the client to find a sense of meaning that transcends the mental, rational and emotional perspectives. The person "plunges within", attains a state of deep awareness and quality of being, that I call "spiritual", and which corresponds to what a person deeply believes in, and that which gives meaning to his existence. This meaning can be shared with others: the "minute of silence", when people with completely different identities and allegiances stand together to share a time of silent respect, is a magnificent example of shared meaning. It shows how people can be in fellowship in spite of the beliefs, religions and values that separate them.

Finally, level 9, **Denominational**, enables the client to attribute meaning in a manner consistent with a vision of the world particular to his faith or ideology. When it is appropriate for the person concerned, working on this ninth level enables him to rewrite the meaning of the here and now in a manner consistent with his religious or ideological tradition—in short, whatever he believes in. The answers from previous levels take on a different tone of sound or color, depending on the meaning the client attributes to this level.

Access to Renewed Coherence

Through these nine specific yet correlated levels of identity, the identity backbone provides an integrative approach to an individual's identity. Though no model, however sophisticated, can give a full account of the complexity or the fundamental mystery of being, the identity backbone provides a valuable frame of reference that helps the coach position his approach, both within his own practice and with respect to other helping

---

[7] See Eric Berne *Intuition and Ego States*, Harper, 1977.

relationships. What is both special and universal about coaching is that it takes into account all the components of identity construction. This integration occurs not only vertically (the nine vertebrae in Fig. 29) but also horizontally (the base of the figure) which represents the different fields of knowledge that can be used to analyze the client's levels of identity and his ecosystem. The coach can thus embrace the different identity levels of the client without confusing them. As he helps his client rebalance his identity, the coach helps his client bring more consistency, more unity, and in the end more meaning to his life (Fig. 30).

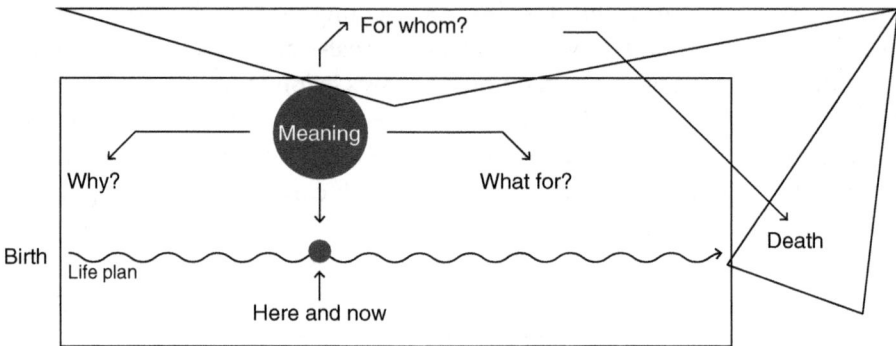

Fig. 30   The existential model of life between birth and death

   As he manages the coaching process, the coach can use the identity backbone to understand where the client's stakes lie. The first five vertebrae (or identity levels) are mainly about the relationships the client has with others. In terms of intervention zones, we are talking of zone 2 (the client's relationship with the coach), zone 4 (the client's relationship with those involved in the problem), zone 6 (the relationship of those involved with the problem) and zone 8 (the client's relationship with the problem). Vertebrae 6 to 9 are more directly related to the person himself. In business coaching, the coach will normally sign a contract to work on the organizational, professional and managerial levels (vertebrae 2, 3 and 4). His work will be distinctive in that it will focus on aligning these three vertebrae and also aim to make them consistent with the client's private life (vertebra 5). Notwithstanding, he will never completely disregard the more intimate vertebrae in the client's identity backbone. Scars from a person's past, or strong ideological or religious convictions can significantly affect how the client considers and experiences his professional relationships. The coach will not attempt to work directly on these more intimate areas: he is there to help the client recognize the different levels in his identity, to understand his stakes at the level of each vertebra, and to define or redefine his priorities as a result. Rarely are professional issues resolved without the client searching inside himself and revisiting these levels, even though this exploration may have nothing to do with therapy. One might even say this inner work is the condition for being able to come up with new ways of thinking and acting.

The identity backbone helps the coach think through and position the coaching relationship with respect to what is "important" or what is "essential". Politics, technology, business and the economy (vertebrae 1 to 4) all lie in the domain of what is important, whilst all that concerns the client's private life—his psychological, emotional and bodily structure, as well as his emotional bonds, his ethical, societal and spiritual convictions (vertebrae 5 to 9)—lies in the domain of what is essential.

The human person needs to be considered as a whole. The coach will endeavor not to reduce one level to another, but will seek to unite them in a common movement that accesses a person's deep sense of meaning. At the same time, even though coaching may open up to adjacent domains, it does not encroach onto those domains. Though a strategy of access to meaning may take the form of interpretation, this is not in the psychoanalytic sense of the term (that of unveiling hidden meaning). The coach bars himself from entering the client's secret garden, but he embraces what the client says at the different levels of meaning that correspond to his identity, and invites the client to listen to himself. Like the osteopath who accompanies his patient, the coach helps his client in the search for a new sense of balance that offers greater consistency, ontological security* and capacity for accepting otherness. By doing this he helps his client stand upright so as to decide and act in a manner consistent with his values in all areas of his life, supported by all the "vertebrae" of his identity.

The identity backbone also helps the coach check, at any given moment, whether what he is doing remains strictly within the limits defined by the coaching intervention, both in terms of competence, and in terms of his own code of conduct. It helps the coach identify at what level his client is questioning himself, thereby avoiding amalgamations and confusion. This may mean that the coach directs his client towards a different kind of helping relationship, when the need that is finally expressed goes beyond the domain defined by the contract or the coach's own competence. The coach needs to be able to take the whole person into account, because moving forward in a particular situation requires taking account of his psychology and beliefs. At the same time, his role should never be confused with that of a therapist or a spiritual guide. If he feels there is a need in these areas, the coach will point his client to the relevant specialist. As such, the nine levels of the identity backbone also help clarify the frontiers between the different helping professions.

The Meaning Molecule

The meaning molecule, now a major part of my practice, has two main sources: Viktor Frankl with respect to meaning, and Donal Winnicott with respect to object relations theory.[8] Frankl's writings and personality profoundly affected me, in particular when I read his first book, *Man's Search for Meaning*.[9] In his book, Frankl, a Jewish psychologist and psychotherapist, testifies of his own hardships and his observation of others' suffering during his internment at Auschwitz during the Second World War. The conclusions he drew from living through this hell on earth became the foundation for Logotherapy which he subsequently developed: amongst the prisoners who remained alive, it was neither intelligence, nor strength, nor riches that determined resilience. Those most likely to survive were those who, beyond the horror and the trauma of their experience, gave meaning to what they were going through.

Object relations theory

deals with relationships between people, especially between the mother and her child. Our key drive is to form relationships with others, and we internalize the objects of our love. Thus we have a relationship with the internal mother as well as an external one.

Frankl's three "avenues to meaning"

In the postscript to his book, Frankl distinguishes three ways of giving meaning to one's experience:

- by what I bring to the world, by creating a work or doing a deed—such as a project, a political or artistic endeavor;
- by what I receive from the world—meeting someone I love, experiencing nature, a work of art, or having a spiritual experience.
- by the freedom I exercise in when facing a fate I cannot change, such as an accident, a traumatic incident, illness or death; paradoxically, the constraints imposed on me, even if I did not desire them, become the opportunity for me to create meaning for my life, and I welcome them and give meaning to them instead of giving in to vain rebellion and denial.

---

[8] See his article *Transitional Objects and Transitional Phenomena*, Int. J. Psychoanal., 34:89–97 (1953).

[9] First published in German under the title *Ein Psycholog erlebt das Konzentrationslager (A Psychologist Experiences the Concentration Camp)*.

For years, I meditated on Frankl's testimony, trying to understand the wellspring behind a sense of meaning powerful enough to keep someone alive. Finally, this reflection gave birth to what I call the meaning molecule, composed of four "atoms", all of which need to be present to meet our fundamental needs—a strong sense of bonding and a relationship with others rooted in our own human identity. My conviction is that we aspire to satisfy our need to belong, in order to live out our deepest nature, that of "beings in fellowship". For this we need an object of love, the capacity to relate, an infinite dream, and enthusiastic energy. For us to give meaning to our lives, all four need to be present: if one of the atoms of the meaning molecule is missing, our whole being is out of balance (Fig. 31).

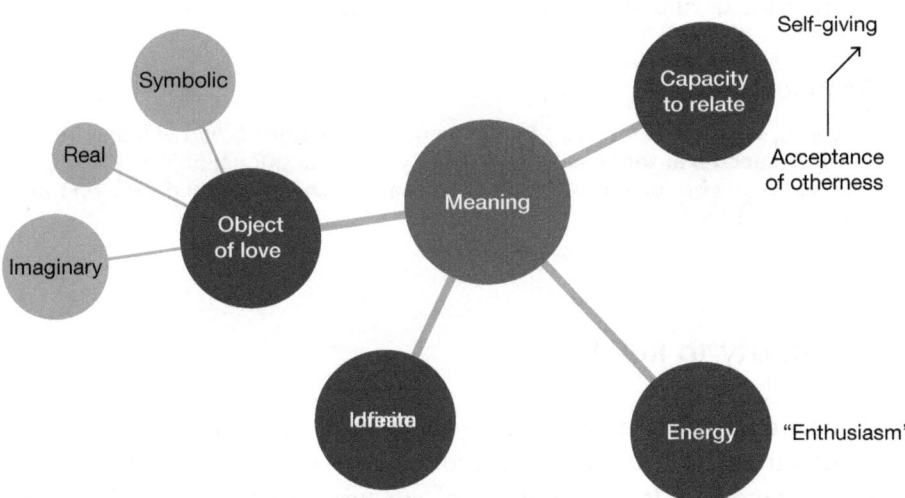

Fig. 31   The meaning molecule

The Object of Love

First of all there is an **object of love.** Frankl eloquently describes how those who survived the Nazi concentration camps were able to hold out because they had an object of their love, whether it was real, imaginary or symbolic.

- The real object may be a loved one, a family, a village or a community to which we feel we belong. Meaning is constructed through the attachment that we have to this object or person that we aspire find again.
- The imaginary object may reside in a dream or project we have. In spite of its virtual nature, it gives meaning to our existence.
- The symbolic object designates something that transcends reality, which links our experience to a greater meaning, such as a work of art or literature, our political commitment, or a belief in the divine.

Donald Winnicott emphasized the foundational role of the object relation in children, in particular that of the transitional object* in the construction of self as a human subject. George Kohlrieser[10] demonstrates that even as adults we need to build our own ontological security* through a bond with an object of love—another person, a community, a place, a goal, a project—that can guide us and structure our sense of meaning.

> **Transitional object.**
>
> An object, such as a teddy bear, that has a quality for a small child of being both real and made-up at the same time. Playing with a transitional object can be an important early bridge between self and other, which helps a child develop the capacity to relate to others.

The Capacity to Relate

Since relating is at the heart of our sense of being as humans, we also build meaning through our capacity to accept otherness. In other words, meaning does not come only from the object of our love, but from the relationship that we have with the object of our love. The final purpose of all personal development and human potential work is to restore or reinforce our capacity to enter into relationships.

My experience in therapy has shown me how the bond with an object of love becomes pathological when it becomes exclusive or symbiotic. A drug addict, for example, identifies the object of love as his "fix": when it is the only thing that counts for him, then his whole life can be reduced to his addiction. This can also happen with food, medication, or other

---

[10] George Kohlrieser, *Care to Dare, Unleashing Astonishing Potential through Secure Base leadership*, Jossey-Bass, San Francisco, 2012.

addictions like work, which alienates people so that little exists for them outside their work. Workaholics find neither time nor satisfaction in social, family or romantic lives. Devoting oneself to a project, an activity, or a passion can be deadly for one's relationships. Identifying a client's object of love is not innocuous, since it points to the way the client relates to others. It can enable the coach to detect his client's toxic or destructive dependence because of his attachment to an object of love. In coaching, this strategy aims to identify whether the client's object of love alienates him and stops him finding more fulfilling relationships and activities on which to bestow his love. In business this could be his career, his exaggerated sense of belonging to his company or the addictive nature of his work.

In the coaching school I run, the participants gradually experience new forms of relating through peer groups similar to those in therapy. In these groups, they practice giving and receiving positive and negative strokes*, and learn to live out their relationships from the richer and healthier perspective of an "economy of abundance". These future coaches free themselves from the more or less neurotic roles they played out because of their cultural or family heritage. They discover other, more satisfying ways of investing themselves in a relationship. They discover the importance of concepts such as inclusion, control, openness*,[11] regulation and metacommunication. They learn to listen differently, to share their emotions, to exercise empathy and to take up the stance of a "resource person" who helps another construct their own identity.

Stroke

In Transactional Analysis, a person gives a stroke occurs when he recognizes another person, either verbally or non-verbally. He gives him a kind of "unit of recognition".

Inclusion, control, openness

From Will Schutz, *The Human Element*. **Inclusion** is the first stage of team development, which consists of the process of each team member being fully included in the team. The team then enables each member to have a say in the

---

[11] These concepts are from Will Schutz, and imbue the whole culture of the *Coach & Team* coaching school I founded.

way it functions, as it moves to giving **control** to its members. Finally, as each team member has the courage to expose his own weaknesses and vulnerability, the team attains **openness**.

Developing one's capacity to relate and to bond is always the result of building (or rediscovering and rebuilding) and accepting otherness. In other words, an encounter with an object of love is not enough, one needs to be able to invest oneself in a relationship, to create a shared space of belonging that results in a healthy and nourishing bond. This will often require significant work on oneself. Even though everyday life can help us move forward, it is often only through focused personal development and indeed therapy that we achieve this openness in our relationships. This openness requires us to face up to and free ourselves from our fears and the defenses we have built to protect ourselves from old hurts and untreated griefs. As we free ourselves from the defenses which have become our psychological, ideological or institutional prisons, we experience a kind of healing and—to paraphrase Freud—"become capable of loving and working".

Creating this bond becomes the anchor for our ontological security*.

Having built or restored a capacity for accepting otherness, we are able to move on to *self-giving*. Viktor Frankl expresses the progression in this way: *Homo Faber* (who defines himself by what he is able to do, his competences and his knowledge), who has become *Homo Amans* (able to go beyond himself through his capacity of relating to others), then attains a fuller sense of meaning and existing by embodying *Homo Patiens*. In the full knowledge of the facts, *Homo Patiens* offers himself up for the common good, even going as far offering up his life for something that transcends him—such as a cause, a community, or an ideal.

It is of course important to remain on one's guard so as not to transform this commitment or relationship into a kind of deviant, unhealthy or alienating dependence—whether in one's business or any other project in which one invests oneself. A company is not a cult; religious faith must not lose itself in fanaticism or fundamentalism; political commitment should not turn into an intolerant ideology. History, and especially the history of the twentieth century, has vividly illustrated the fact that the greatest ideals can give birth to the worst monstrosities. Working on meaning is important because it helps to create the conditions under which the client is able to build a healthy relationship with an object of love, thus meeting his aspiration of greater fulfilment, without veering into extremism.

The Infinite Dream

Beyond the relationship, the object of love needs to generate a dynamic whereby the client seeks to surpass himself, going beyond the rational without ever abolishing it, and opening him up to the mysterious, even infinite dimension of his existence.

If it does not carry a dream, some sort of mystery, or even a spark of folly, the sense of meaning will always fade away. This is why numbers in themselves are never fully satisfying: they lock us into the finite dimension of certainty, and what is quantifiable.

The works of Abraham Maslow, Frederick Hertzberg, Douglas McGregor and, more recently research from the University of Rochester, suggest that the most powerful source of our acts lies in our desire for self-realization, if possible by doing something whose ultimate fulfilment is by definition unattainable. "Hygiene factors", external and material motivation, though necessary, are not enough to move us forward. Access to meaning mobilizes motivators of another order, linked to irreducible elements of our individual human conscience: our need for fulfilment, completeness, recognition and belonging. For Jeremy Rifkin, this represents *Homo Empatheticus;* for me, "a being made for fellowship". Let me make it clear that fellowship is not fusion; it is the Princes(s)' Alliance* that I describe in Strategy 1: *The Person-centered Approach, or Rogerian alliance.* This Princes(s)' Alliance is the energizing connection between the positive parts of people which resonate deeply within each as they relate to each other.

Energy

The relationship with the object of love needs to be **a relationship that generates energy**, the fourth component of the meaning molecule.

What gives a person meaning are the things that help him push out into the river of life, not those which shut him into poisonous relationships, dead ends, or artificial paradises—whether in his personal, social or professional life. When an individual's energy is activated and his potential released, then we can safely say that meaning has been rediscovered. The trigger often comes from outside, such as meeting a charismatic person, having an inspiring boss, getting a new project, being offered an unexpected opportunity or experiencing a "moment of grace". However, it is only through an internal dynamic that an individual can build lasting meaning. He nourishes this dynamic by connecting to his internal resources, his successes, his self-confidence or his faith—in other words, when it awakens the Prince(ss) slumbering at the heart of his identity. Each of us is free to choose the Princes(s)' name, depending on one's beliefs…or one's doubts.

From Ego to Self: Connecting Anew with the Spark of the Divine

I owe it in large part to Viktor Frankl that I was able to include the existential dimension in my professional and personal life. His contribution helped me place my profession in the context of an integrative view of human nature: my client, like me, is made up of finite elements, which at the same time are open to the infinite—the infinite nature of love, and the infinite dimension of the fellowship that is the Princes(s)' Alliance. The existential opens the way to the spiritual, and even to the denominational dimensions in our lives.

Taking this perspective has helped me make my professional activity, and even my life, a time and place to help my fellow humans in their journey as they seek the treasure that lies in their deepest being. Of course, I always respect the existential and spiritual dimensions specific to each of my clients, which may be centered on a religious belief in transcendence, or the belief in the self-transcendence of the humanist or atheist. Whatever the case, I am convinced that, as human beings, we only fulfill ourselves when we surpass ourselves.

Helping the other put what is essential back into the heart of what is important, helping to restore his capacity to fully live in a relationship: this, for me, is a way of building "humanity" anew with my client. I live out this approach because I believe that helping another means literally to rediscover a kind of "enthusiasm",[12] or a means of communing with the divine which is at the heart of our being, in a mysterious way, far beyond any religious discourse.

"Intimior intimeo meo—he who is in me is more intimate with me that I am with myself", wrote Saint Augustine of Christ. This echoes St Paul's cry:

---

[12] Enthusiasm comes from the Greek *en theos*, literally "in god".

"It is no longer I who live, but Christ who lives in me." In my experience, this notion of fellowship has a strong link with Eastern wisdom, in particular the teaching of Shankara in the Vedanta. This great philosopher and Hindu mystic believed the world, space and time are only mental perceptions, and the only real identity is in the "Self". For me, the Prince(ss) I speak of in this book is none other than this Self—or, for the Christian, Christ who lives within.

As I practice my profession, I assume responsibility for my beliefs, but I ensure that I am never sectarian or proselytize. I do not hide my faith, but I only share it in exceptional circumstances and with the greatest reserve, with an attitude of the deepest respect for the other's frame of reference.

The integrative helping relationship

In my book *At the Heart of the Helping Relationship* (available only in French) I share a model called *Weighted Integrative Therapy* (WIT). This is closely linked to the concept of the identity backbone*, and is based on the following observation: a number of different schools of therapy coexist with different approaches to the "patient". Each approach has a number of presuppositions that form a "therapeutic paradigm"—in other words, each school has a certain vision of what it means to be "healed". This vision reflects a certain vision of health, which in turn reflects a certain vision of what it means to be human.

This led me to classify seven approaches, outlined in the table below, along with the concept of health that underpins them.

Approach	Underpinning Concept of Health
Traditional Western medicine	Suppress symptoms.
Psychoanalytic	Resolve unconscious conflicts.
Humanistic	Restore the ability to grow.
Systemic	The capacity of the system to resolve the problem by itself.
Existential	Find renewed meaning in one's problem, one's life, one's death, one's existence.
Spiritual	Find meaning in one's suffering or one's life as a result of one's spiritual journey.
Weighted Integrative	Weight each of the above approaches according to the patient's need, whilst making sure no approach is excluded.

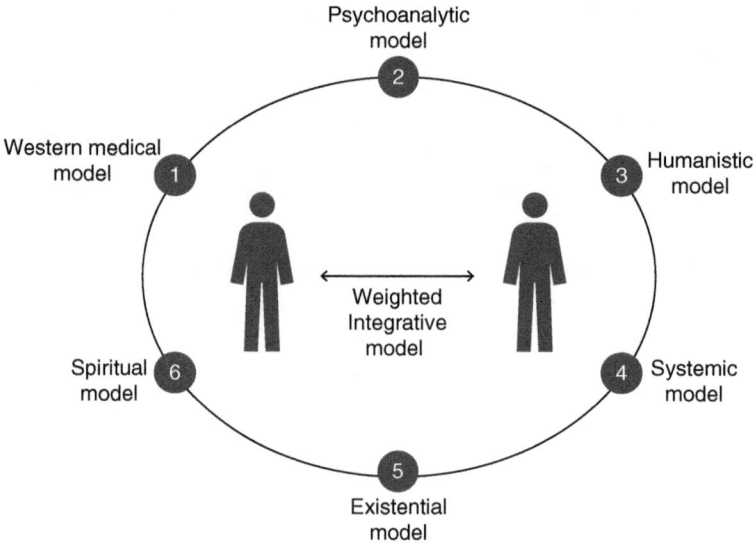

Fig. 32   Weighted Integrative Therapy

These approaches are not mutually exclusive: I show in my book how there are no fundamental contradictions between them. Each therapeutic paradigm opens up a specific perspective on the complexity of what it is to be human. They are all partial theories in that they represent different statements about one aspect or another of our humanity, and they have developed operational models and work plans in consequence. Each model by itself represents a simplistic view of reality; their complementarity appears when one take a "meta" stance that goes beyond each partial vision. I call this "meta" stance Weighted Integrative Therapy (Fig. 32). It attempts to understand human beings in a holistic, and not just analytic manner.

Let us take the image of cutting precious stones. A diamond shines from all directions once all its different facets have been cut. In the same way the integrative therapist aims to work on—or at the very least, to embrace—all the different facets of his client. For change to be sustainable, it needs to occur in the different dimensions that make up a human being: body, emotions, thoughts, behaviors, the psyche, as well as his existential and spiritual dimensions. Treating a patient in any other way only generates partial, and therefore inadequate solutions. Depending on the individual, the problem, the specific needs, the moment in time, and the progress in the therapeutic relationship, the therapist mobilizes the most appropriate approach without ever losing sight of the wider perspective that includes the other approaches.

Though it does not address the same issues as Weighted Integrative Therapy, integrative coaching as I see it is based on the same integrative view of the human person. It considers each human being as an open and complex entity, with different, but inseparable levels of identity that constitute a whole that is greater than the sum of its parts. When faced with his client and his client's problems, the coach does not stop at the "objective" symptoms:

- he welcomes the other with all his emotional intelligence and psychological depth;
- he puts his client face to face with the responsibility for his own growth—in the humanistic paradigm, a "healthy" individual is not someone without problems, but someone who is working on his problems;
- he takes into account the systemic dimension of situations, in other words the "pathologies" and issues in the overall relational system within which his client operates;
- he concerns himself with the end purpose of those involved, and considers them first and foremost as "growing subjects" for whom meaning is primary.

Key Points and Pause for Reflection—Access to Meaning

The questions below will help you think through how you use access to meaning in the helping relationships that you manage. These questions are designed to help you search inside yourself, so it is important to take your time. Even if you only deal with one question, take the time to reflect fully on it, rather than simply going through a "checklist" exercise.

1. How aware am I that the notion of meaning represents much more than an objective, or even values?
2. To what extent do I make sure that I identify the factors that condition the energy and the awareness of my client?
3. How do I contribute to the emergence and construction of consistency in my client's consciousness?
4. How do I help my client specify at which level of meaning he has a need?
5. How do I help my client understand and establish his priorities, what is essential, important and urgent?

Strategy 7: The Client's Path

How does the current stage fit in my client's journey?
Where is my client coming from? What is his past?
Where is my client going? What does the future hold for him?
What transition space should he consider?

A "Waypoint" in the Client's Personal Journey

We are all in a state of becoming, and our identity constantly changes as we seek to find ourselves in our existential journey. We often stumble over obstacles, and sometimes get lost or end up in dead ends. When this happens, we may call upon the services of a coach to help us set a new direction, or define anew the path we choose to tread.

The coach's role is to help his client gauge the path he has already trodden, discern its meaning and importance, and understand the significance of the stages he has been through. His role is also to help the client identify the path(s) that are now opening up before him, to visualize the tracks he may follow, and to spot the difficulties he is likely to encounter. In the light of this discussion with the coach, the path the client treads takes on new coherence.

© The Author(s) 2017
V. Lenhardt, *My 10 Strategies for Integrative Coaching,*
DOI 10.1007/978-3-319-54795-4_9

The strategy of the client's path positions the time of coaching as "waypoint" in his personal journey. The questions the coach explores in this strategy are:

• What is the meaning and importance of this place and this time for the client?
• How did the client get to where he is now (*flash back*)?
• What future lies before him (*flash forward*)?
• What transitions are needed?

We have already seen various strategies that enable us to define the time and space dimensions of coaching, the difference stances the coach can take, the intervention options, the client's stakes and the decisions that need to be taken. Here, the objective is to position the present moment in the light of the past, the current context and the future that is emerging so that the client can

> *fulfil the future that is emerging in the present moment, rather than "fix objectives to solve a problem".*

For this, the coach needs to look at managing any transition period(s) that may be needed, so the client can give himself the means to fulfil his future, with the necessary protections* and permissions*—everything he needs to free up his potential and his energy.

If we lack the means to achieve our objective, we may need to adapt our objective to our means.

As he envisions his future, the client may realize that what he wants to achieve is currently beyond him. The strategy of the client's path integrates three elements to help the client move forward with the means at his disposal;

• the lever for transformation, which I call third-order suffering*;

Third-order suffering The suffering associated with growth, comparable to what the caterpillar goes through as it transforms into a butterfly.

• the client's space-time context—in other words, the stage in life that represents his "here and now", which is the result of the path he has taken in the past and represents his potential for the future;
• the transition space he needs to put in place to enable his transformation.

Inevitable Losses

The path of growth is not always a "long quiet river". As a person goes through changes in his identity, he may need to go through a grieving process for beliefs, relationships, and goals that he gives up as he sets out on a new path with a new logic, new ways of working and new projects. He will also need to free up energy he spends in other areas in order to invest it in new ambitions. Transformational work takes on different forms and has different rhythms with different individuals, but it almost always involves difficulties and heartbreaks. Changing one's skin is rarely easy—the butterfly knows something about the challenge of moving from incremental to transformational change!

The strategy of the client's path requires the coach to have both practical experience and a solid theoretical understanding of what constitutes and conditions change. The coach needs to understand and take into account the nature of the change and the level of change involved (see the different levels of change, described in Strategy 1: *The Rogerian Alliance*). He also needs to be able to deal with the client's resistance to, and fear of change—we build our defense mechanisms to protect ourselves from primal fears. The coach will need to help the client to dismantle his fortresses, go beyond his fears and center himself on the positive dimension of his transformation. This entails accepting a particular kind of suffering that is consubstantial with transformation.

My experience as therapist, coach and teacher has led me to distinguish three different types of suffering.

First-order suffering that we are all familiar with, comes from life's knocks and bumps: a physical accident, the pain of injury, illness, addictions, ageing and death—sooner or later we lose someone close to us, or we become aware that we need to consider our own demise. It is the stress generated by our personal difficulties, our relationship problems, or situations and events that we had not wished to happen, but which we need to face as we journey through life.

Second-order suffering that we are also all familiar with, is born of separation or confinement. This is the suffering of the person separated from an object of love—such as a loved one, family, or country. It is also the suffering one who feels he is far from his dreams and aspirations, a stranger to what he would like to be, to accomplish or to experience in terms of relationships. It is the suffering of the person who does not know how to get out of a situation, and feels imprisoned, physically or virtually: he may be unhappy at work, but feeling stuck because there is a family to feed; locked into an unhappy marriage or family from which he can see no escape; paralyzed by psychosomatic illness, for which there seems to be no "cure".

Third-Order Suffering: the Price of the Return to Life

Even though the first two orders of suffering can help us to grow, and can even be used to give meaning to our lives, it is better to avoid them if possible.

What I call third-order suffering* is of an entirely different nature. It is related to identity change, and in that sense is also inevitable. We need to learn not to avoid, but to meet with, and to accept this suffering that is associated with the growth that can occur at any of the levels of our identity.

Those who go for therapy normally do so in order to rid themselves of psychosomatic illnesses, psychological distress, relationship issues, or other symptoms that bring suffering to their lives. Their hope, or belief, is that they will be healed of their suffering and become less vulnerable in the future. What a surprise when they realize that things are not so simple! The process of change itself, and the state of heightened sensitivity that comes with it, leads them to experience unexpected suffering: some of their defenses have been dismantled, and trying out new behaviors generates new risks. Having for years lived in protected isolation, they now find themselves faced with a paradox: therapy, through which they were seeking a means of alleviating their suffering, leaves them more vulnerable because they have dismantled their defenses and become more open. Removing their protective shell makes them more aware and more open, but also more sensitive and more fragile. They discover that the price to pay for the journey towards "healing" is that of exposing old wounds and reliving painful events that they had repressed or suppressed. They need courage to encounter their own fragility in the very place they had built the protective wall of defensiveness and fear. They need to make sense of this suffering in order to support the work of restoration and construction.

We experience third-order suffering when, more generally, we see a limit within ourselves—a rigidity, pathology, unease, or anything that stands in the way of our fulfilment—and we go beyond this limit in order to open ourselves up other possibilities. Fear and grief often accompany this experience. As we leave behind a certain comfort in our ideas and our reassuring defense systems, we recover the capacity to accept otherness. This letting go—intellectually, psychologically, physically, emotionally, existentially and even spiritually—can be frightening, and even painful. As we forsake our physical or relational dependencies, we are faced with absence and emptiness before we find new balance. This experience generates pain and deep turmoil at the moment when our energy is released, but this energy is then free and available again for us to use.

I often compare this pain to the pain one feels when blood begins to circulate again freely in a frozen hand or a stiff leg: it is the pain of returning to life.[1] Third-order suffering represents the price of growth, the price to pay for greater life, freedom and responsibility.

Herein lies the greatness of the relationship the coach proposes to his client: to be a companion as he treads this path. To do this, the coach needs to take the measure of his client's ability to come to terms with change, and evaluate how feasible it is for the client to undertake the work of identity deconstruction and restoration with all that this entails in terms of the difficulties that the client will need to face. The coach helps him question his comfortable habits, face his fears, take difficult and sensitive decisions, and dare to live out new situations that express the change he has made.

In order to achieve this, the coach takes great care to prepare a development plan with his client that identifies the transition periods needed, along with the appropriate protections* and permissions* for each period. As the coach does this, the client becomes free to make sense of his suffering, and to continue on the path of fulfilment as a human being.

> ### When the caterpillar resists becoming a butterfly
>
> In the early 1990s, one of my clients, a brilliant man in his fifties from France's elite school, the "Polytechnique", and in charge of a subsidiary of 800 people, was asked to become vice-president of one of the biggest companies (10,000 employees) in the industrial group he was working for. This change represented a significant promotion and recognition of his capacities. At the same

---

[1] Spiritually, third-order suffering corresponds to the journey that St John of the Cross calls the "dark night of the soul", the darkness represents the believer's hardships and difficulties of renouncing his own life, forsaking the world, and opening himself to otherness and divine love.

time, he needed to move from the position of a hierarchical, somewhat authoritarian order-giver, to that of a non-executive vice-president in the role of a "super coach" whose responsibility was to prepare the whole organization for change. In his previous role, any decision he made was immediately executed by his subordinates; in his new role, he needed to expend considerable effort to negotiate actions with those who needed to do them, and thereby establish his influence. He had a gratifying title and status, but he felt disillusioned and insecure. In his new job, he had to take up another stance, and he was acutely uncomfortable with this change, much as the caterpillar "suffers" during its metamorphosis into a butterfly. In one of our sessions, when I remarked that he was turning into a butterfly, his response was: "Well, I must admit that my life as a caterpillar was much less frustrating!"

My client was living through third-order suffering. His humorous resistance eloquently illustrated his dream of returning to a former, less gratifying, but more comfortable situation.

The Space-Time Dimension

Each client comes to coaching with his own situation—a dream, a life project, decisions to take, relationships to examine, or a profession or job to question. The issues discussed always have a dual perspective: on the one hand, the client's path over time, and on the other hand the place from which his questioning emerges: his education, his culture, his family or ethnic roots and, of course, his script*—his basic psychological structure, his primal way of functioning and the partially unconscious life plan within which he may be imprisoned.

The coach seeks to understand not only all the contradictions and dead-locks within which the client is more or less consciously confined, but also everything that has contributed to his development, and helped him become who he is today: his key stages in life, his multiple personal and professional experiences, his many and varied competences. Re-evaluating the client's past enables coach and client to explore "re-decision" moments together; they will bring to light the way the client built up his resilience through the difficulties he faced on his journey. They will then go further and deeper: some of the major decisions that we take in our lives belong to our script*, that is to say the largely unconscious life plan we have programmed. Other decisions reveal a counter-script, or a programme that our parents or other significant authority figures decided for us, and that we have internalized without being fully conscious of it. Yet other decisions stem from an anti-script, or a life plan that is the result of our rebellion against our past and the place we belong—we are actually playing their scripts out in reverse, though of course we would vigorously deny it!

This clarification and discernment is a significant piece of work, and needs to occur right through the whole coaching process.

When considering the client's future, the coach first needs to avoid prematurely predetermining it by focusing too early on objectives. Until the client has sufficiently "cleaned his spectacles", learned to "listen" to his desires and needs, and become aware of his deep aspirations, he remains conditioned by the compulsive repetition and the internal messages of his Superego, or his Ideal Self. The coach needs to be acutely aware of the danger of looking at the future with the spectacles of the past. Some over-simplified existential approaches fall into this trap, and prematurely fix objectives before defining how the client wishes to fulfil himself through his profession, his projects, or his activities.

I personally have been deeply influenced by Viktor Frankl's thinking. Frankl reverses the reading of an individual's history and choices by taking an existential stance with a focus on end purpose rather than causes. When looking to the future in this way, waking dream techniques can be extremely revealing and helpful. The coach may use the exercise of the "epitaph on the tombstone" and invite his client to imagine what would be written on his tombstone, and what he would like to be written, after his death. A variation of this is imagining what his colleagues say about him when he retires.

Widening the range of possibilities in this way by visualizing the end of a person's working life, or the end of his physical life, is often more fruitful than specific questioning about the desires and objectives in the client's immediate future. In all cases, the coach needs to understand how well the client's future aspirations are consistent with his past.

The current space-time context of both the client and the coaching intervention is another key indicator to adjust the strategy of the client's path. If the client has questions, for example about his profession, or wishes to change companies, it is important to ask if this questioning occurs in an environment and ecosystem that are favorable and are ready to embrace it. Some ways of calling a client into question, though necessary, may be too brutal or premature given the client's family, relational or professional situation. It may even be advisable to maintain an unwanted situation for a few months until the client is able to achieve some sort of reconciliation with certain key elements in his current situation and defining factors of his past. In this way, the coach gives the means and the time for the client's deepest desire to emerge, a desire which will often have been masked, repressed or even suppressed.

Is now the right moment to change? Or is now the moment to prepare a future change? These are questions the coach needs to ask, along with his client, in order to avoid rash, premature acts that may simply be a way of escaping anxiety and uncertainty through violent and impetuous action.

The questioning process often directly or indirectly impacts all aspects of the client's ecosystem. The client may sometimes get confused with the many interacting things going on at the same time: his own attitude to change and the losses it implies, the impact of the past, material uncertainty, or doubts about his underlying desires. These may get mixed up in his mind, and as a result, the client may become uncertain as to his own desire for change.

One way of reframing the situation is to get the client to think through the means he currently has to achieve the desired change. Does he have a clear project? Are the conditions right for implementing his project? Does he have the needed competences to implement his project, or the technical, financial, psychological, relational support he needs to manage the transition? "Adapting the objective to the means" implies an objective analysis of the situation and the context, a subjective analysis of the desires and needs of the client, and careful thought about the "ecology" of adapting the client's need to the feasibility of the project.

The Transition Space

Three weeks to "manufacture" a rabbit…but how long to "make" an elephant?

One difficulty in the practice of coaching relates to how much time is needed for the emergence of the desire to change, and the time required for implementing the change once decided. Depending on the scope of the change, the period of gestation may be more or less long. During that time, the coach needs to ensure that his client has access to one or more transition spaces. For example, the client wishes to start his own business, but he lacks a number of objective elements as to how he will exercise his new responsibility. Training as a business owner may be essential for the success of his project. An over-preoccupation with efficiency or a desire to face up to his fears may prompt him to take decisions prematurely. He will then look to his coach, not to confirm whether or not his plans are robust and realistic, but for a validation of his "compulsive" decisions. The coach will refuse to give that validation, since he realizes that his client needs reassuring because of his fear of a vacuum, and that he is not adequately taking account of the internal listening process needed for the emergence of his real desire. The client has probably become aware of what he does not want to do, but does not yet have access to what he really wants to do. The coach will create the time and space to fulfil the conditions required for the client to listen to his true desire. He will then put in place the protections* and relationship framework for the transition.

The strategy of the client's path integrates these three components—third-order suffering*, the space-time dimensions of the situation, and the transition space. But it is also based on the coach's assessment of the client. The rhythm at which he works, and the form the coaching takes, depend on the client's maturity—his capacity of calling himself into question, his access to his real desires, how he embraces his own fragility, and how he achieves his freedom with a view to taking on greater responsibility.

A number of typical situations a client may face

Professional orientation
The client questions his professional future, his choice of direction, his potential or his aspirations. With regards to coaching, many come to me to seek advice about training as a coach and to assess themselves as potential coaches. Whatever their profession and their experience on the ground, they generally realize that most of the problems in business are not about technical matters, but are really human factors such as issues of identity, relationships, power, hierarchy and teamwork. One thing they often need to develop is their capacity for empathy: beyond being able to relate to people, beyond any expertise developed in the helping profession, the trainee coach needs to prepare himself above all as a "being in fellowship", in other words to embody the humanizing dimension that is probably the source of every individual's deepest motivations. Strategy 9: *Humanization* deals with this subject in more detail.

Crisis
Facing a crisis, in the widest sense of the word, often has the advantage of revealing something of the deepest aspirations in an individual. In these kinds of situations, the coach's support enables the client to better understand the stakes involved, the intensity of the conflict he is living through, and what he needs in terms of protections. The crisis will often reveal the inadequacy of an individual's stance. The situation into which he has put himself may testify to a disregard for his own aspirations, or to a denial of contextual elements that he was unable, or unwilling to see.

Outplacement
The client may use a coach to transform an outplacement, often seen as a symbol of failure, into a situation that favors his individual and professional fulfilment. The strategy of the client's path can be extremely useful here to help the client

experience this stage in his life, not as a dramatic and unexpected separation, imposed from the outside and misunderstood, but as a stage in a journey that can become a path to growth. This is possible, even if it is a bumpy road, with idle periods and sometimes uncomfortable twists and turns in the road.

Changes in the ecosystem
Working through the client's transition space inevitably leads to the reconfiguration of the client's ecosystem. This reconfiguration will entail a questioning of the client's relational system, both professional and personal, as well as his own personal history.

A Constructivist Logic

Much coaching work is done using a constructivist* logic, in which the client's development takes the form of an emergence that the coach embraces step by step—like the horizon which "retreats into the distance" and reveals further landscapes as we move forward in our journey. This emergent process may take the form of several approaches:

- the trial and error approach enables constant reconfiguration of the client's strategy as a function of his experience;
- the "occurrence" approach enables new and unexpected events to upset and change actions plans;
- the "vision/rear-view-mirror" approach, where future direction is determined by the path already trodden, and enables the future path to be defined by looking into the rear-view mirror;
- the scenario approach, where action is defined by navigating between a number of pre-designed scenarios;
- the visioning approach, where people project themselves into the future, from three months, to three years, or even—using their intuition—to twenty years.

The constructivist approach is by definition uncomfortable, because it does not offer the security and certainties—real or presumed—of a planned strategy. It corresponds to the logic of a post-industrial business, a logic of complexity, where the mechanical thought processes and actions of planned implementation no longer suffice. In the linear perspective inherited from Taylorism, goals are designed, the business plan is written, specific objectives are defined, and then a process is determined to establish the path to achieve those pre-defined objectives. Business leaders are today aware that in a global civilization characterized by endemic uncertainty and the instant circulation of information, this elegant mechanism is woefully inadequate.

Paradoxically the will to plan at all costs creates the risk of losing the capacity for strategic monitoring, missing the weak signals that are essential to continually adjust a strategy to its environment. Business leaders also need to learn the delicate alchemy of

> *combining the logic of objectives AND the logic of constructivism.*

Because coaching is deployed in this in-between space, it can serve as a model, not just for individuals, but also for organizations. When people move into enaction*, they build transient representations under constant redefinition, whilst making them as relevant as possible to the experience of individuals, teams and organizations. Within this logic of emergence and recursiveness (the whole generates the parts and the parts generate the whole), the helping relationship becomes a vector for transformation for both clients and coaches. This transformational process is never linear: more or less spectacular advances are followed by backward steps or moments of inaction…which serve to prepare further advances. As we will see in the following chapter, this circular process nevertheless involves a number of necessary phases.

Points and Pause for Reflection—The Client's Path

The questions below will help you think through how you use the client's path in the helping relationships that you manage. These questions are designed to help you search inside yourself, so it is important to take your time. Even if you only deal with one question, take the time to reflect fully on it, rather than simply going through a "checklist" exercise.

1. As I identify my client's situation, to what extent am I contextualizing his present moment in the light of what he experienced yesterday, what has brought him here today, and the possibilities open to him tomorrow?
2. To what extent am I able to balance operational realism with the existential dimension of my client's journey?
3. How do I discern what relates to "objective" time (*chronos*) and what relates to the "opportune" time (*kairos*), that of intuition and grace?
4. Beyond the past and future, to what extent am I able to help my client reserve a "transition space and time" for himself today?
5. So that my client has the means to achieve his objective, how do I help him adapt his objective to his means, and then identify and put in place the support, protections and permissions he needs to move forward?

Strategy 8: Identity Construction

> *What does my client need in terms of his identity?*
> *Deconstruction? Restoration? Construction? Reconfiguration? All four?*
> *What balance between actions, relationships and searching for meaning?*
> *How to align what is important (profession) with what is essential (personal life)?*

Finding more unity in one's life and identity takes time. There is a path to tread, it is often wise not to tread it alone…and at the same time important to discover and respect one's own rhythm. When helping a person on this journey, the coach needs to be deeply aware that

plants do not grow better when you pull them.

Beyond helping a person to get going, and to solve any specific problems (the coach can also help in problem-solving) the coach always looks to help his client become who he is, and to construct his own identity. Doing this involves raising a number of questions:

- What does the person need in order to forge his complex identity in a complex environment?
- What does he need to deconstruct?
- What restoration work is needed?

© The Author(s) 2017
V. Lenhardt, *My 10 Strategies for Integrative Coaching*,
DOI 10.1007/978-3-319-54795-4_10

- What does he need to construct?
- How can he prepare himself for continual reconfiguration?
- How can the coach structure the different phases and dimensions of this "construction site"?

Identity construction holds a special place in the range of coaching strategies, especially in Europe. In the Anglo-Saxon world, coaching has historically been focused more on results and less on the client's identity. Though one does not exclude the other, in my view:

> *the strategy of identity construction is the center of gravity of the helping relationship.*

It is at the heart of all the other strategies, and underpins all the coach's interventions and stances. In this sense it is transverse and holomorphic*.

The models I share below, born of my experience, will help a coach implement the strategy of identity construction.

The DRCR Model

Identity construction has four main phases: Deconstruction, Restoration, Construction and Reconfiguration (Fig. 33). Its dynamics are recursive and complex: a person may simultaneously be going through deconstruction in one area of life and construction in another, and these two areas will interact with each other.

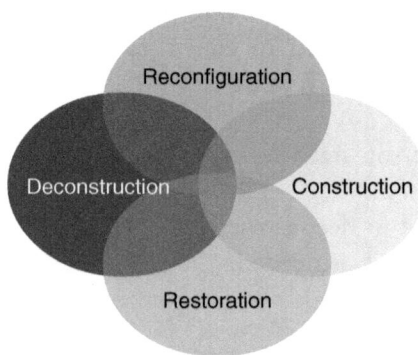

Fig. 33 Simultaneous deconstruction, restoration, construction and reconfiguration

I use the term **deconstruction** in Jacques Derida's[1] sense of the word. Each of us is more or less a prisoner of our own frames of reference— ideological, political, cultural, religious or professional. For any true change to happen, we need to "deconstruct" our ways of thinking which all have underpinning presuppositions and inherent contradictions. It is when we come face to face with the contradictions and dead ends that characterize our current thinking, that we open ourselves up to other realities.

No real transformation occurs if we do not start by freeing ourselves from our mental prisons or dead ends. Our beliefs, the way we represent the world, other people, ourselves, our current identity and status, are often maladjusted and outdated, since they were constructed in another place and at another time, based on other stakes than those of today. Our primal and largely unconscious scripts* serve to structure our personality and organize our "life plan", though theses scripts may no longer be relevant. Even ways of thinking and acting that were effective in the past and made us successful may not meet to the needs of our "here and now" situation. Yet we remain attached to them, as if they were a part of our very identity. If we wish to change, we need to break away from them; this means identifying flawed scripts, unlearning them, and deconstructing some of what we have learned throughout our life.

These kinds of issues are present in all coaching scenarios. Take, for example, a client who has forged his professional identity through learning and practicing his trade. If he is to freely learn a new profession, take on a new function, or adopt a new management culture, he will need help to deconstruct the parts of his identity that are no longer adapted or relevant to his new profession. He will need to accept the loss of some of what he has already, and discard past ways of functioning that no longer correspond to his current situation and issues. Or take a business leader, who undergoes a different kind of deconstruction when he gives up his knowledge, experiences the competence paradox*, becomes a "leader as resource-provider" and breaks out of the prison of his hierarchical status. This is never easy. It requires highlighting the areas where he gets stuck, accepting a diagnosis and possible challenges from the coach, and giving up certain things that may be dear to him, before he is able to step out and take hold of his own freedom.

---

[1] Jacques Derrida, *Speech and Phenomena and Other Essays on Husserl's Theory of Signs.* Northwestern University Press, 1973.

Competence paradox

It is by focusing his energy on developing the competence of others at the cost of developing his own technical competence that the leader becomes more fully competent.

Restoration follows hard on the heels of deconstruction and may even occur at the same time.

This is not restoration in the sense of rebuilding the walls of the prison we have just demolished, but addressing the deficiencies or hurts, hidden until now, that need specific treatment. When a person removes his outer shell, he finds himself naked and exposed, with all his inadequacies, imperfections, weaknesses and vulnerabilities visible for all to see. Now is the time to start work on these weak points that were previously covered up or denied. This involves working on needs and emotions, managing stress and daring to experience an openness where one can show one's frailty without shame or fear. I have often seen business leaders refuse to share their worries and needs, and close themselves to any form of criticism—or even compliment—out of fear of exposing parts of themselves that they had carefully hidden behind their defenses. Overcoming this fear of being exposed in one's own eyes and the eyes of others often requires specific help.

Becoming aware of one's weaknesses and sensitive areas, then undertaking the work of restoration is a first step. A person then needs to develop new "muscles", and identify new ways of operating that correspond to today's and tomorrow's concerns.

Construction involves acquiring these new codes of conduct, new behaviors, new attitudes, new habits and new competences that enable the client to act differently and more appropriately in his current environment. He will learn to step out of his comfort zone—for example, by accepting moments of silence in a conversation—and find the subtle balance between protections* and permissions*: knowing how and when say "no" as well as "yes". He will learn to accept challenges and how to metacommunicate—all in all, to experience more open and enriching relationships.

Reconfiguration is where he learns to continually evolve, and live out the dynamics of constant transformation, because the situations in which he finds himself are constantly evolving. The client who has been able to break out of his old habits, and has developed new behaviors in a given context, will need to invent and improvise anew, using situational intelligence*, when the context changes again. Often, the person engaged in a process of transformation realizes that his current ecosystem is holding back or stifling the change he wishes to make. He will then change parts of his ecosystem, by changing roles, changing profession, changing company or even changing country—thus changing his environment and his relationship with the environment. A person who moves to another continent, or a business leader who decides on a radical career change, goes through this kind of identity transformation. He gives up his old "map of the territory", creates a new one, and then practices continually changing it. As Heraclitus said long ago: "No man ever steps in the same river twice". And we all know, as Heraclitus also said, that "there is nothing permanent except change".

A Relationship of Equals

The strategy of identity construction combines all four phases of transformation. The coach helps the client to become aware of what needs to be deconstructed, restored, constructed and reconfigured. He is also aware that he will often need to work simultaneously on all four phases. This is complex and subtle work, and brings a number of paradoxes, contradictions and ambivalent attitudes to light. The coach needs to be extremely alert and highly sensitive if he is to appreciate the path trodden by his client at the same time as remaining focused on one or other aspect of change. And because the world continues to change as coach and client tread their path together, the coach continually cycles round all four phases.

Another fundamental point is that the deconstruction-restoration-construction-reconfiguration process is not just about the client. The coach needs to continually revisit it in the context of the coach-client relationship, and also go through the cycle for himself. Assisting change in a person requires a certain parity between helped and helper. As the agent of change, the coach contributes to the dynamic of transformation in his client. In return, as he listens to his client, he receives inputs that enrich him in turn and nourish his own change dynamic. In turn, the coach does this work on himself, and the way he does it becomes a model for his client: experiencing this process for oneself constitutes an invitation to the other to do the same. In the same way, the business leader in an organization who takes up the stance of internal coach and becomes a model for change, generates a change dynamic in those around him.

Envelopes of the Self: The Four Identity Zones

I often use the DRCR model in conjunction with that of the four identity zones. It considers a person's identity as a more or less stable balance between four components, or four zones, which structure a person's identity (Fig. 34).

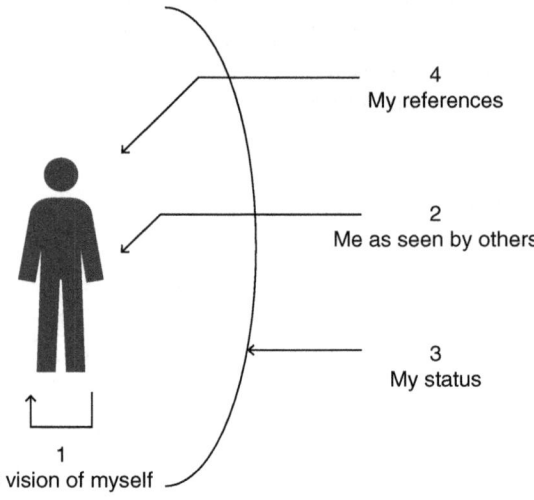

Fig. 34   The four identity zones, or four "envelopes"

Zone 1—**Internal recognition**. This is the **vision we have of ourselves**, the image we have created of who we are, the way we see ourselves, how we identify our strengths and weaknesses, and how we imagine that other people see us.

Zone 2—**External recognition.** This is the **vision others have of us**, the image that others have created of who we are. We perceive them through a number of indicators such as their behavior towards us, their feedback and the signs of recognition they give us.

Zone 3—**Status.** I call this zone the "**Skin Ego**".[2] It is composed of relatively objective elements of one's identity such as one's bodily structure, the way one dresses or one's "look", one's diplomas, one's professional status and responsibilities, or how much one earns.

---

[2] Expression borrowed from Didier Anzieu, See his book: *The Skin Ego,* Yale University Press, 1989.

Zone 4—**Personal Reference Points** are the different elements with which a person builds his vision of the world, or his frame of reference. They include his beliefs, his Ideal Self or Superego, his values, and his role models. These elements give meaning and coherence to his life and activity, as we saw in Strategy 6: *Access to Meaning.*

This simple model does not fully reflect the dynamic of a person moving from "ego" to "Self", from mask and "Frog" to "Prince(ss)"—in other words fully becoming a subject, beyond all the definitions that the external world tries to impose on who we are. Nevertheless, it can be very helpful: once an identity issue comes to light, it is almost always correlated with one of the four zones, or with a misalignment between them. In a business context in particular, a manager's identity cannot develop properly if the four zones are out of balance. The role of the coach is to identify which zones need to be reinforced, and then to put in place a coaching process that will help re-establish balance and consistency between them.

Dissonances between zones can be many and varied. One person may have a high opinion of himself, judge himself competent and capable, yet may not feel properly recognized by others—his bosses, his colleagues or his clients. On the other hand, a person may have a good reputation in the eyes of others, but his lack of self-confidence and self-esteem makes him fragile, in both his professional and personal life. Remember, Marilyn Monroe did not think she was beautiful! Dare I suggest that this gives hope to many of us?

Zone 3 (status) often needs attention. The person believes he is competent, and has a good reputation and good feedback from others, but feels a gap between his external status and his intrinsic worth. For example, not having certain diplomas (or not daring to say that one is self-taught), or not having the responsibilities and salary that he regards as his due ("I'm good at my job, the others know it, but I am underpaid and my job is too small"). When this happens, a person will tend to seek compensation elsewhere, either in another company, or in the trappings of power and the dynamics of narcissism.

In my view, zone 4 (reference points) is the most important, and the most deeply challenging. If a person has not built strong and meaningful reference points, he will be uncomfortable when challenged on any of the other three zones, and will be thrown off balance. For example, someone who loses his job and becomes unemployed may be unsettled materially, and also in the image that his family and social circle have of him. But without reference points, he will be deeply destabilized and will lose confidence in himself.

This often occurs in certain outplacement situations. If a person has not established a strong meaning molecule (see Strategy 6: *Access to*

Meaning) that gives him strength and stability in spite of difficult circumstances, the experience of calling himself into question will be extremely painful.

This is where coaching is so valuable. Beyond the operational aspect of helping a person find a new job, it is the work of support and reconfiguration of a person's identity, along with the accompanying emotional burden, that is paramount for the client in these circumstances.

Without a balance between these four dimensions, the client will feel destabilized in his ecosystem, and to protect himself—like the lobster—he may build a shell to compensate for his lack of backbone.

The coach's objective, in the first instance, is to help the client become aware of any imbalances. Only then can he work on restoring the client's ontological security*.

Growth rings

The four-zone model deals simultaneously with the different zones. Another model represents identity envelopes as they layer on to one another over time. Rather like the growth rings on a tree trunk, the stages which build someone's identity are gradually built up. They are composed of four parts: his *personality*, forged through his individual and family history; his *education*, which corresponds to knowledge he has acquired by learning or experience; his *profession*, which he has developed throughout his professional life and the different jobs he has held during his career; and his *function* in the current organization along with the stakes attached to it.

Each of these identity strata may be marked by traumas or inadequate development. The strata and zones affected will manifest themselves again and again in the client's "here and now", rather like a scratched record, in the form of a hindrance, a barrier or a dead end. Someone who was deeply hurt when fulfilling a certain role will reactivate this pain when asked to play a similar role, or to interact with others playing this role. In the same way, a big gap between the different levels of identity of a person—his personal life and his work, or his training and his job description—means that he will face difficulties in specific professional situations. Clients often have difficulty identifying or accepting these contradictions, but can find in the coaching relationship the resources they need to analyze, then overcome these issues, either by learning to live with non-alignment, or by finding ways of realigning them.

Linking to the Identity Backbone

These models are closely linked to the identity backbone* described in Strategy 6: *Access to Meaning*. The coach needs to consider what, in the client's identity construction, appears either lacking or incongruous with respect to the elements above, and to consider what might need to be adjusted or reconstructed. It is not enough to take into account all the "vertebrae". Coaching is about identifying and treating the vertebrae that are weak, bringing them into systemic coherence with each other, and then using the work done on one of the vertebrae to reinforce the whole backbone, in a holomorphic* manner.

Balancing Action, Meaning and Relationships— the Autonomy Deployment Tree

The autonomy deployment tree extends the thinking about autonomy in Strategy 2: *Fish/fishing rod—His frame/my frame*, by describing the balance between three poles in our lives.

As I listened over the years to the many clients that I had the privilege of coaching, I realized that we are torn between three kinds of self-fulfilment.

- The first is **action**. We project ourselves into the world, and seek to transform it through what we do, and "leave our mark", or our "value-add".
- The second is **meaning.** We try to find meaning in our action, and this search for meaning sometimes leads us to step back, withdraw from our activities, and set aside places and times to rediscover our inner resources and to seek deep within ourselves the foundations of our identity.
- The third is **relationships.** All through our lives, we need others, and we spend time and energy to maintain these bonds.

Each of us can, and will benefit from finding his own balance between these three poles. Some veer more towards action, others towards a search for meaning, and yet others towards relationships (it will come as no surprise that coaches and others in the helping profession veer towards the latter). This balance may change as we grow: the person who, at a certain stage in his life is more focused on action, will at a later stage prefer to retreat into himself, or on the contrary open up to others. The balance of autonomy deployment may even change during a single day, according to our mood (Fig. 35).

In all cases, and at any given moment in a person's growth, it is vital to integrate and balance these three vectors, and not to identify oneself exclusively with one or other of them.

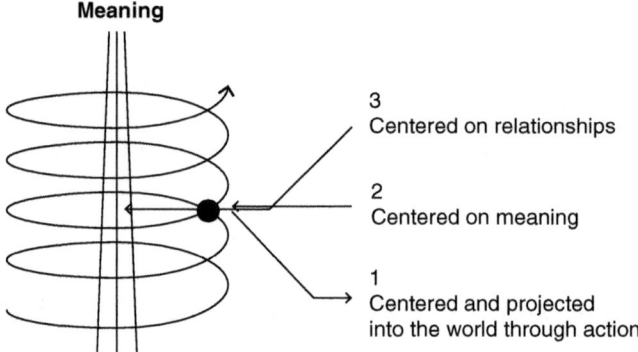

Fig. 35   The autonomy deployment tree

The person who is ceaselessly active risks losing himself—hyperactivity is often the expression of an unanalyzed "compulsion". Similarly, a person who is compulsively and continuously searching for meaning may simply be running away from the world. And the person who throws himself body and soul into transient relationships may simply be afraid of being alone. Irvin Yalom speaks of the fear of solitude that is in fact the anxiety of coming face to face with oneself. This fear is so frequent that many people, tend to avoid the risk of deeper, open and satisfying relationships, and multiply "pseudo-relationships" to shield themselves from their loneliness.

The first vector is the one we most often encounter in business coaching. It is the "action-man manager's" favorite: he is a "doer" who wants to show that he is committed to a project, that he is capable of acting on his environment, and even of co-creating the world as he engages passionately with it.

For his stability, and to give meaning to all he is doing, it is important that he does not lose contact with the second vector—that of the "column of meaning" (or the meaning molecule described in Strategy 6: *Access to Meaning*). Failing that, he risks identifying himself with his actions to such as extent that he becomes a hostage to his work, a workaholic who sacrifices everything, including his private life, to his job.

The third vector is where a person's investment in relationships and his emotional competence play out. He cannot dispense with this vector, if he wants his actions as a manager, and indeed his life, to result in success.

The support offered by the coach creates a space for dialogue and for raising awareness of these issues, opening the way for the client to work on rebalancing these three aspects of his life.

Integrating Different Perspectives

The reader will by now have understood that, in my view, the helping relationship stems from an intersubjective* dynamic whose end purpose is to

deploy an integrative and constructivist approach to our human condition*

Fig. 36 provides an end-to-end model for this humanistic project. It describes three basic dimensions of human development—the capacity to master content (competence, knowledge, and know-how), process (or relationships) and meaning—and links them to two fundamental aspects of identity construction:

Dimensions of development		Content and "profession"	Process and relationships	Meaning and vision
What is "important" ?	Professional Managerial Organizational Societal	Manager as order-giver	Manager as resource	Meaning-bearing leader
What is "essential"	Denominational Spiritual Existential Psychological Private	Homo Faber	Homo Amans	Homo Patiens
		Being to develop one's talentS	Being in relationships	Being in fellowship
Type of human being		Centered on oneself	Centered on the other	Centered on the community

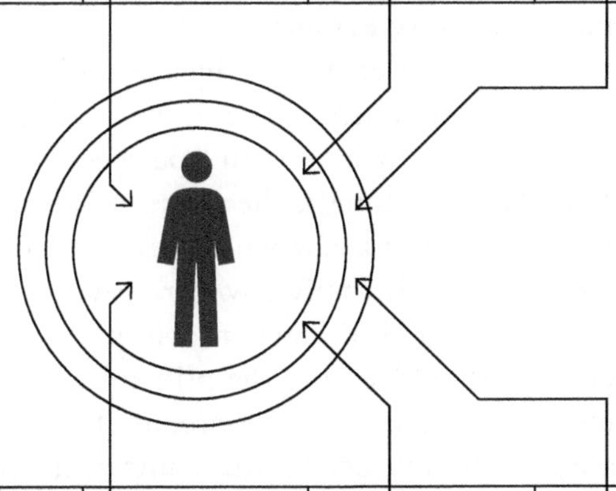

Fig. 36 Summary of identity construction

- on the one hand, what is "important", represented by the professional, managerial, organizational and societal levels in the identity backbone*;

- on the other hand what is "essential", represented by the personal, psychological, existential spiritual and denominational levels.

From the perspective of business coaching (whether individual, team or organizational) the key question is: What are the stakes involved from the angle of what is "essential", and from the angle of what is "important"?

What Is Important: Managerial Stances

From the perspective of what is important, the key challenge today in organizations is how to implement Collective Intelligence*.[3]

In a business, or any other collective structure considered as a living organism, the different players cannot be reduced to simple doers. Each and every employee is called to become a bearer of the DNA of the organization, that is to say the common vision that everyone has co-constructed. Each and every one can live in alter-dependence[4] with the others, and consider himself vested with the organization's stakes and responsible for its performance and sustainability.

Functioning with Collective Intelligence* requires people in the organization to have made the journey from a mechanical view of the organization and their place in it, to a systemic perspective, and finally to an open, holomorphic* vision. As long as the actors, and primarily those with management responsibility, do not change their representation of what is going on and how they position themselves with respect to their identity, an organization will be ill-prepared to take the leap into managing in a complex environment and implementing the principles of "Freedom Incorporated".[5]

Exercising leadership in an environment of Collective Intelligence requires being at ease with complexity. In this context, the role of a business leader in an organization can no longer be limited to being the "locomotive that pulls the carriages". Whilst he continues to take decisions, define and drive strategies, the business leader needs to generate a dynamic of responsibility in those who work with him in everything they do. To do this, he becomes a "talent developer", who ensures that each shared project becomes the

---

[3] I wrote a book on this subject with Philippe Bernard, *L'Intelligence Collective en Action (Collective Intelligence in Action)*, Pearson, second Ed., 2009—available only in French.
[4] Alter-dependence is described in Strategy 2: *Fish—fishing rod/His frame—my frame.*
[5] See Carney and Getz, *Freedom Inc: Free Your Employees and Let Them Lead Your Business to Higher Productivity, Profits, and Growth*, Crown Publishing Group, 2010.

opportunity for growth for each of those who work with him, and through them, an opportunity for growth for the whole organization. As he does this, his main concern becomes to manage, intelligently and appropriately, multiple stakes involving many areas, processes and levels of meaning. He goes beyond a purely hierarchical attitude, and progressively enriches it to achieve an integrative managerial stance. This "meta" stance enables him to exercise his responsibility at the heart of complexity, and to assume the paradoxes and contradictions inherent in managing several logical levels simultaneously.

In order to do this, the leader of a community of work—whether it is a small team or a large organization—needs to have been through identity transformation, which is necessarily destabilizing to start with. In my book *Coaching for Meaning* I describe in detail these "quantum leaps" by which the expert becomes a manager, and the manager becomes a leader, or, from another perspective, the "manager as order-giver" becomes a "manager as resource-provider", and finally a "meaning-bearer". I describe them briefly below.

From Expert to Manager to Leader

One perspective on management development sees it as a journey from expert to manager to leader.

The **expert** has developed a competence in his profession that makes him an authority, a "subject-matter expert". He is centered on the content ("What to do?") and the basic techniques of management and integration of different professions that enable the production of added value for the business.

The hierarchical **manager** deploys the competence of others. He focuses on the process—the relationships between people, work instructions and action plans ("How to do it?"). He chairs meetings, ensures teams communicate with each other, puts in place the required internal and external interfaces, and makes sure everything works. He also ensures that people are motivated, and that different management systems (Strategy, Finance, Sales, HR, Operations, etc.) are integrated and consistent.

The **leader's** primary concern is with meaning, values, and end purpose ("Why, and for what?"). He focuses on company vision and strategy definition, and oversees the overall alignment of processes and major strategic thrusts.

Developing into a leader as meaning-bearer requires going through the two previous stages. Progressing from one stage to another implies managing incompetence thresholds: a highly competent specialist does not become a good manager overnight. It also implies going through a grieving process, as a person loses some of the attributes of his previous identity.

If these stages have been part of a gradual process of maturing, all three can be simultaneously present, in varying degrees, in every leader. Indeed, a fully-fledged leader has integrated all three stages: he is a specialist (he knows his profession), a manager (he knows how to get people to do things) and a meaning-bearer who gives coherence to an organization from both an internal and external perspective.

From Order-Giver to Resource-Provider to Meaning-Bearer

A further perspective on management development is from the point of view of a journey from order-giver to resource-provider to meaning-bearer.

The **manager as order-giver** plays the role of decision-maker, supervisor and hierarchical leader who is focused primarily on results, and only secondarily on developing his people. His professional identity consists of his expertise in one or several professions. He is also competent as a generalist, fulfils his role as manager (by ensuring alignment of objectives), and assumes his role as leader (by defining certain operational objectives). The function of order-giver is essential in an organization, and each and every manager needs to assume it to some degree. It also has its risks: the manager may identify himself with his roles, and lock himself into expert or supervisor status that in turn maintains his people in a state of dependence instead of encouraging their growth. At the same time, mastering these professional competences enables him to become a resource used by others when they need him.

The order-giving function is not abolished in the **manager as resource-provider.** However, he takes on a new managerial identity as he begins to pay at least as much attention to relationship processes and helping his people take on responsibility, as he does to technical content. He has gone beyond purely hierarchical modes of functioning: even though he knows how to take decisions when needed, he habitually delegates his power and practices subsidiarity*. He has understood that it is in his deepest interest to move from McGregor's theory X to theory Y and to generate intrinsic rather than extrinsic motivation. He listens to his people, trusts them and encourages them to take initiatives and to design their own solutions. Because he is aware of his own limits, he surrounds himself with people more competent than he is in their domain. The manager as resource-provider thus manages cross-functional projects and facilitates the development of each and every person in a logic of collaboration. He has become an enabler through whom others develop their competences. I have had the privilege of coaching a number of business leaders[6] in different national and international contexts and industries; what has always impressed me was the way their very personality embodied the notion of resource-provider. Over and above their competence and charisma, I benefitted greatly from my journey with them—professionally, but also quite simply from a deeply personal perspective.

In the land of Theory Y

The stance of the manager as resource-provider uses the same logic as Douglas McGregor's theory Y[7]: since work is natural to man, and his motivation is mainly intrinsic, the manager's role is to enable people to deploy their motivation; the core management principle is that of self-evaluation. In theory X, motivation is considered to be extrinsic, so a manager needs to motivate people; the core management principle is that of control and sanctions—either positive or negative.

Though the manager as resource-provider does not abolish his role of giving orders, he fulfils his identity at a higher logical level.

- **He presents the stakes involved.** He invites his people to take up responsibility by putting them face-to-face with reality—what Jim Collins calls "the brutal facts".[8] The objective is to establish a relationship between equals and bring people to see and assess the stakes for themselves, instead of being simple "doers", confined within a hierarchical relationship.
- **He defines the rules of the game.** He explains the frame of reference, defines the "relational contract", and establishes the necessary protections* so people are safe to speak up, take initiatives and deploy their competence.
- **He generates a dynamic of "calling oneself to action".** By putting in place permissions*, he invites everyone to propose solutions once they have understood the stakes involved. He is aware that his people are often

---

[6] Three of my books are joint testimonies of a journey together. *Transformational Leadership* with Alan Godard: Palgrave Macmillan, 2000. *Oser la Confiance (Dare to Trust)* Insep Consulting, 1996, *L'intelligence Collective en Action (Collective Intelligence in Action)* Pearson Education, 2009. The last two are available only in Frenchh.

[7] Douglas McGregor, *The Human Side of Enterprise*.

[8] See Chapter 4 of *Good to Great*. Random House, 2001.

more competent than he is when it comes down to their specialism, and so he places them in front of their collective responsibility and their capacity to resolve the issues themselves.

The ocean creates continents by withdrawing

said the poet and philosopher Friedrich Hölderlin. Bertrand Martin said the same thing in a different way: "it is by acting as a resource-provider that the leader makes managers".

- **He supports his people.** For the players involved in this process, moving from dependence or counter-dependence to interdependence means that they will experience identity crises. People need to learn to accept the loss of the (psychologically far more comfortable) status of a simple "doer". They will go through moments of doubt, uncertainty and will sometimes be at a loss as they face the issues that emerge. If he has asked his people to take risks, the manager as resource-provider owes it to them to support them by offering them a listening ear, his own example, protections and permissions*.

- **He welcomes proposals.** The manager as resource-provider guarantees to all his people that all proposals will be considered, even if they are surprising or disturbing.

- **He optimizes decisions and implementation.** Welcoming all proposals does not mean that they will all be accepted and implemented. Some are simply set aside, others need further thought and more in-depth analysis, yet others need complementary studies or further validation before being considered for implementation. It is up to the manager as resource-provider to organize the decision process with the competent people, and then to check implementation directly with those involved.

- **He starts again…**

This spiral-shaped process has fractal* properties. The logic remains the same, whether applied to a project team with a small number of people or to an organization-wide project with many different players, or even to a whole organization.

Fractal

Geometric figures whose parts, at infinitely many levels of magnification, appear geometrically similar to the whole.

In a complex world, the manager needs to enter a third dimension. Beyond mastering content and process, the **leader as meaning-bearer** focuses on building a shared vision with his people, with common values and an end purpose that transcend the organization's immediate objectives. He defines the overall direction, yet remains constantly on the lookout for weak signals and what is emerging in those around him, so as to constantly redefine the vision with them. He uses situational intelligence* to take account of the constraints and opportunities in the environment, the stakes of all those involved, and their degree of autonomy. Through this dynamic of co-construction, the leader as meaning-bearer helps others to develop as much as he himself develops (Fig. 37).

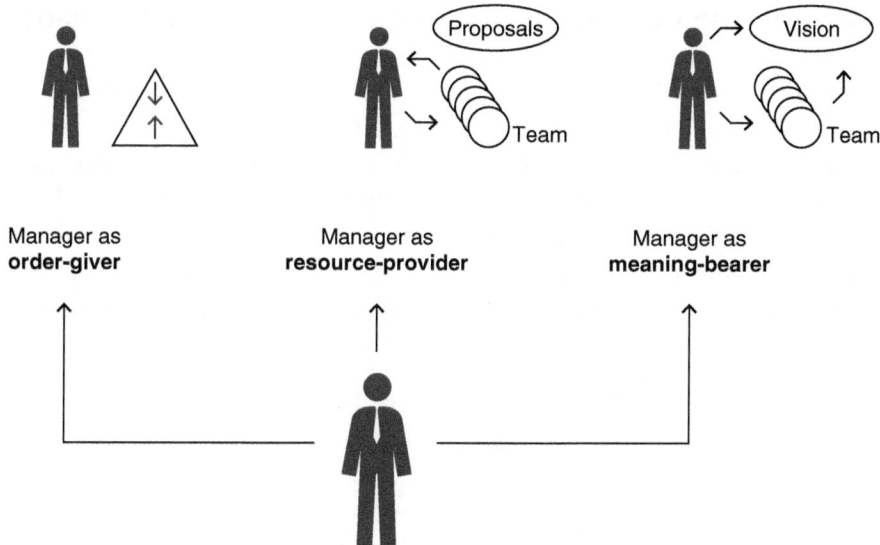

Fig. 37   Stages of management development

According to this model, each level of management development fulfils itself at a higher level: the order-giver fulfils himself as a resource-provider, who in turn fulfils himself as meaning-bearer. The final stage goes beyond the previous stages, whilst including them.

As order-giver, he embodies meaning through generating healthy dependence, for example at the beginning of certain projects. He represents the "North Star" which shows the way, and around which the team assembles (but he does not take himself to be the North Star—a narcissistic trap into which too many managers fall).

As resource-provider, he points to the stars, and helps his people to recognize the stakes involved. He is a talent developer, and also brings each and every one to realize that they can represent a star for others. Each person feels able to lead others in a kind of distributed leadership.

As meaning-bearer, he creates the conditions for the deployment of Collective Intelligence where each player becomes—in his place and at his level—co-producer of a collective vision, and shares ownership of its implementation. Finally, he acts in a holomorphic* dimension: even when fulfilling the role of order-giver, he remains in a "meta" stance, because his intervention is fully underpinned by his vision as meaning-bearer.

Adjusting the Cursor: the Art of Contingent Management

The challenges facing organizations today highlight the need for "contingent" management. In our global digital world, businesses often need to sail by sight and move the tiller constantly one way or the other, towards a logic of control (McGregor's theory X) or to a logic of "letting go", of subsidiarity*, of trust and empowerment (theory Y). Like the coach, the manager, whether of a small team or large organization, needs to continually adjust the cursor to the appropriate place for a given situation, the maturity of the players, the nature of the problem, and its importance and urgency (Fig. 38).

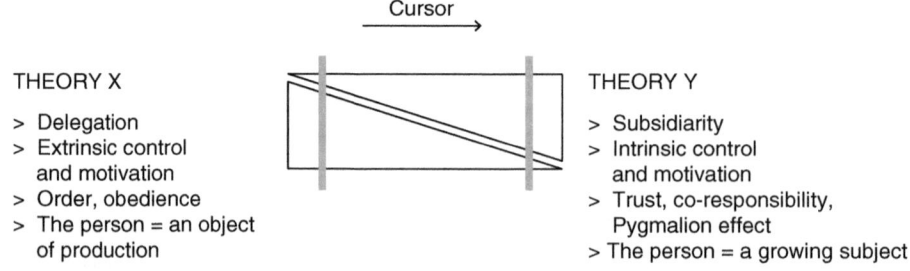

Fig. 38   Managing the cursor between McGregor's theory X and theory Y

If he acts as an order-giver, he is aware, moment by moment, of the contingent nature of this stance, and the need to underpin it with an attitude that develops people and creates meaning. If he acts as meaning-bearer, he does not lose sight of his operational responsibility of steering the project, team or company, since he is accountable for the end results. In this way, he contributes to the necessary agility of the organization he is leading, in a world of constantly accelerating change.

As he integrates these three roles of order-giver, resource-provider and meaning-bearer, the leader will bring one or other of the roles to the fore depending on time and circumstance, but will not set aside the others. The difficulty lies in finding the right stance at any given moment. To enable him to acquire the necessary ontological security* so as not to block the cursor in any one place, a manager needs to learn to deal with identity paradoxes and venture beyond contradictions.

The coach will help a manager to practice the gymnastics of stretching himself through different identity stances, thus developing his flexibility. A coach working with a manager or a business leader will help him revisit the "reality" he perceives (his representation of objective reality). Through the work of deconstruction and (re)construction in the way he represents the world, the coach helps his client change his identity stance.

I call this recursive virtuous loop "transformance" (Fig. 39). It enables the progressive transformation of three elements: the "objective" reality of the problems or stakes at hand; how the client represents this reality (his subjective reality); and finally, the identity of the client. As he works on these problems, that he started off considering as coming from the outside, the client changes his outlook, and transforms himself by assuming responsibility for his paradoxes, inherent contradictions and his own development as manager.

Objective reality exists, but is only accessible to us through the representations we make of it. This representation is conditioned by our identity and stance. As we open ourselves to other possibilities of objective reality, our identity and stance change. As our identity and stance change, the way we represent reality changes, our behaviour changes as a result. Our new behaviour has an impact on that objective reality, and this transformed

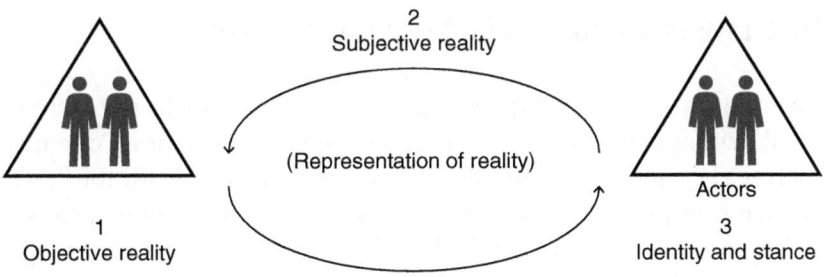

Fig. 39 Transformance

objective reality may in turn transform our identity and stance. A person who has entered the process of transformance is continually questioning which possible realities might be constructed from what he is experiencing, and continually adapting himself to new possibilities.

One cannot go through transformance without experiencing what I call third-order suffering* (described in Strategy 7: *The Client's Path*). The work of deconstruction and (re)construction is no joyride and is painful. Nothing is harder than giving up one's, illusory but "convenient truths" and defenses, and taking the risk of going outside one's comfort zone and protective shell. The leader, as he moves from order-giver to resource-provider and to meaning-bearer, learns to listen, to be silent, to give up certain privileges, and to accept being faced with employees more competent than he is. Yet it is a glorious pain, like that of the mother who pushes her son to leave the family nest, or the master who sees his pupil surpass him. When understood and welcomed, it is a suffering that becomes the means whereby the client goes beyond the identity he has built, and becomes the source of deep joy.

At the scale of organizations, transformance designates a process similar to that of freeing the potential of its people. It corresponds to the work of developing a shared vision through setting in motion all those in the organization by deconstructing, then reconstructing the way they represent the world. From the perspective of organizational development, coaching aims to make the transformation process as fluid and fertile as possible. It contributes to the deployment of Collective Intelligence* by helping people to identify their potential impediments, change the way they look at things, develop concrete change initiatives, put in place ways of regulating conflict, and, above all, create meaning. In this way, it takes objective reality into account without ignoring its complexity.

What is Essential: Self-Transformation

By definition, all management development is conditioned by the client's inner personal development: what is "important" depends on what is "essential".

Conversely, integrating different management stances, with the "quantum leaps" that it implies, can also generate profound transformation at a personal level. The two are intimately linked, and the different stages of management development also embody the identity types that Viktor Frankl distinguished: *Homo Faber, Homo Amans* and *Homo Patiens* (described in detail in Strategy 6: *Access to Meaning*).

The expert and order-giver will identify themselves with *Homo Faber*, who defines himself and builds his identity through what he does. At the beginning, coaching aims to develop one's self-awareness and mastery at this level of identity. Most of the time, without being of aware of it, we are locked into behavioral scripts* and representational systems decided on long ago, and reinforced by our environment. Even though these "programs" may be more or less effective, we have no others. We therefore need to start by recomposing our identity: the fish needs to jump out of the fishbowl. By changing the way he sees himself, the client rediscovers freedom of choice, finds renewed self-confidence, and reaches a clearer awareness of his potential for action and progress. The coach is there to support this dynamic of construction and growth.

The manager as resource-provider is like Frankl's *Homo Amans*, defined by his capacity to relate to others. If the person feels that he deeply exists, with his qualities and competences, he spontaneously constructs his identity through relating, belonging and supporting others—being able to relate is at the heart of being at ease with oneself. Being able to live out relational processes is also a key quality for any person managing a helping relationship. The coach needs to develop awareness of the other, the capacity for accepting otherness (the listening ear, the welcoming arms) and mastery of the web of relationships within an ecosystem. By helping the client to stand back from his own frame of reference, and by reestablishing his ontological security*, the coach helps the client to become more open and put away his masks, his defenses and his rigidity. It is this openness[9] that enables him to recognize and accept other people's frames of reference, to nourish his empathy and to bring to life the Princes(s)' Alliance* that frees up the potential of his relational competences.

One recognizes *Homo Patiens* in the leader as meaning-bearer. He has been through the preceding stages, and is able to link content, process and meaning. He is able to see himself as standard-bearer of a vision, and build a shared project with others that transcends the projects of each individual. *Homo Patiens* is not defined just by his actions and relationships, but by his ability to devote himself to a cause or a project that is greater than he, and to put his interests at the service of the greater common good. In other words, he becomes aware that each of his acts reflects his identity as an individual, as a person in relationships, and as a member of a human community. As a business leader, he can create a dynamic that enables all the members of his organization to make the common project their own, and play their part on

---

[9] In Will Schutz's sense of the word, described in his book *The Human Element*.

building the edifice together. When coaching attains this dimension, the coach's job is to encourage the client to express and develop the qualities that enable him to live under complexity, uncertainty and the paradoxes that are inherent in any human undertaking.

Spiritual Openness

Since a human being is an integrated whole, his existential plans may in turn open up the perspective of spiritual development. Resilience and the development of awareness and ethics also enable a person to enhance his management activities. In general there is a correspondence between the logical levels of management, psychology and spirituality.

For me, *Homo Patiens,* the leader as meaning-bearer fulfils himself in another dimension, that of a "being in fellowship". He is a person capable of giving himself to others or to the common good—to humanity for a humanist, or to a mystical body for one who has religious faith.[10] I have coached a number of leaders, amongst whom were committed Christians, devout Muslims and non-believers with strong humanist convictions. My experience in coaching them has helped me realize that spirituality, in whatever form, if lived out deeply and sincerely, can support values that then radiate into the different management stances. For many, it is their spiritual life that gives energy, meaning and coherence to their personal and professional development. This inner life nourishes a person's whole being, and finds its expression by projecting itself into the world around.

My practice of yoga, and the time spent at Hindu Vedanta centers as well as my experience of monastic life in an ashram and in a Benedictine monastery, has shown me that the approach to being human that is developed in coaching—and that aims to bring coherence between different identity levels—can be lived out through different paradigms that are in no way incompatible.

In a Christian paradigm, a person will strive to live out his life in this world with deep faith, in conformity with his spiritual values, and (for a Roman Catholic) his sacramental life. In this way, he strives to fully live out his incarnation in space and time.

In an atheistic humanist paradigm, people give the best of themselves and devote themselves to a common good that surpasses any individual, selfish

---

[10] Like St Paul who wrote (Philippians 2.17): "But even if I am being poured out like a drink offering on the sacrifice and service of your faith, I am glad and rejoice with all of you."

interests. They may do this in the name of moral values, of an ideal society, or simply in the name of a non-religious transcendence or self-transcendence.

The Vedantic paradigm aims to move from a dualist representation of the world to a unitary, or monist view of human nature: "I am to God what a drop of water is to the ocean." Here the stakes are about disidentifying oneself from one's physical envelope (made up of tensions, physical ailments and suffering), one's energy field (made up of strength, but also of fatigue, agitation and stress), and one's mind (made up of emotions, one's ego, and restless thoughts). Instead, one centers oneself, and finds peace again in one's "Self".

The culture of coaching recognizes the Prince(ss) at the heart of each one of us, though it is often hidden behind the "Frog" who is on a journey and often fighting battles. Whatever the paradigm, it is this same deep dimension of being human that the coach is always, and in all circumstances, aiming to discover, protect and help radiate in his client.

What view of human nature am I co-constructing with my client?

This is the question that lies behind the strategy of identity construction. It is always in the background, always present in the coach's consciousness.

Key Points and Pause for Reflection—Identity Construction

The questions below will help you think through how you use the identity construction strategy in the helping relationships that you manage. These questions are designed to help you search inside yourself, so it is important to take your time. Even if you only deal with one question, take the time to reflect fully on it, rather than simply going through a "checklist" exercise.

1. In the DRCR model (Deconstruction, Restoration, Construction, Reconfiguration), where will I place my needle as an acupuncturist?
2. How do I deal with the paradoxes that emerge when I combine these four phases?
3. Where are the weaknesses and strengths in my client's four identity zones? How will I go about balancing them?
4. As I consider my client's meaning molecule, what process will I put in place to help him learn to build his identity and ontological security*?

5. How do I balance external processes (feedback, questions, information, taking a stand, signs of recognition) with internal processes, where I ensure he activates his resources for himself (his successes, his qualities and his strengths)?
6. What techniques (such as the empty chair exercise or generative questioning) do I use to help my client's internal processes?

Strategy 9: Humanization

> *How can I help my client become more aware of his finiteness, his limits,*
> *and become more himself in all his fullness?*
> *How can I help him find himself by developing his empathy*
> *and his capacity to accept otherness?*
> *How can I help him become freer, fully accept that freedom,*
> *and become more responsible?*

In writing this chapter on humanization, I am deeply conscious of my lack of formal academic training in philosophy and anthropology. My approach is less to try to bring answers, and more to contribute via an open discussion from the perspective of a seasoned practitioner of the helping profession.

I share my thoughts from the perspective of forty years of practice as consultant, therapist, trainer, coach and trainer of coaches, and also from that of my own existential experience, rooted in my personal journey, essentially Christian, but which also includes a number of other paths. I have been deeply enriched by encounters with other forms of spirituality, in particular my experience of Vedanta Yoga, which I continue to practice daily.

This book, and in particular this chapter, reflects my search for coherence, ever fragile, tentative and imperfect, between two poles. On the one hand, my work, my enaction* into the world and my commitment to my relationships; on the other hand, the end purpose and meaning I give to my life.

© The Author(s) 2017
V. Lenhardt, *My 10 Strategies for Integrative Coaching*,
DOI 10.1007/978-3-319-54795-4_11

Following in the footsteps of the great tradition of Saint Irenaeus ("God become man, so than man can become God") and Maurice Zundel[1] ("I is Another", the title of one of his books, borrowed from the poet Rimbaud), François Varillon[2] penned this aphorism, which has inspired and deeply influenced my life:

God makes divine what man makes human.

This is a way of saying that our role as human beings is to make the world more human, and that it is through this humanization, by relating to other human beings, that we attain transcendence. This transcendence can be experienced within a religious approach, or constructed (co-constructed) by one who is not a believer into a form of self-transcendence.

Notwithstanding my daily doubts and failings, my own conviction is that the essential meaning of my journey on this earth is to support a process of humanization—"for and through" those that I coach, "for and through" the Grace that I let into my life, and "for and through" my inner self.

Access to meaning and humanization of individuals and communities repre- sents for me the fundamental purpose underpinning all coaching strategies.

This is the existential dimension of the helping relationship, in the philoso- phical sense of the word. Humanization for me covers everything in the coaching ecosystem that helps clients to become more aware, more humble, and at the same time more ambitious for the common good; everything too, that will help them live with their limits, their finiteness, as well as their infinite potential.

Death As Stage of Growth: Accepting Our Finiteness

We have known since Cicero that "to study philosophy is nothing but to prepare one's self to die". The main axis of humanization, in my view, is accepting one's own finiteness and this fundamental paradox: in order to

---

[1] Catholic priest and theologian, author of the book *Je Est un Autre (I is Another)* Anne Sigier editions, 1986 (available only in French).
[2] *Joy of Faith, Joy of Life.*

live well, we need to learn how to die well. To fully live out our existence, we need to accept the perspective of our own demise. Death destroys us, and the anguish of the perspective of this inevitable end feeds all our other fears. And yet the idea of death paradoxically gives birth to life's meaning—"unless a grain of wheat falls into the earth and dies, it remains alone; but if it dies, it bears much fruit.[3]" Grieving and loss is an integral part of our lives, and is consubstantial with any major change in our lives.

Elisabeth Kübler-Ross[4] was one of the first people to describe the stages of grief, which are the same for physical or symbolic death. She has shown that if this process is properly guided, it can become a profound source of reconciliation of a person with himself, and become a stage in his growth. Palliative care, and all that goes with it, can be seen as an experience of humanization of the dying person and of those close to him. To attach oneself to another until his last breath is a way of preparing for parting, and takes us to another level of awareness and communion.

Symbolic death, or letting go of important things, plays a role in any work of identity construction. One of the most inspiring aspects of the coach's profession is to help the other admit his finiteness. This involves living through the necessary stages of real or symbolic bereavements, forsaking the fantasy of being all-powerful in the eyes of others and in the face of adversity, and accepting the fact of being finite. Furthermore, it involves helping the client to embrace his vulnerability and his deep-seated wounds. Some speak of neurotic wounds (the neuroses we have inherited), others of spiritual wounds (the consequence of sin that, through grace, can become a source of blessing[5]). It is by accepting the gaping wound in oneself that a person can be healed, and help others to heal. This is a doorway into humility, and a doorway into reality. Above all, it is by accepting our own limits and by making them a source of meaning that we as human beings enter into our humanity...that we become, in the fullest sense of the word, "human".

---

[3] St John's Gospel, Chapter 12, verse 24.

[4] *To Live until We Say Goodbye.*

[5] One might add to the Beatitudes "Blessed is the wound", since it in is this very place in we can welcome grace as it comes to meet us.

An Empathetic Consciousness

Another fundamental lever for humanization lies not only in being recognized and loved, but also being able to recognize and love another. Of course, one does not go without the other.

Coaching as a helping relationship cannot avoid what Transactional Analysis calls episcripts* (discussed in Strategy 4: *Contextualization*). The action and stance of the coach, his intervention choices, and the exercises he proposes in the workshops he runs or the training he gives, all represent avenues for the coach to work on himself: they are open windows on what he himself needs to develop.

Creating empathy and accepting the other unconditionally are two qualities that I hope belong to my positive episcript. In this, the permissions* and openings that I help to generate in my clients echo those that I myself need to work through. Recently, in an exercise of inclusion[6] where I invited the participants to listen to each other, I became aware that what I had proposed to them resonated strongly in me. Through what I had proposed to them, I became vividly aware, in my "here and now", of the attention and recognition I had so lacked as a child. My need for recognition, not fully repaired today, and that will surely never be fully repaired, is an open wound, never fully healed, that relates to the significant absence of empathy I suffered with my father, in spite of his relatively kindly manner.

Jeremy Rifkin[7] has shown it is possible to read human history through successive civilizations, including today's progressive emergence of an empathetic civilization, based on a human being's most profound motivation, the need for empathy. We saw in Strategy 1: *The Rogerian Alliance* that the foundation of the act of coaching consists in creating the conditions of a matrix of empathy*—a time and place where the client feels welcomed, nourished and his potential recognized. The Pygmalion effect or the "circle of trust"[8] thus become the norm in a coaching relationship.

I have often experienced this in therapy groups, and it is always both troubling and revealing. One of the participants in regression work opens up

---

[6] When I work with teams or in my training courses, the first part of the meeting always has a time of "inclusion", where the participants share about themselves, what they are thinking and feeling.

[7] *The Empathic Civilization.*

[8] Described in detail in Chapter 26 of my book *Coaching for Meaning*. It described how a virtuous circle can be created by creating protections and permissions, sharing representations of the world, recognizing each other and sharing deeply which then enables a team to work together to produce results, that then reinforce that trust.

a wound, or touches a weakness or point of suffering, and this generates empathy, and often a kind of special fellowship between all the members of the group. The experience of suffering, when listened to and fully heard, deeply welcomed and shared, mysteriously produces healing in the person concerned, and at the same time has a healing effect on the other participants.

In these moments, participants experience deep intimacy: the surroundings fade into the background, and words become futile. The quality of silence in these moments is such, that time seems to touch eternity.

Eric Berne also spoke of this intimacy, shared so intensely in "present moments" where time and space disappear.

All other things being equal, the same process is at work in coaching, even though we do not work at the same depth. Once the matrix of empathy has been created and secured, the coach can listen to what the client says in the same way that a therapist listens to a patient. His verbal and non-verbal expression become the place of access to the client's inner being, the existential open wound from which a person who has accepted his finitude constructs his identity.

"Being comes into existence as a function of the wound that is in the process of being spoken forth" said psychoanalyst Jacques Lacan.[9]

Identity in Three Dimensions

Recognizing oneself as wounded and fallible, and relinquishing one's fantasies of power, does not mean that one no longer projects oneself into the world around—quite the contrary. From this recognition, a person can draw new energy, a will to move mountains and an intelligence that opens up infinite possibilities. A few years ago, I was struck by the profile of the astronauts who had successfully applied to the NASA, in the full knowledge that they would be putting their lives at risk. For the most part, they were not single, but mothers and fathers deeply attached to their earthly existence through the interdependent bonds they had formed. Paradoxically, this emotional bond which gave meaning to their lives, and the awareness that

---

[9] A phrase that his brother, Father Marc-François Lacan, a monk at the Benedictine monastery of Ganagobie, often quoted to me in the conversations I was privileged to have with him.

they might lose it, gave them greater freedom: they were capable of taking extreme risks and being hyper-efficient in their actions, yet remaining solidly anchored in reality. It was because they wanted to return to earth at all costs that they were more likely to succeed in a mission than a young, unattached "hothead". These are the kinds of people that coaching aims to help develop: they may not be future astronauts, but they are individuals who experience themselves, each at their level, as "champions" who are at the same time deeply and irreducibly human—that is to say "beings who relate deeply with each other".

Each time we can help someone bring coherence to an act, a meeting or an event, by connecting them with Viktor Frankl's *Homo Faber, Homo Amans* or *Homo Patiens* (see Strategy 6: *Access to Meaning*), we are participating in human construction.

Emmanuel Levinas[10] showed that relating is at the heart of being. And yet the process of humanization cannot be reduced to the development of our capacity to relate. Human beings not only build their identities through their relationships with others, but also conquer their own autonomy by projecting themselves into, and acting upon the world. It is through my acts in family, profession, social and political circles that I develop myself, increase my sense of responsibility and autonomy, and anchor my life in reality. Beyond my relationships with others, and my actions in the world, I need meaning to develop my identity. If I do not stand back from my action, receive or attribute meaning, I run a double risk: that of being exploited by others, and of exploiting others.

Finding the right balance between meaning, action and relationships is a major challenge, as we saw with the Autonomy Development Tree in Strategy 8: *Identity Construction*.

The pressure of external constraints and the scripts* inherited from our own life histories, puts each one of us in danger of getting lost in our actions or in our relationships. Like some business leaders who are impressive in action, but have no emotional or spiritual lives, some individuals become "lost stars", indefinitely fleeing their terror of death and their existential emptiness through their incessant activity.

Others remain "pure spirit" in their search for meaning, and are completely disconnected from reality, unable to embody themselves in family relationships or in a professional project.

---

[10] See Emmanuel Levinas, *Alterity and Transcendence*, Athlone Press, 1999.

Yet others dissipate their energy in an incessant quest for relationships that go round in circles because they have no sense of meaning, and are not anchored in reality.

The coach's job is to encourage the right balance, and if possible harmony between these three facets of a person's identity. This balance is achieved through acting into reality, relating to others, and searching for (self)-transcendence, which is the deepest wellspring of our quest for identity.

The coach's stance and the relationship he has with his client are guided at all times by this pursuit of coherence. The client needs to have outgrown his wounds, traumas or prisons linked to his personal history if he is to be able to restore his capacity to accept otherness embodied in meaningful human relationships. The dynamic of humanization is a core part of autonomy development (described in Strategy 2: *Fish/fishing rod—His frame/my frame*). At certain times and in certain contexts, some options may appear contradictory on incompatible. For example, moving up the professional hierarchy will give an individual a greater capacity for action. But at the same time, he may need to choose between losing enriching relationships and abandoning a project in which he had felt self-actualized. Even if the coach focuses on developing the relational competences of his client or his capacity to act effectively into his environment, he always needs to balance progression to autonomy with the dimension of meaning.

At Ease in the Midst of Chaos

Integrative coaching in the sense used in this book operates in the domain of complexity, since it deals with human beings and intersubjectivity*. It considers the human person to be an indivisible whole with multiple identities (social, professional, private, psychological, existential and spiritual). These identities are both unique (for himself and others) and "just another object" (from the point of view of the systems and organizations of which he is part). He is in relationships with other human beings, yet interacts with them in an open system, and cannot be reduced to one or other of these dimensions.

Even in the context of business coaching that requires an objective dimension, the coach's view of the client is still conditioned by the mystery of the person in front of him, and his intractable freedom, in spite of the many inevitable double binds* and risks of being exploited that exist. It is this view of the client that enables the coach to place himself in the perspective of sustainable development of the individual, and in this sense, his humanization. Herein lies the complexity and splendour of the coaching profession.

> **Double bind**
>
> A dilemma in communication in which an individual (or group) receives two or more conflicting messages, and one message negates the other. This creates a situation in which a successful response to one message results in a failed response to the other (and vice versa), so that the person will automatically be wrong regardless of his response.

This does not mean that it is impossible to undertake actions to generate change. However, faced with this "human material", the coach needs to be as wary as the psychoanalyst listening to his patient's unconscious, the medical doctor speaking of the life he holds in his hands, or the astronomer who observes stars whose light reaches him through unfathomable reaches of the universe that he will never know, and which may already have disappeared by the time he sees them. The mystery of the human subject invites the coach and his client to enter into a relationship where the "solution" will not come from the expertise of one or the other, but from the meeting of two living subjects, and the realizations that this meeting generates.

More generally, complex objects can only be apprehended with the tools of complexity.[11] An integrative coaching approach incorporates a number of different paradigms, fields of knowledge and views on reality, and is built on the crossroads of a number of theories and professions that deal with human beings. As such it can be looked at as an original construction in complexity—or a transdisciplinary construct, as Edgar Morin[12] would call it. One of the major paradoxes of the helping profession is that to arrive at simple decisions and solutions—by simple, I mean simple enough to generate effective operational action—it is necessary to have gone

---

[11] As per Ashby's law of requisite variety. See his book *An Introduction to Cybernetics*, Chapman & Hall, 1956.

[12] French philosopher and sociologist, internationally recognized for his work on complexity and "complex thought," and his scholarly contributions to such diverse fields as media studies, politics, sociology, visual anthropology, ecology, education, systems biology, and beyond. See his book *On Complexity*, Hampton press, 2008.

through complexity: analytical tools, valid for "complicated" problems, are inadequate for a complex environment.

The same goes for a business in the post-industrial world, where an integrative coaching approach becomes highly relevant. Every organization is inevitably made up of human relationships, and Collective Intelligence* takes account of this living reality: the human factor is part and parcel of technology, and it is living beings who operate human processes. In this context, management based solely on control and hierarchy is ineffective. Only a shared, co-constructed vision can give meaning to action. Once the destination is defined, each player has his own compass, and as long as there is agreement on values and objectives, the twists and turns and contradictions on the way can be managed by each one because the players have found, and shared meaning.

Management under complexity, like quantum physics, has an uncertainty principle. Rigid plans give way to emergent strategies (whose meaning gradually emerges) that are imperfect (do not conform to pre-established patterns) and occurrent (whose course can be changed by unexpected events). These strategies are always surprising and often paradoxical. Exercising leadership in this complex reality requires continually letting go. To paraphrase Tom Peters, "to keep some sort of control over the situation, we need to let go of control to some extent".[13] We need to learn to be at ease with uncertainty, ambiguity, paradox and permanent change, if we are to have any hope of giving meaning to the act of managing. To cope with this complexity, a leader needs to be deeply anchored and stable in what lies at the center of his identity, and what I call the Prince(ss), whose primary quality is his ontological security*.

Complicated is not complex

It is important not to confuse complicated with complex as we make sense of the world around us through our eyes, our sensitivities and our intelligence.

What is complicated can be entirely analyzed, controlled and/or implemented in a rational and predictable manner, as long as we spend enough time and effort on it. An airplane or a computer, though they may be incomprehensible to common mortals, are still mechanical systems that remain in the domain of what is complicated—as are most purely technical artifacts.

What is complex cannot, by its very nature, be controlled: the randomness, disorder and ambiguity of these phenomena are irreducible, and cannot be

---

[13] Tom Peters, *Thriving on Chaos*. HarperBusiness, 1989.

> understood or experienced without accepting their paradoxes and contradictions. All living things, human beings, the unconscious, and phenomena that operate simultaneously at several different logical levels belong to this domain.
>
> In business, producing a consolidated income statement is a complicated task; managing a team or listening deeply to someone is always a complex matter.

The "Scarlet Thread" of Responsibility

We have seen that a major challenge for the coach is his ability to help his client break free from what imprisons him. Each of us, in our own measure, lives in prisons made up of the defense systems we have built. These prisons may be psychological, but may be also family, institutional, ideological or religious. We are impregnated with and structured by a culture that Edward T. Hall's[14] anthropology studies have shown to be largely unconscious. These cultural paradigms guide and significantly limit our way of seeing the world, and the ways we live out our emotions, our relationships and our spirituality. They differ from one individual to another, but we are all in some measure held hostage to them. It is as we become conscious of these prisons that we are able to find greater freedom. The psychoanalyst Alice Miller[15] compared the therapist to the lawyer who stretches his hands out to the prisoner through the prison bars. The same applies for the coach: each time he is able to contribute to the process of liberating his client, at whatever level, he is contributing to his humanization.

The coach's role does not stop there. Viktor Frankl addressed the American nation in these terms: "You have built the statue of liberty on the East coast, you now need to cross the continent and build the statue of responsibility on the West coast." The path taken by an integrative coaching approach goes from helping a person break free from his alienation to helping him to move on towards a logic of responsibility. As we have seen, the coach shifts the cursor of his action according to the needs of his client: his degree of autonomy, the evolution of his personal and professional challenges in his different relationships, and his environment. This constant adjustment of the forms and levels of the coach's intervention is always guided by a scarlet thread: developing the client's sense of responsibility.

---

[14] Edward T. Hall, *The Hidden Dimension*. Bantam Doubleday Dell Publishing Group, 1988.

[15] Alice Miller, *Prisoners Of Childhood: The Drama of the Gifted Child and the Search for the True Self*. Basic Books, 1996.

Having helped his client free himself from his mental, emotional or ideological prisons, the coach creates the conditions needed for him to assume full responsibility for his decisions and his acts. The coach will give permissions* with their associated protections* that are indispensable for a person to exercise his liberty and responsibility without endangering himself. This balance between protection and permission will enable the client to fully and positively free his power and energy.

Each time the coach addresses this trilogy—consciousness of a prison, access to a form of freedom and construction of a sense of responsibility—he activates a process of humanization.

Respecting a client's freedom whilst contributing to the development of his autonomy is a paradoxical proposition—how to help the other dispense with one's help? When the coach challenges the client through feedback, encourages him to take the initiative or suggests he take risks by proposing action options, he always does this with the aim of developing his sense of responsibility. This sense of responsibility comes from within, and is not imposed from the outside. Management writers such as Jim Collins have ably demonstrated that voluntary acceptance of a form of discipline at work never comes from a repressive system, nor from a persecuting form of judgement. It is the necessary result of an educational process that passes through the understanding, then the progressive internalization of self-discipline.

More recently, Frédéric Laloux[16] has published a detailed comparative study of organizations that operate outside the paradigm of hierarchy and procedure. The models he presents confirm the effectiveness of a view of management that is placed under the sign of humanization and Collective Intelligence*. This vision of "Freedom Incorporated" is based on an individual and collective adoption of a culture of personal responsibility and self-governance founded on reciprocal listening, respect for others and collaboration. It thrives on the feeling of fulfilment that being one's real self at work can bring. Until this has become a shared culture, the organization cannot free itself from a hierarchical structure. This individual and collective education to greater freedom and responsibility lies at the heart of any coaching project, as well as all enlightened leadership.

---

[16] In his remarkable book: *Reinventing Organizations: A Guide to Creating Organizations Inspired by the Next Stage of Human Consciousness,* Nelson Parker, 2014.

It is the individual himself, and only he, who is responsible for becoming aware of the change he needs to make, and ensuring that the components of his identity become ever more consistent with the values and meaning which shape his life. For a leader or a manager, developing oneself means first of all developing one's talents, striving to be the best and most competent person in the job. From a systemic perspective, changing oneself is the best way to change the system, or the organization in which one works. But changing, putting what is essential at the heart of what is important, also means changing how one sees other people, and thus changing one's relationship with others. It means seeing in each person in the organization a growing subject as well as an object of production. It also means looking at each individual in the same way that a sports coach looks a champion athlete: he clearly sees his current level of performance, and at the same time he discerns the unrealized potential that lies within. I would add a third dimension: each and every relationship between human beings brings forth a community. To use Bertrand Martin's words, seeing and recognizing the "potential person" beyond his current limits is a way of humanizing the world.

For a manager to go through such a change represents a real existential commitment. Such a manager does not try to remove managerial or structural ambiguity, but recognizes and lives with it. Such a manager accepts the necessarily contingent, incomplete and random nature of any management project. Such a manager understands that it is impossible to lead human beings unless one learns to manage the latent contradictions between inclusion (I respect and recognize each person), control (I decide how to free up talent) and openness (I encourage people to work together and share representations of reality). By refusing to exploit others and renouncing the illusion of being all-powerful, such a manager (or coach, or trainer) offers the support needed for others to move forward. Moreover, it is by acknowledging his own incompetence that he opens up the space for others to develop their own competence.

The coach or leader needs a solid backbone to live through these paradoxes! An integrative coaching approach offers an ideal opportunity to undergo this identity transformation and to accept the frustration and losses it implies. By accepting frustration, I mean recognizing that nothing ever happens completely as planned, that imperfection is at the heart of human nature and that there will always be an irreducible gap between desired and actual situations. Accepting these losses is to give up the narcissistic benefits associated with each stage of one's identity development, and leaving them behind in order to progress to a higher level.

Individuation: Uniqueness in Universality

In concluding this chapter, I will add that the integrative coaching approach leads individuals and teams towards individuation*. Individuation is not asserting at all costs one's "self" as being different and distinct from others. It is the gradual acknowledgement by an individual of the contradictory and conflicting elements that make him an "entity" who is psychologically, emotionally and physically unique. This process enables each individual to develop his own personality, whose uniqueness participates, paradoxically, in a certain universality.

> **Individuation**
>
> Refers to the development of the individual from the universal or the determination of the individual in the general. It is the process by which individuals in society become differentiated from one another.

This is the wonder of a work of art, which awakens something universal in us through the expression of an artist's uniqueness. As coaches, in particular through the Princes(s)' Alliance*, we help our clients gain access to their uniqueness, and to this deepening and widening of awareness that opens possibilities. One way of describing what happens in individuation is what the French novelist André Malraux described as "transforming the widest possible experience into awareness". This means helping the stone mason who is cutting a stone to become aware that he is building a cathedral. As we saw when discussing the meaning molecule in Strategy 6: *Access to Meaning*, the aim of the coach is to help an individual co-construct with others his own particular stance with regards to the world, to others, and to his own existence, and through this stance to find wholeness.

In the domain of organizations, the work of individuation is often necessarily limited, since a business is no substitute for the essential areas of an individual's family life, private life or his approach to transcendence. And yet, even if the workplace represents "what is important" rather than "what is essential", these two dimensions can, and should be made consistent with each other. This shared conviction is at the heart of the EVH CEO Club[17] in which I actively participate. The challenge is to co-construct a new reality.

---

[17] *Entreprises Vivantes par et pour des Femmes et des Hommes Vivants* (Living Enterprise for living women and men), founded in 1992 by Bertrand Martin, CEO of CCM Sulzer.

In this way, the workplace can become a space for the construction of individuals' identities, since it is formed of multiple relationships focused on a common objective of producing wealth by working together.

Complexity and responsibility when coaching in an organization

In the business world, coaching (of an individual, a team or an organization) normally takes the form of a trilateral relationship between the sponsor, the individual and the coach. This relationship is sometimes multilateral, involving others such as the individual's immediate manager, trainers, consultants or HR.

Coaching is normally focused on an agenda that represents the synthesis of the best interests of the individual and the organization. First and foremost, the individual needs protection: not only does the coach respect strict confidentiality concerning what is said between him and the individual, but he also does not report on progress to the sponsor unless it is within the limits agreed with the individual. Notwithstanding this, he remains at all times aware of his responsibility with regards to the wider community that is impacted, directly or indirectly, by his intervention.

It goes without saying that the challenges facing individuals are not always aligned to those facing the organizations they work in. Some interests coincide, but there is often a difference, and sometimes a conflict between them. For example, the career ambitions of an individual may contradict the career path the organization has laid out for him. The coach needs to ensure consistency between the coaching process for the individual and the life of the system he is in, with the limits that it imposes. He is not there to reinforce antagonisms, tensions or contradictions that would exclude the individual from the organization, nor is he there to be exploited by the organization.

Over and beyond the trilateral contract, the coach needs to continually contextualize his interventions. Since he positions himself with respect to a common vision and final purpose, he transcends irreducible (and often legitimate) differences between his stakeholders. To do this he needs to be constantly aware of the constraints, customs, culture and context of the organization.

One could say that an integrative coaching approach has a role in reconciling individual purpose and collective ambition. The coach will distinguish the best interests of the individual and of the organization, will intervene without confusing the two and will "act in the best interests of the overall system", as per coaching's code of ethics. The coach is not there to encourage an individual's fantasy self-identification with the business, nor is he there to align individuals to production requirements, and he is certainly not there to be the "strong arm" of the CEO or the executive team.

Integrative coaching in the sense used in this book acknowledges the holomorphic* dimension of a person in an organization. An individual is seen, not as an isolated and undivided entity, separate from the world, but as a complex being who relates with others within a complex environment, constituting an ecosystem that only tools designed for complexity can handle.

Key Points and Pause for Reflection—Humanization

The questions below will help you think through how you use the strategy of humanization in the helping relationships that you manage. These questions are designed to help you search inside yourself, so it is important to take your time. Even if you only deal with one question, take the time to reflect fully on it, rather than simply going through a "checklist" exercise.

- As he builds plans for his development, is my client ready to accept his finiteness? In other words, does he accept his limits, and the fact that he is incompetent in some areas? Does he let go of things, is he ready to grieve, and does he accept that one day he will die?
- Where is my client in terms of his own "liberation struggle", his capacity to assume his freedom, and his willingness and ability to take up a position of responsibility?
- To what extent is my client opening up to, or interested in the "human element" and, as a consequence, treading the path of humanization?
- How do my client's approach, the direction he is taking and the decisions he is making, contribute to bring greater coherence and unity to his life history, his present context, and his identity?

Strategy 10: Crystallization

How can I help my client become the architect and owner of his solutions and decisions? And avoid doing things in his place!

In the twelfth-century Persian poem *The Bird Parliament,* a group of birds, having crossed seas and deserts, think they have reached their destination and go to meet Simorgh, their king, who possesses all power and knowledge, in order to show him their devotion. But all they find is a lake in which they see their own reflection. They realize, as the poem says, that "Simorgh is them, and they are Simorgh", and a voice tells them: "You have gone on a long journey, and you have arrived at your own door".

> *Pilgrim, Pilgrimage, and Road,*
> *Was but Myself toward Myself: and Your*
> *Arrival but Myself at my own Door.*[1]

This long journey that enables the traveler to "arrive at his own door" is for me a beautiful metaphor of coaching.

How can I help my client to change, to open himself up to his "space of the possible", yet ensure that he remains the owner and accountable for his

---

[1] Farid ud-Din Attar, *The Bird Parliament,* translated by Edward Fitzgerald, Macmillan, 1889.

© The Author(s) 2017
V. Lenhardt, *My 10 Strategies for Integrative Coaching,*
DOI 10.1007/978-3-319-54795-4_12

own solution? It is by adopting a stance that I hope the reader will now recognize:

> *The coach never decides for his client. He never chooses in his place. He is content to contribute to "crystallizing" the client's choice—and therein lies the humility and greatness of the coaching profession.*

Crystallization is another term taken from Transactional Analysis. It designates a particular kind of intervention, whereby the coach brings the client face to face with his different options, and helps him make a lucid, free and responsible choice.

On the psychoanalyst's couch, the key intervention is interpretation. Here it is different: once the client has become aware of the life script* in which he is imprisoned, the coach invites him to experiment new behaviors, beliefs and attitudes that he has sufficiently identified and reinforced to be able to put them into action and to assume them completely. Once the client has freed himself through working on himself and has become relatively autonomous, crystallization puts him face to face with two possible outcomes: continue to function as if he was still executing his script, but no longer identified with, or imprisoned by it; or detach himself completely from it, and learn to function differently.

Taking the Risk of Opening up the Future

At a certain moment the coach, in his role as "accountable for framing the relationship", places his client before a choice: repeat past actions and decisions, or take the decision to strike out freely to new horizons. In essence, the coach is saying to the client:

> *You are free to reproduce yesterday's behavior that has, in a certain manner, protected you until now. You now see that you also have another option, which you may already have tested in a different situation. This new solution for this situation may open up a new future for you, if you decide to take a calculated risk. The choice is yours. Are these two options clear for you?*

Here is an example, taken from a business leader I coached.

My client comes for coaching in order to stabilize his professional situation. He has changed jobs several times over the past few years. Most of the time, it was he who decided to change, after conflicts with his bosses. He realizes that when he disagrees with authority figures, he systematically dramatizes the situation, and ends up impulsively quitting. With my help, he understands that this repeated behavior corresponds to a script* where dramatic action enables him to avoid facing up to and managing conflict. In the past he had preferred to rebel and run away rather than manage his frustrations. Other options are now available to him. Instead of running way, he can attempt to face the situation differently, work out joint solutions, or find different ways of relating, including metacommunicating with authority figures. He now begins to work through these options with me.

In a therapeutic relationship, the client's current issues would surely hark back to past experiences with authority figures (starting with parental figures) with wounds which had not yet healed, and hence generate massive transferential* phenomena in a professional context. In coaching, though these past scenes may be mentioned, we never propose a work of emotional regression, but remain focused on the situation in the here and now.

During one of our coaching sessions, the client tells me how his boss, once again, had provoked him and humiliated him in an intolerable manner. In these circumstances, he asks me, his coach, to approve his decision to quit. As the session progresses, he gradually realizes that if he does this, he is reproducing the very behavioral script that he was seeking to free himself from when he sought my help through coaching. He also realizes that, over the past few months and the individual coaching sessions over that period, there were times when he was able to avoid escalations in conflict with his boss. In spite of the circumstances, he was able to remain patient, listen, manage his emotions and in the end avoid taking dramatic action.

There is a subtlety here. The decision that the client should take is not necessarily to stay put in his job. It may be that the stakes being played out with his boss are such that the right decision is to quit the company. The point is that by bringing my client to crystallization, I as coach help him to realize that he is capable of assuming his frustration and staying in his job if he so wishes. If he decides to leave, it is a decision based on free choice, and not, like on previous occasions, the repetition of a compulsive script.

You see, you no longer feel a prisoner of your impetuous desire to quit your job. You are now aware that you have a real choice between staying and leaving, and that if you choose to leave, it is by free choice, not dictated by your script, but chosen because it seems to you to be the most reasonable and fair decision to take. You are now in a position to take a decision that is fully yours.

The coaching process enabled my client to become aware of, and test out, new behaviors, and led him to make a real choice. In this case he realized that he was free to leave without being carried away by his old emotions, but finally decided knowingly to pursue his career by staying in his job.

A Meta-Strategy: The Stance of Crystallization

In the coaching process as it unfolds over time, crystallization comes after a series of interventions and exercises, over a number of sessions. Though it is a specific intervention within a logical sequence, one can also consider it as a permanent protocol in any coaching relationship that extends over time. From this perspective, crystallization is a strategy that underpins all the others, like a "groundwater table" that permeates the whole coaching process. It is a meta-strategy that nourishes and spans all the others, with a holomorphic* dimension, beyond the sense used in Transactional Analysis.

For me, to "crystallize" means to invite my client to break out of the walls of his prisons—psychological ideological, institutional, cultural, spiritual—and dare to take the risk of taking hold of his freedom and responsibility. I do this, having first of all created a relationship with him, forged an alliance with him, and helped him to step back from his current position. As a coach, I crystallize the possible choices by leveraging my client's position, so that I am always slightly ahead of my client with respect to his level of autonomy, and am able to help him move on to the next stage.

The resulting stance and intervention require high-quality listening and extreme caution on behalf of the coach, especially in business coaching. Sometimes the client, at least for the time being, does not want to change, and that is his right. Sometimes he cannot change, because the company or team in which he works do not give him sufficient autonomy. In this case, the surrounding system is stronger than the individual's will to change, and the coach needs to take this limit into account. The coach is not there to point out what to do, but simply to be the key that opens the possibility of choice. If crystallization is an objective for the coach, he needs at all times to be at the right level of energy and to intervene at the right level of identity, in order to help his client take possession of his freedom and his responsibility. This applies to the way he communicates, to the way he sees himself, to his attitudes towards others and towards life, and of course to his acts. This is why we speak of a meta-strategy.

The contract (more on this later) will have documented explicit objectives and defined the duration of coaching, thus enabling a work plan to be drawn up. It will have specified the respective roles and responsibilities of coach and client, thus providing the framework within which the overall strategy can be implemented in each coaching session. Nevertheless, before each crystallization the coach needs to check that there is mutual consent between him and his client, and that this consent occurs, in Transactional Analysis terms, between Adult and Adult. Even though the coach is far from a neutral bystander, and may sometimes be directive with respect to the process to follow, or even the meaning and stakes involved, he never confuses his role with that of his client.

For crystallization to occur, significant work is needed upstream. The client needs to become aware of his behaviors, and their underpinning dynamics, in particular any compulsive repetitive behaviors. The coach brings these to light gradually by supporting his client as he works through alternative options with respect to behaviors, thoughts and emotions. The coach remains conscious of the behavior patterns in which the client risks imprisoning himself, both as he develops them, and at key decision points. During this process, the coach needs to ensure that the relationship between them supports the development of the client's autonomy. What is at stake is moving from a kind of dependence that, at the start of the coaching relationship, runs the risk of becoming unhealthy (confused, ambivalent or passive-aggressive), to a healthy dependence characterized by the client accepting the principles of metacommunication and being willing to listen to what the coach has to say.

As well as crystallization, the coach's perspective is that of helping his client to pass through the different stages of autonomy (described in Strategy 2: *Fish/fishing rod—His frame/my frame*) and to achieve a level of interdependence, or even alter-dependence with the coach. The coach, using the various means at his disposal, will gradually bring his client into a relationship where they experience each other as equals. Only when this occurs will the client be truly the author of decisions he takes during the coaching. The decisions may have been co-constructed, and the coach may even sometimes have given his point of view, but the client, and the client alone, commits himself and shoulders the responsibility for his choice. In each and every coaching session, the coach needs to have internalized a stance of crystallization that continually frames, or reframes, the relationship for which he is accountable.

The Necessary Ethics of Change for the Coaching Profession

As in all professions that deal with the human person, coaching demands an unreserved commitment to a code of ethics, based on certain prerequisites. The strategy of crystallization poses the question of deontology, which applies to all helping professions. For crystallization to happen, four essential conditions have to be met.

- A **will to change** must be present in the client. Without it, the client will not consent to enter into a relationship which is likely to challenge his beliefs and behaviors.
- The will to change needs to be expressed in the form of a **request** made to the coach, even if it is confused and ambivalent to start with.
- The request needs to result in a **change contract**, that includes setting up a secure and confidential intersubjective* space that enables each party to create and live out the coaching relationship, with all its difficulties and inevitable frustrations.
- Finally—and this is more a prior condition—the coach needs to have **worked on himself** if he is to have the inner freedom and ontological security* that will enable him to welcome his client and accept him unconditionally.

An Obligation of Means

The objectives of coaching may be many and varied. They may aim to resolve short-term problems, or provide long-term help to an individual, team or organization in order to achieve deep-seated transformation. Whatever the objectives, the coach uses all the means at his disposal to enable the achievement of the desired results, in the context of the client's request. However, his commitment extends only to provide the means, not to achieve the results. There are two reasons for this: firstly, he can in no way force his client to change; and secondly, he has no "magic change pill" that he can dispense to those who come to see him.

I would add that it is rare for the resulting change to perfectly coincide with the change expected at the beginning. Clearly, like any sports coach, the coach desires to see his "champions" improve their performance at all levels. But, contrary to the sports coach, he is not accountable for the results of his client. If he was, he would run the danger of being exploited by others, or of exploiting them.

Giving up the Illusion of Omnipotence

The individual is always more important than the objectives. Coaching practice is founded on total respect for the human person: the client is unconditionally accepted, as he is. It is this respect for the other, along with the clarity of the intervention framework (limits, permissions* and protections*) and the strong stimulation achieved by freeing up the client's positive energy, that gives potency to what is being done.

Given that coaching is not based on motivation or influencing techniques, the coach should all the more exclude the use of any form of abusive influence that might result from his position. The limits with respect to seduction, power and money need to be clearly stated upfront, and remain inviolable.

Who is a manipulator of souls or spirits? It is someone who, by encouraging transference*, takes advantage of the intersubjective relationship to establish his power over the other. He is aware of holding sway over the other, and experiences a narcissistic pleasure in seeing the other regress, make an unconditional emotional commitment, and plunge into dependence.

Coaching is—and owes itself to be—the complete opposite of this kind of practice. The coach's primary and final concern is to contribute to the autonomy and freedom of his client. When he is faced with a request which often resembles a call to take responsibility for the client and put him in the position of rescuer*, the coach can respond in a healthy manner because he has given up his fantasy of omnipotence.

The "Out of bonds" Field of Therapy

Coaching is not amateur or disguised therapy. Like all helping relationships, it has a therapeutic dimension, since a helping relationship will generally create a virtuous circle that leads an individual to be more confident, to feel better, and to experience relationships in a healthier and more peaceful manner. Beyond the answers to the situation that his intervention brings, the helping professional activates zones of healing energy in his client, at different levels of his identity and his relationships.

At the same time he does not directly touch the deeper levels of the client's psychology and personal identity, which remain "out of bounds" and represent the limit of coaching with respect to therapy. The complex, always ambiguous, subtle and intimate dimension that a coaching relationship implies, requires great caution, and absolute renunciation of the temptation to respond to the client's request at a level other than that determined by the coaching contract. If the client's request does not appear to be manageable in the framework thus defined, the coach should refer his client to other helping professionals.

The Alliance for Change

Whatever the case, coaching requires a climate of trust such that the client feels at all times respected and safe from any form of manipulation or perversion of the relationship. It also requires a tacit agreement on the level of reciprocal commitment from each party ("How far are we willing to go together?"). This "Alliance for Change" is far more than a simple legal contract. It has an irreducible dimension of intellectual, psychological and emotional complicity, from both a personal and a social perspective. At the same time, a certain formality is needed, and is embodied in a contract that guarantees a protected time and place where individuals accept being challenged, being put back in their place, or being jostled, in order to progress with the coach on the path of change. By contractually formalizing the relationship, its means and its success criteria (where, when, how, who sponsors and who pays), the coach and the client(s) establish their shared responsibility with regards to the outcomes.

Trilateral contracts in the context of a team of coaches

As we saw in Strategy 9: *Humanization*, in business coaching the relationship will generally be trilateral (sponsor, client and coach) or multilateral (multiple stakeholders). The coaching contract and ways of working need to be adapted for each type of contract.

One procedure concerns the referencing work done by the person accountable for establishing a team of internal or external coaches, and defining how the team functions. Setting up a series of trilateral contracts is a prerequisite here: firstly, by identifying the stakes for each of the players, then by establishing a clear contract with each party, and ensuring each person's approach is compatible. For each individual coaching, it is up to each coach to ensure that the consistency of each trilateral contract is preserved.

Cleaning One's Spectacles

If the coach remains prisoner of his ego, script* or frame of reference, he cannot generate the Pygmalion effect—that gaze that sees the client's Prince (ss) behind the Frog's defenses and scripts, and enables the crystallization of the conditions for the client's growth. The coach's personal work aims to activate the coach's own Prince(ss) within, and can rarely be done without having a place of therapy, or at least a place of regulation, supervision or resourcing.

This is because the coach needs to have gone through long and rigorous self-reflection, in order to learn to refuse to play the games into which his client will attempt to draw him, often unconsciously. In order to avoid symbiotic relationships, and the traps and excesses that always threaten a relationship, let alone another person's manipulations, the coach needs to take care not to become his own plaything. It is doubtless impossible to "control" one's unconscious. Nevertheless one can remain attentive to it, so as to detect and analyze how one is reacting to positive or negative transference, one's own counter-transference or parallel processes* (described in Strategy 4: *Contextualization*), which sometimes almost completely invade the space of the intersubjective encounter between coach and client.

More generally, the coach needs to "clean his spectacles". This means getting rid of his prejudices, ideological presuppositions and pre-established frameworks, so as not to be carried away by his own grey areas, and so as to be able to accept the other's frame of reference. He needs to get rid of his own blinkers if he is to constantly stay at the right distance in the relationship, to understand at each moment what the client needs, and to intervene in the right place, at the right time, in the right way, and with the right rhythm.

What Should One Expect from a Coaching Course?

Coaching needs a solid code of ethics. But it also needs a solid teaching program to launch the coach into the profession. Business coaching also requires the coach to have a solid experience in the workplace and in business.

Today, there is a wide choice of coaching schools across the world. Some are more generalist, and other specialize in certain domains such as sports coaching, life coaching or team coaching. However, their difference mainly resides in two main approaches that lie behind them.

The first is to put the emphasis on a purely operational, or even "instrumental" approach. The focus is on assimilating methods and techniques—"how to do" rather than "how to be". This results-orientated approach is characteristic of many schools in the Anglo-Saxon world. The second approach seeks to work more on the construction and deepening of the coach's identity, without neglecting the pursuit of effective results. The premise of these courses is that the coach will function better when he has strengthened his ontological security* and developed his openness to others.

The coaching course I created in 1988, and that is taught in the Coach & Team network in French-speaking countries, clearly espouses the second approach. It is one of the most active advocates of this approach in the French-speaking world. The appendix summarizes the principles and philosophy on which this course is based.[2]

The Paradox of Power

With regards to the coaching ecosystem, speaking of strategies has a paradoxical aspect. Contrary to the consultant, who is hired to bring solutions to his clients—sometimes before the client has even asked any questions—the coach's primary calling is not to propose solutions. This does not stop him intervening, and even being a force for proposals when needed. But when he intervenes, he strives to remain "empty", that is to say available, in relation with and embracing what comes from his client.

Such an attitude may at first sight appear to be completely "anti-strategic". Yet the vacuum that the coach creates in himself, and between himself and his client in order to make it the place where the other is fully received, is not a space where there is nothing, like the Newtonian void. It is a "quantum vacuum*" or energy field from which emerge new particles of matter[3] which in turn generate new worlds. For me, this quantum vacuum represents the intersubjective* space of the encounter between two partners, two subjects, whose energy will interact and mysteriously, magically, bring forth solutions

---

[2] The book *Devenir un acteur de l'entreprise libérante* ((*becoming a actor of a business that frees its people*), Interéditions, 2017 (available only in French) provides a detailed description of the principles and constituent elements of this course.

[3] We know, since Einstein and his famous equation $E = MC^2$, that energy and matter are the same.

that come neither from the coach, nor from the client, but from their interdividuality*.[4]

> **Quantum vacuum (or quantum fluctuation).**
>
> The temporary appearance of energetic particles out of empty space, as allowed by Heisenberg's uncertainty principle. In these circumstances, conservation of energy can appear to be violated, but only for small times. This allows the creation of particle-antiparticle pairs of virtual particles, which may have been very important in the origin of the structure of the universe.

One needs to have learnt much and practiced much to go to one's client with all one's learning, all one's resources, all one's experience, and then to set them aside in order to make oneself totally available to meet him—like a spinning top or gyroscope that is in constant movement whilst giving the appearance of being immobile. The coach is at work, even when he appears to be doing nothing—and in truth, he does not intervene as one commonly understands the term. The power of the relationship proceeds entirely from this paradox. The coach has renounced the illusion of omnipotence in order to live out a relationship in total acceptance of both the other person and himself, with their respective limits. He has also learnt to remain solidly upright on his axis, even though he is in spinning constantly, like the top. As he faces his client, the different strategies described in this book enable him to mobilize the accumulated energy at the right level, and so activate the potential of his client in line with his stakes, his objectives and the means at his disposal.

The power of this process does not come solely from the coach's energy. It is the result of the optimization of three energy systems: the coach, the client and their interaction in the complexity of relating. The coach, as owning the relationship, is responsible for creating this synergy.

Depending on the objectives, priorities and situations, this optimization will sometimes occur through a directive intervention: the client may not have enough energy, or may generate negative energy and thus need an impetus from the outside. It will also sometimes occur when the coach appears to do nothing, as he lets the client bring his potential to the relationship. Here, action takes the form of non-action—a look, a silence or a listening ear are sometimes the best way to free up the client's power in a

---

[4] As per Jean-Michel Oughourlian's expression, discussed in the introduction.

helping relationship: in appearance, the coach "brings" nothing, but by his attitude he creates the conditions whereby his client frees up his own energy. This approach is both effective (it achieves results) and efficient (it achieves them with an economy of means).

Like all the coaching strategies, crystallization operates in a relational space with four poles: the coach, the client, the relationship between them and the context. Depending on how the coaching progresses, and according to the time and circumstances, the coach will focus his interventions on one or other of these poles. But focusing at a given moment on one pole does not mean he will disregard or neglect the others: the coach continually scans the whole relational field.

It is here that the coaching approach, that of generating an intrinsic dynamic for problem resolution, differs from consulting practice. It is unique in that it constructs a relational space that becomes the place from which solutions emerge. In this sense, coaching takes the humanistic view according to which "it is the relationship that heals". The relationship, this intersubjective space, becomes the place of healing and transformation. It is here that the contract is designed, the request is made explicit, the need is dealt with, the parallel processes* are identified and dealt with, possibilities are experienced, and change is crystallized.

All ten strategies in this book are organized around the implementation of this intersubjective dynamic, which in turn presupposes that the coach has come to terms with the fundamental paradoxes of coaching:

- the **paradox of education**—how to help the other do without one's help;
- the **paradox of autonomy**—how to progressively create interdependence through dependence;
- the **paradox of competence**—how to dissolve one's competence into the development of the other's competence.

As coaches, we only have access to the emergent part of the iceberg of a person's identity. What is essential comes to the surface, and materializes in what is most visible: a person's behaviors. Nevertheless, peoples' deep structure, the scripts* they have inherited, their intimate wounds, the cultures to which they belong, their existential and spiritual choices—all this remains out of sight, below the waterline. Hence a particular difficulty: helping the other to change, whilst operating at a distance, like the nuclear engineer who has to handle nuclear matter at a safe distance through protective screens and levers, in order to release energy in a controlled manner.

Coaching brings a specific response to human issues. It rests on a professional practice that integrates many diverse, yet complementary disciplines, and is accompanied by a rigorous ethical stance.

Key Points and Pause for Reflection— Crystallization

The questions below will help you think through how you use the strategy of crystallization in the helping relationships that you manage. These questions are designed to help you search inside yourself, so it is important to take your time. Even if you only deal with one question, take the time to reflect fully on it, rather than simply going through a "checklist" exercise.

1. To what extent am I conscious of the inevitable paradox of the helping relationship: helping the other to do without my help?
2. How do I keep a permanent watch on the paradoxes that condition all relationships under complexity:
   – partially letting go of control, so as to keep control of the part that I need to manage;
   – accepting and recognizing the area of my competence, so as to accept the infinite area of my incompetence;
   – rejoicing in the existence of the areas of my total or relative incompetence, because they are the place from which my client develops his competence.
3. To what extent am I ready and mobilized to intervene at any moment, yet also comfortable (like the rapidly spinning top that apparently remains immobile) to move aside and let the other take up his place, in the knowledge that, for my client, my conscious presence is his best support?
4. To what extent am I able, through the trust I show, to help my client find, or rediscover confidence in himself and in life, without ever taking his place?

Appendix: Training, The "Coach & Team" Way

Each school in the Coach & Team (CT) ecosystem has its own particularities, but all the training courses have a common curriculum that represents our "minimal shared cultural envelope". These consist in a set of values, teaching principles, theoretical content and implementation methods, which all share a common end purpose, and are embodied by specific vocabulary and teaching methods. At the end of the course, what participants have learnt is validated by a certification process. This way of teaching is both highly structured and very flexible, and is based on a few key principles, outlined below.

Training "Through and For" Complexity

The course prepares future coaches to live, work and coach others under complexity. Whether from the conceptual perspective of understanding complexity or from the operational perspective of knowing how to manage complex situations, it develops their capacity to evolve in a world that is no longer in the domain of the "complicated" (which can be controlled, objectively named and predictably implemented), but that of the complex, which cannot be mastered.

A Generic Training Course

The CT approach is generalist in that it proposes an integrative approach to different kinds of coaching and their application. It is also generative in the sense of developing the coach's identity, rather than just giving him

© The Author(s) 2017
V. Lenhardt, *My 10 Strategies for Integrative Coaching*,
DOI 10.1007/978-3-319-54795-4

recipes or a set of techniques. The course has a clear operational dimension, and at the end of the course the participants have learnt to use a "toolkit" that will be useful to them for the rest of their professional lives. But, fundamentally, the course trains them to find the "right stance" that they can then adapt to widely varying situations.

Identity Construction

Over and beyond the knowledge acquired, along with specific coaching practice and group exercises, identity construction is the guiding thread throughout the course. The aim is to take into account the individual as a whole, his quality of being and his capacity to relate, and not just his competences in the technical sense of the word. The way the course is taught aims to develop ontological security*, not with the aim of forming omnipotent and omniscient beings: on the contrary, it aims to enable future coaches to accept their fundamental identity paradoxes, starting with the competence paradox*: to support their clients' competence, they need to recognize and accept their own areas of incompetence.

Informing Theory with Practice, and Practice with Theory

The fourth major principle of the course is to set aside times and places which enable constant to-ing and fro-ing between on the one hand "reflective" work on content, process and meaning, and on the other practical exercises. Specific methods are used to help participants plunge into, and evolve in complexity. For example self-organization (participants are treated as "already coaches"); or alternating teaching, internalization, explanations and practice sessions (a professional coach knows how to inform theory with practice, and practice with theory); or again through holomorphism* (each participant nourishes the dynamic of the course, which nourishes each participant). In this way, the training course aims to give each participant the means of being fully autonomous as a coach, whether he aims to exercise his profession as a full-time professional or whether he simply wants to internalize the coaching approach as he exercises another kind of helping relationship or management function.

Peer groups

Peer groups are one of the key vectors of the 18-month CT training journey. They meet two to three times between each module (modules are 6 weeks apart), right through the course. Each peer group consists of five to ten (maximum) people who meet when and where they themselves decide, with the objectives and agendas they determine. For example: to learn to self-organize, to help each other in their professional development, to coach each other, to share what they read, to share their experiences and to prepare for the final examination.

These groups are at the heart of the course. As their name indicates, "peer groups" are formed of people who consider themselves as peers, without a leader designated from the outside. This particular relationship and the limited size of the group make it an extremely fertile ground for learning the profession and stance of coach, and, from a wider point of view, of experiencing the life of a group in all its complexity. Often, these peer groups continue to meet after the course has finished, as they build on the trust and understanding that have formed between the group members. They represent a place where individuals can exchange their experiences of coaching, and they can also serve as professional or personal support networks.

A Place of Therapy

No-one can hope to practice an effective helping relationship unless he has learnt to cope with his own limits and wounds. For this deep dive, the future coach needs a space, outside the training school, where he can engage in the deconstruction, restoration, construction and reconfiguration of his frame of reference and his scripts*. Any therapeutic approach can be appropriate, but I recommend therapeutic approaches that integrate several dimensions—cognition, the body, emotions, behaviors and relationships.

Supervision

Throughout the training course, the coach is supported by a supervisory framework. This requirement does not disappear when the coach enters the profession. A peer or other qualified and experienced person in the helping relationship can fulfil the role of supervisor. The light that this person can shed will enable the coach to take a step back, unblock situations by opening other intervention paths, stabilize a coaching relationship in the face of strong disruption, or help discover answers to ethical issues. The supervisor is also an experienced correspondent with whom the coach can build a space of encounter and exchange so as to take a bearing on his practice, as well as enrich and deepen his approach as he develops his professional know-how.

Glossary

Alliance. There is an alliance between client and coach when mutual trust, along with the agreement on the objectives and approach, enables both parties to overcome the frustrations along the way without calling the relationship into question.

Collective Intelligence. A dynamic of co-responsible players, interconnected culturally and organizationally through an alliance around a shared vision.

Complicated vs. Complex. A complicated problem can be resolved by analytical methods has "a solution", and its future states can be predicted, given enough time, work and brain power. A complicated system (such as a space rocket) can be mechanically repaired, with predictable consequences. A complex system has multiple autonomous parts interacting in many ways, and constantly adapting to each other. The relationship between cause and effect cannot be discerned, nor can future states be predicted. Unpredictable phenomena emerge out of the interaction between the many different elements of the system, and the behavior of the whole is different to that of the sum of the parts. Social groups or the coach/client relationship are examples of complex systems.

Competence paradox. It is by focusing his energy on developing the competence of others at the cost of developing his own technical competence that the leader becomes more fully competent.

Constructivist. Based on the belief that people construct their own realities and find meaning based on life experience. In other words, experience constructs reality, affecting our knowledge and understanding of the world and our place in it. Constructivism focuses on human meaning making and promotes a person's proactive participation in his or her life in order to create change.

Double bind. A dilemma in communication in which an individual (or group) receives two or more conflicting messages, and one message negates the other. This creates a situation in which a successful response to one message results in a

© The Author(s) 2017
V. Lenhardt, *My 10 Strategies for Integrative Coaching*,
DOI 10.1007/978-3-319-54795-4

failed response to the other (and vice versa), so that the person will automatically be wrong regardless of his response.

Ego state. Transactional Analysis splits the different ways we express different parts of our personality into three main ego states: Parent, Adult and Child (written with capitals to distinguish the states from actual parents, adults and children). The Parent corresponds to that part of the Self that was formed under the influence of one's parents and other close parental figures. The Child corresponds to our spontaneous self, or our obedient self. The Adult corresponds to our rational self.

Enaction. Enaction, in its most basic sense, denotes a movement or action made manifest in the world. It is a dynamic process of world-constitution that is always intimately linked to a particular bodily identity and situated within a greater field of interpenetrating relationships. It can be summed up in the pithy verse of the Spanish poet Antonio Machado who inspired Varela: *Wanderer, the road is your footsteps, nothing else; There is no road, you lay it down in walking.*

Escape hatch. Term in Transactional Analysis that describes extreme behavior that is activated when our essential needs are not being met. People access extreme choices from their script and therefore archaic decisions, which are not reflective of the here-and-now situation.

Fractal. Geometric figures whose parts, at infinitely many levels of magnification, appear geometrically similar to the whole.

Frame of reference. Everything that constitutes a person's paradigm. A person's paradigm includes ways of representing the world, culture, social groups, values, past history, mental maps, psychological structure, competences and resources.

Free floating attention. The coach will not try to comprehend every detail as his client tells it. Instead, he relies on his subconscious and inner thought processes to handle the data, which will, at a later point when there is more information to draw upon, compute the meaning and relationships among the stored data.

General semantics. In general semantics, it is always possible to give a description of empirical facts, but such descriptions remain just that—descriptions—which necessarily leave out many aspects of the objective, microscopic, and submicroscopic events they describe. According to general semantics, language can provide people with a structural 'map' of empirical facts, but there can be no 'identity', only structural similarity, between the language (map) and the empirical facts as lived through and observed by people as humans-in-environments.

Gestalt. In Gestalt psychology, Gestalt refers to the integrated structures or patterns that make up our experience. These structures have specific properties which cannot be derived from its individual elements, nor are they the sum of these elements.

Heteronomy. Subordination or subjection to the law of another or action that is influenced by a force outside the individual. It is a term used by Kant for those laws which are imposed on us from without.

Holomorphic. From the Greek *Holos* "whole" and *Morphos* "form". When the parts have the same form as the whole, in the same way that each cell of a living organism contains all the genetic information of the organism of which it forms a part.

Humanistic psychology. Not to be confused with humanism. Humanistic psychology studies the whole person, and the uniqueness of each individual. The humanistic approach emphasizes the personal worth of the individual, the centrality of human values, and the creative, active nature of human beings. It helps the patient gain the belief that all people are inherently good, and pays special attention to such phenomena as creativity, free will, and positive human potential. Humanistic psychology acknowledges spiritual aspiration as an integral part of the human psyche. Humanistic psychology rose to prominence in the mid-twentieth century in response to the limitations of psychoanalytic theory. Carl Rogers and Abraham Maslow were two important figures in humanistic psychology.

Identity backbone. A tool I have developed for the coach to help align the different levels of his identity. At the base is the client's social identity, on which rests his organizational, then managerial and professional identities. Above that the identity he has in his private or family life, then his intimate psychological identity. Finally there are the existential, spiritual and denominational levels of identity. The coach will help the client align these different identities, like the osteopath realigns the backbone of a patient who has back problems.

Imago. An imago is an unconscious idealized mental image of someone, especially a parent, which influences a person's behavior.

Inclusion, control, openness. From Will Schutz, The Human Element. Inclusion is the first stage of team development, which consists of the process of each team member being fully included in the team. The team then enables each member to have a say in the way it functions, as it moves to giving control to its members. Finally, as each team member has the courage to expose his own weaknesses and vulnerability, the team attains openness.

Individuation. Refers to the development of the individual from the universal or the determination of the individual in the general. It is the process by which individuals in society become differentiated from one another.

Interdividual. According to Jean-Michel Oughourlian "Interdividual psychology is the study of the types of interaction that take place between psychological entities". This interaction, and the relationship between people, is characterized mainly by mimesis, where each party imitates the other.

Intersubjectivity. The sharing of their subjective states (emotions, attention, intention…) by two or more people. A focus on intersubjectivity gives primacy to reality as experienced by subjects, rather than attempting to define "objective reality".

Introjection. The unconscious internalization of another person's behaviors, ideas, values, or points of view. A person who picks up traits from their friends (e. g., a person who begins frequently exclaiming "Ridiculous!" as a result of hearing a friend of theirs repeatedly doing the same) is introjecting.

Level 5 leader. According to Jim Collins, a level 5 executive "Builds enduring greatness through a paradoxical blend of humility and professional will… Level 5 leaders channel their ego needs into the larger goal of building a great company. It's not that level 5 leaders have no ego or self-interest. Indeed, they are incredibly ambitious, *but their ambition is first and foremost for the institution, not themselves.*" (Collins' italics).

Metacommunication. A term brought to prominence by Gregory Bateson to refer a way of communicating about how one is communicating that enables both parties in a conversation to distance themselves from and understand what is going on between them. It can include "all exchanged cues and propositions about (a) codification and (b) relationship between the communicators".

Modeling. By modeling I mean the manner in which the stance and the whole set of behaviors adopted by the coach with his client will serve as models for the client, who will be able to introject, then reproduce them in other relational situations.

Object relations theory. Object relations theory deals with relationships between people, especially between the mother and her child. Our key drive is to form relationships with others, and we internalize the objects of our love. Thus we have a relationship with the internal mother as well as an external one.

Ontological security. Ontological security is about being secure at the core of one's being (ontology is about the nature of being). This security is a key anchor for the coach when faced with complex and sometimes difficult coaching situations.

Parallel process. A parallel process occurs when the client's unease or issues in relation to his ecosystem are reproduced in his relationship with the coach. The client "relives" the problems he has in his own relational system by projecting them onto his relationship with the coach.

Princes(s)' Alliance. When the Prince(ss) at the heart of the client meets the Prince(ss) at the heart of the coach, a special, powerful alliance is created that generates solutions for the issues facing the client.

Protection, permission and potency. A term coming from Transactional Analysis. To offer someone permission, the coach provides him with new messages about himself, others and the world. These messages realistically describe the person's grown-up resources and options. He can use them to replace old restrictive or destructive messages that he may have perceived his parents as giving her in childhood.If the client does take new permissions, he may experience this change as risky. Without being fully aware of it, he may look to the coach for protection. This requires also that he perceives the coach as having enough potency—enough power—to provide the needed support and protection.When he acts on the permission with the required protection, and succeeds, he himself acquires a feeling of potency.

Quantum vacuum (or quantum fluctuation). The temporary appearance of energetic particles out of empty space, as allowed by Heisenberg's uncertainty principle. In these circumstances, conservation of energy can appear to be violated, but only for small times. This allows the creation of particle-antiparticle pairs of virtual particles, which may have been very important in the origin of the structure of the universe.

Rule of St Benedict. A book of precepts written by St. Benedict of Nursia (c. 480–547) for monks living communally under the authority of an abbot.

Script. Eric Berne describes scripts in the following terms: "Each person decides in early childhood how he will live and how and how he will die, and that plan, which he carries in his head wherever he goes, is called his script (Eric Berne, *What do you say after you say Hello ?* Corgi, 1975, p 51). We all write our own life stories in early childhood, and finesse them throughout our lives. This life story, which is based on the decisions we made in our childhood and on parental programming, is continually reinforced, and is like a play with a beginning middle and end. It is buried in our memory, out of range of our consciousness, which means that we are not aware that we are the author of our own script.

Second Industrial Revolution. The second industrial revolution came about with the discovery of oil and the combustion engine, electricity and the telephone. All of these required significant capital, and implied central, hierarchical organization of materials and labor.

Situational intelligence. Knowing what to do in a given situation, then doing it, based on understanding what is going on, rather than applying ready-made solutions.

Socratic questioning. Socratic questioning is used to help uncover the assumptions and evidence that underpin people's thoughts in respect of problems. For example: "Why do you think that?... And why is that?.... Are you aware of another explanation?".

Stroke. In Transactional Analysis, a person gives a stroke occurs when he recognizes another person, either verbally or non-verbally. He gives him a kind of "unit of recognition".

Subsidiarity. Subsidiarity is "the principle that decisions should always be at the lowest possible level or closest to where they will have their effect, for example in a local area rather than for a whole country" (Cambridge English Dictionary). It differs from delegation in that the local decision maker has full authority and does not need to refer up the chain or report the decision to a higher authority.

Systemic. A manner of understanding how things influence each other within a complex entity, or larger system, by taking into account the relationships and interactions between its parts (as opposed to an analytical approach that breaks up the object in order analyzes its individual component parts). Systemics refers to an initiative to study systems from a holistic point of view.

Third Industrial Revolution. Rifkin characterizes the third industrial revolution as the coming together of peer-to-peer communications through Internet with peer-to-peer energy through distributed energy generation, an intelligent infrastructure through the Internet of Things, and distributed production through 3-D printing. In this context the cost of communication, production and distribution are close to zero, putting severe pressure on the capitalist paradigm of margin and profit.

Third-order suffering. The suffering associated with growth, comparable to what the caterpillar goes through as it transforms into a butterfly.

Transference, counter-transference. Transference is a phenomenon characterized by unconscious redirection of feelings from one person to another. It involves a reproduction of emotions relating to a client's previous relationships onto the coach. For example, a young client may reproduce emotions relating to his father or mother if the coach is older than him. Countertransference is where the transference of the client generates emotions in return by the coach. For example, the coach might remember problems with his adolescent son and project those feelings into the coaching relationship.

Transitional object. An object, such as a teddy bear, that has a quality for a small child of being both real and made-up at the same time. Playing with a transitional object can be an important early bridge between self and other, which helps a child develop the capacity to relate to others.

Bibliography

Anzieu, D., The Skin Ego, Yale University Press, 1989.

Ashby, W.R., An Introduction to Cybernetics, Chapman & Hall, 1956.

Bennis, W., Sample, S.B., Asghar, R., The Art and Adventure of Leadership. Understanding Failure, Resilience and Success, John Wiley & Sons, 2015.

Berne, E., Games People Play, Ballantine Books, 1964.

Berne, E., Intuition and Ego States, Harper, 1977.

Berne, E., Principles of Group Treatment, Grove Press, New York, 1966.

Berne, E., The Structure and Dynamics of Organizations and Groups, Ballantine Books (reprint), 1984.

Berne, E., What Do You Say After You Say Hello? Corgi Books, 1975.

Carney, G., Getz, I., Freedom Inc: Free Your Employees and Let Them Lead Your Business to Higher Productivity, Profits, and Growth, Crown Publishing Group, 2010.

Collins, J., Good to Great, Random House Business; 2001.

Derrida, J., Speech and Phenomena and Other Essays on Husserl's Theory of Signs, Northwestern University Press, 1973.

Din Attar, F-u., The Bird Parliament, translated by Edward Fitzgerald, Macmillan, 1889.

Drucker, P., Management Challenges for the 21st Century, Routledge, 2007.

Drucker, P., The Post-Capitalist Society, Routledge, 1994.

Dusay, J., Egograms and the "Constancy Hypothesis", Transactional Analysis Journal, 2, 37–41, 1972.

Frankl, V., Man's Search for Meaning, Beacon Press, 2006.

Frankl, V., The Unconscious God, Simon & Schuster, 1976.

Goulding, B., Goulding, M., The Power is in the Patient, Barnes & Noble, 1979.

Hall, E.T., The Hidden Dimension, Bantam Doubleday Dell Publishing Group, 1988.

© The Author(s) 2017   **235**

V. Lenhardt, *My 10 Strategies for Integrative Coaching*,

DOI 10.1007/978-3-319-54795-4

Hamel, G., The Future of Management, Harvard Business Review Press, 2008.

Herzberg, F., 2-Factor Motivation-hygiene Theory, 1971.

Herzberg, F., Motivation to Work, John Wiley and Sons, 1959.

Jullien, F., A Treatise on Efficacy, University of Hawaii Press, 2004.

Kahler, T., The Process Therapy Model: The Six Personality Types with Adaptations. Taibi Kahler Associates, 2008.

Karpman, S., Fairy Tales and Script Drama Analysis. Transactional Analysis Bulletin, 7(26),39–43, 1968.

Kohlrieser, G., Hostage at the Table: How Leaders Can Overcome Conflict, Influence Others, and Raise Performance, John Wiley & Sons, 2006.

Kohlrieser, G., Goldsworthy, S., Coombe, D., Care to Dare, Unleashing Astonishing Potential Through Secure Base Leadership, Jossey-Bass, San Francisco, 2012.

Kohut, H., The Analysis of the Self: A Systematic Approach to the Psychoanalytic Treatment of Narcissistic Personality Disorders, University of Chicago Press, 2009.

Kübler-Ross, E., To Live until We Say Goodbye, Simon & Schuster, 1997.

Laloux, F., Reinventing Organizations: A Guide to Creating Organizations Inspired by the Next Stage of Human Consciousness, Nelson Parker, 2014.

Lenhardt, V., Au coeur de la relation d'aide (At the Heart of the Helping Relationship). Interéditions Dunod, 2008.

Lenhardt, V., Coaching for Meaning, Palgrave, 2004.

Lenhardt, V. Ed., Devenir un acteur de l'entreprise libérante (Becoming a actor of a business that frees its people), Interéditions, 2017.

Lenhardt, V., Godard, Transformational Leadership, Palgrave Macmillan, 2000.

Lenhardt, V., Bernard, P., L'Intelligence Collective en Action (Collective Intelligence in Action), Pearson, second Ed., 2009.

Lenhardt, V., Martin, B., Oser la Confiance (Dare to Trust) Insep Consulting, 1996.

Levinas, E., Alterity and Transcendence, Athlone Press, 1999.

Maslow, A., A Theory of Human Motivation, Wilder Publications, 2013.

Mayar, V., Employees First, Customers Second: Turning Conventional Management Upside Down, Harvard Business Review Press, 2010.

McGregor, D., The Human Side of Enterprise, McGraw-Hill Professional, 2006.

Meinniger, J., Success Through Transactional Analysis, Mass Market Paperback, 1974.

Miller, A., Prisoners Of Childhood: The Drama of the Gifted Child and the Search for the True Self. Basic Books, 1996.

Morin, E., On Complexity, Hampton press, 2008.

Ogden, C.K., Richards, I.A., The Meaning of Meaning', Harcourt Brace, 1989.

Oughourlian, J-M., Notre troisième cerveau (Our Third Brain—not yet translated), Albin Michel, 2003.

Oughourlian, J-M., The Genesis of Desire (Studies in Violence, Mimesis, and Culture), Michigan State University Press, 2010.

Panikkar, R.,The Trinity and the Religious Experience of Man: Icon-person-mystery. Orbis Books, 2009.

Peters, T., Thriving on Chaos: Handbook for a Management Revolution, HarperBusiness, 1989.

Pierrakos, J., Core Energetics: Developing the Capacity to Love and Heal, Life Rhythm Publications, 1990.

Rifkin, J., The Empathic Civilization: The Race to Global Consciousness in a World in Crisis, J P Tarcher/Penguin Putnam, 2010.

Rifkin, J., The Zero Marginal Cost Society: The Internet of Things, the Collaborative Commons, and the Eclipse of Capitalism, Palgrave Macmillan, 2014.

Rogers, C., Encounter Groups, Penguin, 1973.

Rogers, C., Freedom to Learn, Prentice Hall, 1969.

Rogers C., On Becoming a Person, Constable, 2004.

Ruesh, J., Bateson, G., Communication: The Social Matrix of Psychiatry, Transaction Publishers, 2008.

Schutz, W., Profound Simplicity, Thorsons, 1979.

Schutz, W., The Human Element, Jossey Bass, 1994.

Serres, M., Latour, B., Conversations on Science, Culture, and Time. University of Michigan Press, 1995.

Sinek, S., Leaders Eat Last: Why Some Teams Pull Together and Others Don't, Penguin, 2014.

Symor, N-K., Actualités en Analyse Transactionnelle (Transactional Analysis News), AAT, 7, 27, July 1983 (not translated into English).

Varela, F.J., Ethical Know-How, Stanford University Press, 1999.

Varela, F.J., Principles of Biological Autonomy, Elsevier, North-Holland, New York, 1979.

Varela, F.J., The Embodied Mind: Cognitive Science and Human Experience (with Evan Thompson and Eleanor Rosch), MIT Press, Cambridge, 1991.

Varillon, F., Joy of Faith, Joy of Life, Paulines, 1993.

Weick, K.E., Sensemaking in Organizations, Sage, 1995.

Whitney, D., Cooperrider, D.L., Stavros, J.M. Appreciative Inquiry Handbook: For Leaders of Change, Berrett-Koehler Publishers, 2008.

Winnicott, D., Transitional Objects and Transitional Phenomena, Int. J. Psychoanal., 34, 89–97, 1953.

Woelfe, N., The Living Organization: Transforming Business to Create Extraordinary Results, Quantum Leaders Publishing, 2011.

Yalom, I., Existential Psychotherapy, Basic Books, 1980.

Yalom, I., Staring at the Sun, Piatkus, 2011.

Zundel, M. Je, Est un Autre (I is Another) Anne Sigier ed.

Index

A

Ambiguity, 13, 21, 38, 58, 59, 61, 73, 76, 94, 141, 142, 203, 218
Appreciative Inquiry, 23, 51, 86
Autonomy, 27, 71
    autonomy Deployment Tree, 179
    degree of, 57, 58, 68, 70, 75, 95, 140, 187, 214
    and humanization, 201
    and meaning, 79
    paradox of, 205

C

Challenging, 27, 42, 114, 118, 130, 205, 218
Change, 8, 17, 20, 46, 139, 166, 173, 202, 206
    agenda, 97
    alliance for, 95, 218
    barriers to, 42
    and bereavement, 70, 77
    capacity for, 94
    management, 6, 44, 141
    right moment, 166
    sustainable, 156
    will to, 96, 105, 163, 214, 216

Coaching alliance, 214, 218
Coaching culture, 2, 22, 69
Coaching relationship, 16, 68, 102, 124, 133, 175, 178, 198, 201, 212, 214, 215
Coach's stance, 14, 25, 61, 75, 123, 125, 128, 188, 198, 201, 212, 214, 223
Collective Intelligence, vii, 2, 6, 8, 21, 139, 142, 182, 190, 203, 205
Complexity, 12, 14, 20, 31, 67, 76, 90, 95, 107, 138, 139, 168, 182, 192, 201–203, 208, 225
Constructivism, 18, 28, 111, 168
Contextualization, 108, 111
Contract, 10, 28, 53, 78, 83, 88, 92, 93, 97, 130, 208, 215, 216, 218
Crystallization, 27, 60, 81, 119, 212

D

Decisions, 7, 16, 27, 57, 81, 114, 132, 160, 164, 166, 202, 211, 213, 215
Diagnosis, 56, 69, 80, 84, 94, 130

© The Author(s) 2017
V. Lenhardt, *My 10 Strategies for Integrative Coaching*,
DOI 10.1007/978-3-319-54795-4

Double bind, 202
Drivers (Transactional Analysis), 115

E
Ego States, 50, 51, 86, 128, 129, 134
Emotional intelligence, 138
Empathy, 23, 40–42, 49, 95, 119, 151,
     167, 195, 198
Enaction, 37, 42, 60, 69, 111, 124,
     169, 195
Escape Hatch, 132
Ethics, 2, 20, 51, 88, 141,
     208, 216, 223
EVH CEO Club, 6, 20, 207

F
Frankl, Viktor, 31, 50, 79, 144, 148,
     154, 165, 200, 204
Freedom, 195, 205, 214

H
Holomorphic, 9, 28, 35, 70, 94, 102,
     111, 139, 172, 179, 188, 208
Homo Amans, 152, 190
Homo Faber, 152, 190
Homo Patiens, 152, 190
Hostage taking, 15
Humanistic psychology, 1, 23, 39

I
Iceberg, 14, 29, 222
Identity, 42, 101, 155, 159, 171, 173
     of coach, 67, 220
     construction, 175, 181, 197, 199,
          206, 226
     crises, 186
     development, 5, 13, 73,
          129, 140, 190
     envelopes, 178
     facets, 201, 206
     issues, 25, 115, 126, 132
     levels, 104, 106, 145, 214
     managerial, 142
     paradox of, 141
     search for, 72
     strategies, 25
     transformation, 21, 77, 162
     zones, 176
Identity Backbone, 26, 79, 106, 142,
     155, 178, 181
Individuation, 207
Integrative coaching, 13, 18, 37, 69, 86,
     156, 201, 202, 208
Interdividual, 12
Intersubjectivity, 3, 40, 52, 61, 69, 101,
     111, 181, 201, 216
Introjection, 71, 96

K
Kübler-Ross, Elisabeth, 70, 197

L
Leadership, 7, 14, 15, 20, 40, 81, 138,
     173, 182, 183, 203
     level 5 leaders, 21
Listening, 2, 17, 39, 42, 49, 57, 62,
     124, 138, 186, 205, 214, 221
     third-order listening, 29, 49, 68, 118
Lobster complex, 142

M
Matrix of empathy, 40, 49, 198, 199
McGregor Theory X & Y, ix, 43, 184,
     185, 188
Meaning, 79, 119, 137, 138, 144, 148,
     153, 159, 171, 179, 191, 196,
     203, 206
Metacommunication, 33, 62, 64, 81,
     151, 213

N

Non-directiveness, 17, 39, 124

O

Object relations theory, 148
Ontological security, 21, 119, 150, 152
  of client, 147, 178, 189, 191
  of coach, 48, 94, 105, 126–127,
    142, 216, 226

P

Paradox, 11, 13, 21, 94, 197, 203
  of autonomy, 205, 222
  coach's stance, 61
  of competence, 127, 173, 206,
    222, 226
  of education, 69, 222
  of identity, 141, 226
  of power, 220
  of therapy, 162
Parallel processes, 13, 25, 69, 99, 110,
    112, 114, 117, 133, 219
Permissions, 25, 49, 58, 131, 160, 174,
    186, 198, 205, 217
Person-Centered Approach, 36
Princes(s)' Alliance, 37, 41, 47, 105,
    154, 191, 207
Protections, 25, 49, 58, 95, 105, 131,
    160, 174, 186, 205, 217
Pygmalion effect, 42, 188, 198, 219

Q

Questioning, 69, 86, 107, 129, 165,
    166
  socratic, 50, 129

R

Relationships, 119, 150, 152, 153, 179,
    191, 200
Rescuer, 52, 56, 96,
    113, 217

Responsibility, 6, 20, 27, 182, 185,
    204, 208, 214
  of client, 37, 57, 76, 94, 134, 156, 205
  of coach, 14, 132
Rifkin, Jeremy, vii, 41, 139, 153, 198
RPNRC, 24, 83, 91, 102, 105, 111

S

Scripts, 50, 115, 132, 164, 173, 191,
    200, 213, 219
Second Industrial Revolution, 5, 139
Silence, 39, 57, 124, 126, 144, 190,
    199, 221
Situational intelligence, 58, 67, 97, 187
Space-time context, 160, 165, 167
Strategy, 9, 58, 77, 94, 108, 147, 168
Stroke (Transactional Analysis), 151
Supervision, 3, 108, 219, 227

T

Therapy
  boundary with coaching, 46, 48,
    106, 217
  for the coach, 52, 95, 152, 227
  gestalt, 50, 133
  logotherapy, 50
  reasons for, 162
  Weighted Integrative (WIT), 155, 156
Third Industrial Revolution, vii, 5, 139
Third-order suffering, 160, 162, 164,
    167, 190
Transactional Analysis, 51, 70, 86, 113,
    115, 132, 198, 212, 215
Transference, 13, 69, 96, 117, 217
Transformance, 189
Transitional object, 150
Transition space, 28, 159, 160

U

Unconditional acceptance, v, 39, 42,
    75, 221